DATE DUE

JN 28 '87			

A History of Italian Literature

A History of Italian Literature

Volume 2

Eugenio Donadoni

With additional materials on Twentieth-Century Literature by Ettore Mazzali and Robert J. Clements

Translated by Richard Monges

New York: New York University Press
1969
London: University of London Press

Library of Congress Catalog Card Number: 68-13026
Manufactured in the United States of America

8.

The Nineteenth Century

General Considerations on the First Half Of the Century

The last years of the eighteenth century and the first of the nineteenth saw Italy occupied by French arms. In Milano, in Romagna, in Naples, Genoa and elsewhere, these same years saw the rise of those republics which were realizing, or seemed to be realizing, the ideals of equality and fraternity preached by the writers of the Enlightenment (*Illuministi*) of the preceding century. It was more a demagogic than a democratic triumph. Amid the din and uproar of poets and writers celebrating the new liberty, the recognition of error by the best minds was equally prompt; the wisdom gained by past experience made them carry on the Alfierian anti-French tradition. The Napoleonic domination and empire found greater favor. Napoleon undoubtedly deserved much credit for having reawakened the military spirit in Italy; after his fall, it was from among former Napoleonic soldiers that there came the first Italians to dedicate themselves to the revival of the nation – the *Risorgimento.* But the Italians became aware soon enough that Napoleon had taken from them far more than he had given. They saw him make Italy a French province, a *département.* A reaction set in against him in Italy and throughout Europe which, passing from effects to causes, displayed itself in hostility to materialism and violence, which were no less basic to the revolutionary governments than to the Napoleonic empire. In France, the Viscount of Chateaubriand and Madame de Staël were the standard-bearers of this insurrection against forms of thought and of government which had shattered the most venerated religious and philosophic traditions of humanity. But under the Napoleonic oppression each nation found itself, its appearance, its past, and its poetry; wherefore in the very period of French domination, which lasted until about 1815, a political and spiritual reaction grew and ripened. An exaltation of the individual and of feeling invaded all branches of speculation; in the more properly literary field it was called *Romanticism.* In Germany, England, Italy, and later, in France, this reaction called Romanticism flourished up to mid-century, magnificent in its spontaneity. It took the most varied forms, and it met with some strong resistance, not all of which was of an aesthetic nature. In the first half of the nineteenth century, then, two literary periods are distinguishable, which correspond to two different moments in the collective life: the French period, covering the revolutionary literature and lasting until about 1815, and that of the literature of the Restoration, or Romanticism, from 1815 to 1850.

Vincenzo Monti

His Life

The figures of two poets dominate the first period, in complete antithesis one to the other: Vincenzo Monti and Ugo Foscolo. The former expressed in abundant and ringing verse the public enthusiasm or aversion to the great events that pressed fast one upon another. He was entirely exterior; he sensed what was striking, glamorous, and illusory in the times, not what was great. The other was all inwardness, all passion, all Italian spirit and feeling. A follower of the tradition of Alfieri and Parini, he was perhaps the first real poet of Italian contemporary literature.

Vincenzo Monti was born at Fusignano near Alfonsine, in Romagna, in 1754. As a boy he was put in the seminary at Faenza. He learned the entire *Aeneid* by heart and felt himself to be a poet. He went on to the University of Ferrara to study law or medicine, but there he devoted himself to poetry and, following Varano, aimed at the standard of Dante. When he was twenty-two he published the *Visione d'Ezechiello;* Cardinal Borghese, then legate at Ferrara, noticed him, appreciated him, and brought him to Rome. The *Prosopopea di Pericle* [*Prosopopoeia of Pericles*], written in honor of the discovery of a bust of the hero near Tivoli and ending with great praise of Pius VI, won for him the post of secretary of Duke Braschi, that Pope's nephew. Then, in enjoyment of those honors and leisures, he composed poems which became famous: the little *Il pellegrino apostolico* [*The Apostolic Pilgrim*] about the unsuccessful diplomatic journey of Pius VI to the secularizing Emperor Joseph II in Vienna; *Le bellezze dell'universo* [*The Beauties of the Universe*] for the wedding of Duke Braschi and Lady Costanza Falconieri; and the *Ode* to the Montgolfier brothers, inventors of the aereostatic balloon, a warm eulogy of the miracles of science. In Rome he began the little poem *Feroniade* on the draining of the Pontine marshes, and he composed the tragedies *Aristodemo* and *Galeotto Manfredi;* also the *Basvilliana,* against the Revolution and in praise of the Papacy.

The new ideas had fascinated Monti. In 1797 he fled

Rome, leaving behind his very beautiful wife Teresa Pickler and his little daughter Costanza who, however, rejoined him later. After various ups and downs, the new republican, no longer the abbé, but now Citizen Vincenzo Monti, landed in the central city of the French movement: Milan, the capital of the Cisalpine Republic. There he found old and new literary enemies, with whom it was necessary to come to terms. Out of hatred for him, a law was enacted which excluded from any public employment those who had previously lauded the old governments. In one of the many demagogic journals, Monti repudiated his *Basvilliana.* He wrote ultrarevolutionary and antireligious poems: *Il pericolo* [*The Danger*], *La superstizione, Il fanatismo* [*Fanaticism*]. In a *cantata* for the La Scala theater he celebrated the anniversary of the execution of Louis XVI. He went so far as to curse the cross, preferring to praise the tree of liberty in its place. Even all this was not sufficient to dissipate the distrust floating around the former poet of Catholicism. Only Ugo Foscolo rose up boldly in his defence. The whirlwind invasion of the Austro-Russians in 1799 drove Monti, along with many other liberals, into France.

In the journey through Savoy he suffered great privations. He found a way to subsist, modestly, in Paris. And in Paris he took revenge on the demagogues who had made life hard for him in Milan by writing *La Mascheroniana,* and completing the *Caio Gracco.* By now demagogy was on the way out; henceforth the world would see a restorer in Napoleon. The victory of Marengo reopened the gates of Italy to Monti. He greeted the fatherland with a tender and impetuous ode which concluded with the apotheosis of the conqueror. Napoleon took notice of him and appointed him professor of Italian eloquence at Pavia. But Monti's lectures, begun in 1802, were more concerned with Italy than with France. He was called back to Milan where he was appointed court historiographer (or poet, or panegyricist: it was all one) and Knight of the Iron Crown. Citizen Monti became the courtier Monti. Then he began the long series of poems and compositions in praise of Napoleon: *Il beneficio* [*The Benefice*], *Il bardo della Selva Nera* [*The Bard of the Black Wood*], *La Spada di Federico* [*Frederick's Sword*], *La palingenesi politica* [*Political Regeneration*]. His translation of the *Iliad*, previously begun at Rome, gave him more honor.

The final vicissitudes and the fall of his Napoleon did not inspire him to write a single line of poetry, and the return of the Austrians to power in 1815 caused him to lose all his public offices and his stipends. The poet hastened to remedy the situation by hailing the new masters with *Il mistico omaggio* [*Mystic Homage*], *Il ritorno d'Astrea* [*The Return of Astrea*], *L'invito a Pallade* [*The Invitation to Pallas*]. However the Austrian government made no show of appreciating him highly; he had sung the praises of too many masters. In this final period of his life he devoted himself entirely to linguistic problems and, in collaboration with his son-in-law Perticari, published *Proposta di alcune aggiunte al vocabolario della Crusca* [*Proposal to Make Some Additions to the Dictionary of the Crusca Academy*]. As the struggle between Classicists and Romanticists was already ardent, Monti found himself to be the representative of the former, espousing their program in the *Sermone* in defence of mythology (1825). But grave misfortune struck him: the threat of blindness and paralysis. Yet he continued to write: affectionate things, such as the poem celebrating the name day of his wife; and he continued to perfect the old mythological poems which he had left unfinished. He died in Milan in 1828.

Lyric Poems

Throughout his long life Monti was a productive lyric poet. We have already touched on some of his more famous lyrics. Among his youthful writings are: the *Elegie* and the *Pensieri d'amore,* delicate pages filled with a melancholy and even desperate sadness, echoing notes of English poetry and of *Werther;* and the Sapphic ode *Invito di un solitario a un cittadino* [*Invitation of a Lone Man to a Citizen*] which, like some others, is a lamentation against the French atrocities, against the impious "New Enceladi" [Enceladus, slain in the mythical War of the Giants, and buried by Athene beneath Sicily, which still shakes when he turns over]. Not so felicitous are the forced and rhetorical lyrics written during the Revolution and the Empire. The *canzone* which precedes *Il Congresso di Udine* (1797), the congress at which the fate of Italy was to be determined between Napoleon and the Germanic states, is one of the noblest of its kind; but the *Cantata per la pace di Campoformio* is repugnant to Italians when they consider that the Peace of Campoformio meant sacrificing the oldest and most Italian of the republics to Austria. The odes, *Ierogamia di Creta* [*Sacred Marriage in Crete*] of 1810, and *Le Api panacridi in Alvisopoli* [*The Panacridian Bees in Alvisopolis*] a year later, celebrate with elegant profusion of mythological allusion the wedding of Napoleon and Marie-Louise of Austria and the birth of the future king of Rome. Monti was once more really poetical in the lyrics of his last years when he was able to listen to his heart, both as man and father. Even in that period, however, there was a superabundance of futile poems for special occasions, which the famous poet could not refuse any illustrious petitioner.

The Short Narrative Poems

Monti was more at ease in the short narrative poem, which requires less impetuosity and offers more expedients. We shall touch on the more significant compositions of this type in chronological order, beginning with the *Basvilliana.*

Hughes de Bassville, a secretary of legation in Naples, had come to Rome to disseminate revolutionary propaganda there. The mob killed him in January, 1793, and only intervention of the Pope kept his wife and child from being slain. Monti was a friend of the agitator and for this reason, among others, it was opportune that he should turn suspicion away from himself by writing a poem, which he did, against the French Revolution. However, moved by a kind and Christian thought, he imagines that Bassville dies forgiven by God. But, guided by an angel, he must in penitence see with his own eyes the crimes and the enormities of the revolution of which he had been one of the fosterers. It was the author's plan for the poem to follow, step by step, the gigantic event, to be the poetic chronicle of the Revolution, sung by a hostile and religious spirit. It was to have appeared in monthly cantos, but it remained unfinished after the fourth canto. The two spirits are present at the slaughters in Marseilles and at the irreligious action in Avignon. Then they reach Paris, surrounded by allegorical figures: Mourning, Trouble, Madness, Hunger, Discord, War, Atheism. There they witness the execution of Louis XVI, dragged upon the scaffold by four famous regicides of French history. The ghost of Hugues kneels before the soul of his king, begs his forgiveness, and tells about himself, his death, and the unconquerable power of the Church. The king forgives and rises to heaven. Sinister shadows, but for the intervention of a cherub, would drink of the blood of the executed monarch. Among these shadows are Voltaire, Diderot, Helvetius, Rousseau, and D'Alembert, believed to be the author of the *Système de la Nature,* an atheistic book. Under the threat of God's vengeance and the resistance with which England, Spain, and Piedmont are preparing to oppose French power, the story stops. The tercets of the *Basvilliana* seemed Dantean; the poet was even called a "refined Dante." Certainly the *Basvilliana* has power to evoke images, magnificence of sound, and oratorically eloquent passages, such as the one that extols the majesty of Catholic Rome facing the Revolution.

In Rome Monti began two other poems in blank verse: *Prometeo* [*Prometheus*], in 1797, and the *Feroniade*. The *Prometeo,* in three cantos, describes a journey of the divine spirits upon the earth and gives a prophecy of the future glories of humanity. When the poet published the first canto, he had already passed over to the French cause and found means of inserting high praises of Bonaparte in it. The *Feroniade,* which takes its name from the goddess Feronia formerly worshipped in Latium, was suggested, as we said above, by the draining of the Pontine marshes attempted by Pius VI. Like the *Prometeo,* it rests upon a mythological apparatus: the anger of Juno against Feronia beloved of Jove. It is considered the most exquisite of Monti's short poems, just as the *Prometeo* is surely his richest in philosophic meditation.

The *Mascheroniana,* composed in Paris, continues the Dantesque meter and manner of the *Basvilliana.* First it narrates the death of the poet and mathematician Carlo Lorenzo Mascheroni, mourned by the moral and civic Virtues and by the Muses. The deceased then rises upward through the heavens, for they are all desirous of greeting him; but he is looking for his former earthly friends. Then the French mathematician Borda comes to meet him and leads him into the constellation of Orpheus where the poets dwell. There he perceives Parini, who sternly deplores the triumph of demagogy which he saw in Milan, and from which kindly Death freed him. Borda assures Mascheroni that Italy is safe. Then come the extravagant praises of Napoleon: the invasion of Egypt, the coup d'état, Marengo; liberty has returned. But Parini nurses his doubts: he would not care for the liberty he had already seen. Now two fellow citizens come to confirm his doubts: Pietro Verri and Cesare Beccaria. Pietro Verri has returned from a journey in spirit to the Italian republics: Milan, Ferrara, Bologna; everywhere he has found moral and civil degradation, the populace raised out of its place and the good and worthy men driven out. A voice announces that, by virtue of Bonaparte, peace and justice have returned to the world. Then Beccaria, the man best acquainted with the subject of justice, as author of the book *On Crimes and Punishments* undertakes to speak on the matter. Here, at the end of the fifth canto, the poem is interrupted. In its fundamental theme, and in its most eloquent pages, the poem amounts to an accusation against the demagogy which so oppressed the poet during his years in Milan. In composition it reduces to a series of declamations interrupted by some spectacular episodes, such as the appearance between the second canto and the third of the throne of the eternal, and the vigorous description in the fifth of a whirlwind which devastated the territory of Bologna.

Of Monti's Napoleonic poems, the most famous was *Il Bardo della Selva Nera,* in seven cantos in various meters. It has frequent echoes of Ossian, a subject which Napoleon liked, and recalls in some passages Gray's *The Bard.* It is imagined that, on the eve of the surrender of Ulm, a wounded French soldier (Terigi) is taken in by the bard of the Hercynian forest, Ullino, and his daughter Malvina. The bard is not half wild, like those of antiquity, but civilized and a lover of knowledge and enlightenment. However, he is no less inspired than those of ancient times, and at times he sings, to the accompaniment of his lyre of the approaching, merited defeat of his people. But these lyrical chants are mainly for ornament. The substance of the poem lies in the story of Terigi during his convalescence. He tells of himself and his mother, a fervent Italian of the department of the Var, married to a Frenchman; above all he speaks of Napoleon, under whom Terigi had served. In this way the first war of Italy is talked about and also the Egyptian expedition, whose scientific importance and civil significance are stressed. The coup d'état of 18 Brumaire is narrated; all the arguments in favor of a despotism are brought out afresh, and strong language is used against, the Revolution and Reign of Terror. In Napoleon's second expedition to Italy, Terigi found his home destroyed and in its ruins discovered his mother, who died of joy on seeing him. Of all Monti's poems this is the most adulatory: the invectives against Austria, Russia, and England sound coarse and unbecoming. Italy is not felt; rather: *"Italia bella Dirà: 'Di Bonaparte ecco l'ancella!' "* ["Fair Italy will say:/'Behold Bonaparte's maidservant!' "] The true and warm love of Malvina occasions some fine pages. The end of the first canto was highly praised for its description of the evening after the battle. Perhaps the most epical passage is a fragment of the eighth canto, which conjures up the ghost of Hannibal on the Alps.

More discussed, even by its admirers, was the *Palingenesi politica* of 1808, a poem in blank verse dedicated to Joseph Bonaparte, King of Spain. Naturally, the palingenesis, or regeneration, is the civilization which the noble Spanish nation will receive from Napoleon's brother. The central image of the poem is the chaos of matter, overcome and changed into beauty by the work of the divine spirit, while the chaos of the world's nations is brought to order by Napoleon's spirit. The *Palingenesi* was to be a part of the *Bardo*.

The Theater

Monti's ambition was too great for him not to try his hand at the genre that brings an author closest to his public: the drama. In 1787 his *Aristodemo* was played in Rome and was a great success; today it is put on only by college groups. The action is based on the remorse of the king of Messene, Aristodemus, who has killed his daughter because of lust for power and finally commits suicide. The torments, the anxieties, and the delirium of the king recall those of Alfieri's *Saul.* His *Galeotto Manfredi* is a tragedy of jealousy, which develops in a fifteenth-century court. The figure of the mischief-making courtier Zambrino smacks of Shakespeare's Iago. The *Caio Gracco,* finished in Paris in 1800, a more important piece, was inspired by the same antidemagogic hatreds as the *Mascheroniana.* Caius Gracchus, the true lover of the people, is abandoned by the masses, who are made to believe that he is their enemy and exploiter. From this a massacre results, which ends with the suicide of Caius, who takes his own life rather than be stained with the blood of the people. The drama is magnificent; the speeches of Gracchus to the populace are warmly eloquent. Mention may be made also of the play, *Teseo,* which was performed at La Scala in 1804. Athens and Trezene fall prey to crimes and disorders during Theseus' absence. He returns and restores liberty and peace: a clear allusion to Napoleon and the creation of the Italic kingdom in opposition to the disorders of the Cisalpine Republic. Equally allusive to Napoleon as savior of Italy is the melodrama with music by Paisiello, *I Pitagorici* [*The Pythagoreans*], performed in Naples.

The Translations

The lengthy and yet quite incomplete listing of the poetic works of Monti could not have a more fitting conclusion than a mention of his translations. In this field he had only to entrust himself to his stylistic virtues, and in those he was a master. In his republican years he translated the satirical poet Persius, the briefest and the most obscure of the Latin poets. He rendered some of the satires into an equal number of Italian verses: this was a display of virtuosity rather than art. In his hours of leisure he turned Voltaire's most scabrous poem, *La Pucelle,* into very successful Italian stanzas. He kept this effort of his secret, however, and it did not appear publicly until 1878. His *Iliade* was a masterpiece that caused the fairly numerous other Italian *Iliads* to be forgotten: the pedantic one by Salvini, the plebean one by Ceruti, and Cesarotti's falsification. Monti knew little more than the rudiments of Greek and helped himself with the literal Latin versions [Guido Mazzoni remarks that Foscolo mocked Monti as "the great translator of the translators of Homer" in *L'Ottocento,* I, 1949, 82]. His very ignorance, however, allowed him to work with a spontaneity, a liberty, a warmth, and an eloquence which he perhaps would have lacked if he had kept his eyes fixed on the Greek text.

Prose Writings

Monti's prose writings are far from negligible. Some of the many lessons that he gave at the University of Pavia are still extant. His lecture *Sull'obligo di onorare i primi scopritori del vero* [*On the Obligation to Honor the First Realists*] is a eulogy of Italian glories ignored by foreigners. His lessons on Socrates are noble, as are those against the sophists, extolling that moral conscience which, at least in theory, Monti considered as the source of eloquence. But Monti's principal prose work, as mentioned above, dates from the late years of his life: *Proposal of Some Corrections and Additions to the Dictionary of the Crusca Academy* published in 1818. Italian philologists for centuries had been bickering over the "question of the language." Naturally, the Crusca Academy held tenaciously to the Tuscan speech as the norm, and Father Antonio Cesari — of whom more later — went further than most in the *Giunti veronesi* [*Veronese Additions*] which he made to that vocabulary. On the other hand, the *Istituto nazionale* [National Institute] of Milan proposed attainment of the Italian language by criteria much more generous than those of the Crusca; that is, by taking advantage of writers from all parts of the peninsula and giving due importance to the language of philosophers and scientists. Monti adopted as his own the principles espoused by the Institute, made fun of purism, the Crusca, and Cesari by insisting on the fundamental idea that the "noble Italian idiom," outlined by Dante in the *De vulgari eloquentia,* is not at all the language of the *plebes,* or even that of Tuscany, and that it would be ridiculous today to bring back into use obscure and ignoble words current in the first centuries of the vernacular. The work, including the linguistic remarks, is shrewd and witty. Polemical letters, prefaces, and other means make agreeable a material that is abstruse in nature. The dialogues inserted here and there, some of which had been published previously in the *Poligrafo,* are among the liveliest and most spirited works in Italian didactic prose.

Ugo Foscolo

His Life

Ugo Foscolo was the firstborn (1778) of several children of a Greek mother and a Venetian father on the Ionian island of Zante, one of the few dominions remaining to Venice in the East. His father, a doctor, moved later to Spalato [called in England, Split] where Ugo received his earliest education in the seminary; this, and, perhaps even more, the sorrowful travail of his first years, awakened in the child mystical tendencies which never entirely disappeared. His father died and his widowed mother moved the family to Venice, where they lived in indigence. The youth soon entered into the literary life of the city. He cultivated friendly relations with the noted writer Isabella Teotochi Albrizzi, with Pindemonte and with Cesarotti. He became an avid reader of Ossian and of Young, and dashed off poems filled with sadness. Then he strengthened his style by reading Parini, as is apparent in some lyrics of high civil significance. He adored Alfieri, and on that model he wrote his *Tieste.* The success of this tragedy in the Sant'Angelo Theater made the young author a celebrity in Venice.

In that same year 1797, Venice saw the last of its Doges and saw enacted a new constitution modeled on the many which Bonaparte was imposing on Italy. Because he was suspected of revolutionary ideas, Foscolo sought refuge in Bologna, capital of the Cispadana Republic; from that city he sent out the ringing ode *A Bonaparte liberatore.* Then he returned to Venice, where he became secretary of the municipality. Although his distrust of Bonaparte and the French was unconcealed, he took up arms along with the most ardent patriots. The Treaty of Campoformio turned his distrust into hatred and turned him into a revindicator of Italian spirit and continuer of the anti-French sentiments of Parini and Alfieri. He came to Milan as editor of the *Monitore.* There he was close to Monti at a time when demagogy and envy were unleashed against him and, as told above, he came nobly to Monti's defence. He venerated the aged Parini. When the *Monitore* was suppressed as too Italian in that capital of the Cisalpine Republic, he returned to Bologna to seek a living as a law clerk in the Criminal Section of the Department of the Reno. He was engaged in writing his *Jacopo Ortis* when news of the Austro-Russian invasion came: again he took up arms, this time as a lieutenant in the national guard. He saw action at Cento, where he was wounded in the thigh; at the Trebbia, under General MacDonald; at Novi. He reached Genoa, where there were gathered such of the French and Italian militiamen as had fled before the invaders. During the siege, magnificently defended by Masséna, Foscolo performed the duties of a soldier, as well as those of a gallant and a poet, composing an ode to Marquise Luigia Pallavicina, who was thrown from her horse while riding. He republished his ode to Bonaparte, but added a letter reproving him for selling out Venice and cautioning him against becoming a despot.

When Genoa fell, its heroic defenders were transported to Antibes on English vessels. The victory of Marengo, though, had already opened the gates of Italy to them. Foscolo hastened to Milan, where he was assigned to the staff of General Pino. As a staff officer he traveled widely. In Florence he became acquainted with young Isabella Roncioni, affianced to a Marquis Bartolomei, whom she did not love. Foscolo fell in love with her and, to tell his love, he undertook to complete the *Ortis,* of which a horribly adulterated edition was circulating in Italy. But the success of the young officer did not keep step with the success of the young novelist. His book was too hostile to Bonaparte and the French, just as the *Orazione* for the *Comizi* (Assemblies) of Lyon sounded like an overly harsh accusation against French sympathizers. Perhaps the *Orazione* was too revealing of the autocratic ambitions of the Restorer. Besides, he was leading a very irregular life: gambling, running up debts, and distinguishing himself among the fair ladies.

There is no point in recalling all the women beloved by Ugo in his richly active career; nor is there any need to be too scandalized by certain usages of those commonly unbridled times. Here it is enough to say that he had already forgotten Isabella Roncioni; that he was madly in love with the very beautiful and famous Countess Antonietta Fagnani Arese and that this passion is documented by a whole sheaf of Ugo's ardent letters and the marvelous ode *A l'amica risanata* [*To a Friend, on Her Recovery*]. A change offered itself: participation in the enterprise which Bonaparte was attempting against Italy by assembling an army on the coasts of Normandy and Picardy. Foscolo, who had finally attained the rank of captain, was ordered to Boulogne-sur-Mer, where he passed the time translating the humoristic English author Laurence Sterne's *Senti-*

mental Journey and prefacing it with a *Notizia su Didimo Chierico* [*Note on Didimo Chierico,* a pseudonym which Foscolo adopted also for other satirical writings] in which he expressed his whole philosophical, moral, and literary credo. As the expedition dragged on – it was finally abandoned – Ugo obtained a short leave of absence. He went to Paris, where he met the young Manzoni, and made a long visit to Venice, where he once more saw his mother and relatives.

He visited Pindemonte in Verona, where it may be that he heard that poet read the first canto of his poem on cemeteries. He returned to Milan with no desire to stay on in military service. Fortunately a General Caffarelli took him under his wing and allowed him to devote himself to writing. The happiest and most productive years of his life followed. He cast light on the works of Raimondo Montecuccoli for the noble purpose of restoring the memory of old fames now forgotten. In April, 1807, he published *I Sepolchri* [*Sepulchres*] at Brescia, which increased his stature as a poet. When in 1803 he had published an Italian translation of *The Lock of Berenice* of Callimachus, (fl. c. 265 B.C.), a little poem turned into Latin by Catullus, supplementing it with ample philological, critical, and aesthetic notes, he had already established his status as a scholar. As a result, in 1808 he was appointed to the chair of eloquence at the University of Pavia, previously occupied by Monti. Now, finally, prosperity, dignity, and liberty seemed to be within his grasp. But Napoleon did not take kindly to thinkers and philosophers; he preferred the exact sciences. The chair was suppressed, together with others of philosophical disciplines. Of Foscolo's teaching, only a few lectures were left, and also the splendidly eloquent inaugural speech: *Dell'origine e dell'ufficio della letteratura* [*On the Origin and the Function of Literature*]. The discontinuance of his professorship reduced Foscolo to near poverty, a special hardship for him a lover of life in the grand style. Upon the fallen man his many enemies broke loose. On that fallen man, who would not praise the *Palingenesi politica,* flashed the bolt of vain Monti's anger.

Foscolo responded provocatively, and he tried to express his whole being and portray the times allegorically in a tragedy, *Aiace* [*Ajax*], which was awaited with such intense curiosity and by such a large audience that it had to be performed at La Scala (1811) . It was a failure, not only because of dramatic deficiencies in the work, but because of the intrigues of his adversaries, who claimed to see in it irreverent allusions to Napoleon (certainly represented by Agamemnon) and to his feared Minister of the Interior, Fouquet, of whom Foscolo probably had not even thought. The play was forbidden, and Foscolo was "invited" to take an eight-month furlough.

He chose Florence, which seemed to him to be the only city still Italian. Here he moved among those who frequented the salons of the more reactionary than ever Countess of Albany, Alfieri's companion; but there too he met the only woman who ever really loved him: the *Donna gentile,* the "Kind Lady" as he always called her in his letters: that is, Quirina Mocenni of Siena, wife of a certain Ferdinando Magiotti, demented and ill, whom she took care of religiously. In that calm environment Foscolo felt his poetic inspiration renewed. He completed publication of his Sterne translation. He composed a passionate tragedy, *Ricciarda,* and the love affairs and the elegances of Florentine society inspired the poem *Le Grazie* [*The Graces*]. But when the Napoleonic power was shaken to its foundations by the battle of Leipzig (October 16–19, 1813), Foscolo returned to Milan to fight under the viceroy Beauharnais whom he liked and, in common with others, would have liked to see made king of an Italian kingdom. After Waterloo, the Austrians occupied Milan. Marshall Bellegarde sought to influence the new government in favor of the writer, who had been so hostile to the spirits of the French government. He proposed that Foscolo should direct a new periodical, to win Lombardy to the régime. Foscolo resisted the temptation. He, who had not sworn fidelity to the French government, would not swear fidelity to the Austrian government. Also, with desperate foreboding of the fate of Italy, and convinced that Italy had neither the moral nor material forces to become a nation, he resolved to save his dignity as a man and writer by exile.

He disappeared from Milan the evening of March 30, 1815. He wandered around Switzerland, then settled near Zürich. From there he published for a few friends the satire, or libel, in verses in the biblical manner, *Dydymi Clerici prophetae minimi Hypercalypseos liber singularis* [*On the Hypercalypsis of Didimo Chierico, Minimum Prophet, One Single Book*], leveled against the critic Lampredi and the latter's friends, but chiefly against Monti — scorned as a poet, abused as a husband. Much more important for knowing Foscolo's political ideas and his pessimism concerning the revival of Italy, are the *Discorsi sulla servitù d'Italia* dating from that time but published posthumously. Persecuted by the Austrian police even in Switzerland, he went on to England.

The years that the poet spent in London were years of great dreams and greater disappointments. He threw himself into writing articles on literature for the reviews, obliged to neglect more noble undertakings such as the meditated publication of all the Italian classics with full commentary on the lives and times of the authors. However, in what may have been his most wretched years, he wrote his *Saggi* [*Essays*] on Petrach and the *Discorso* on Dante, which even today remain fundamental for an understanding of the two poets. In 1822 he met his illegitimate daughter, Floriana, fathered by him at the time of the expedition at Boulogne-sur-mer. She had a small inheritance with her, some three thousand pounds sterling, left to her by a grandmother. Her father might have found solace for his embittered soul and his economic difficulties, but—it is painful to say—with those three thousand pounds, which were to have been the sustenance of that lost girl, he undertook to build and furnish a villa, which finally buried him under debts. Santorre di Santarosa, the valiant Piedmontese refugee, came to visit him in London and found the daughter alone: her father had hidden for fear of creditors. He had many close and faithful friends among the Italian exiles and aid from generous English noblemen was not lacking; from Lord Russel, Lord Dacre, Lord Hudson Gurney. He died September 10, 1827; a few years later Floriana died of tuberculosis. Lord Gurney Hudson had a tombstone placed on the grave of the poet in the cemetery of Chiswick. In Italy that death was passed over in silence. But later came the apotheosis: in 1871 the remains of the poet were carried to Santa Croce to the temple which he had extolled with immortal words.

The *Ortis*

Foscolo's youthful production reached its highest point in the novel *Ultime lettere di Jacopo Ortis* [*Last Letters of Jacopo Ortis*] which, after a falsified edition of the first part by a certain Angelo Sassoli of Bologna appeared anonymously in its definitive form in a second edition in 1802—certain passages concerning Bonaparte would have caused trouble for the author. In fact, these passages were eliminated from all editions published during the rule of the dictator. *Ortis* is a love story in the epistolary form in use in the eighteenth century, like the *Nouvelle Héloïse* of Rousseau and the *Sorrows of Young Werther* of Goethe, with which the *Ortis* has many points in common, even in the makeup of the story. The author imagines that the letters of the student Ortis, a suicide, addressed to his faithful friend, Lorenzo Alderani (that is, the poet Niccolini, a great friend of Foscolo), have been collected by him; he interrupts sparingly to narrate that which can not be told in the letters. The outline of the novel is quite simple. Jacopo Ortis is one of the many young Venetians whom the Treaty of Campoformio drove from Venice. He lives in a small village in the Euganean Hills, an inactive and discouraged spectator of what he sees happening in Italy. There he meets Teresa, the daughter of another refugee, noble-minded, not rich, and fond of Jacopo. However the times are bad, the morrow uncertain, and he has arranged to give his daughter in marriage to a certain Odoardo, a wealthy young man who will enjoy a safe position. Odoardo is often away on business, and Jacopo has more and more chances to see Teresa, with whom he falls madly in love. But he knows she is betrothed to another man, and even if she were free he would not marry her, so wretched is his situation and that of his country. Instead, he goes off on a journey in Italy to forget. He touches Florence, where he worships at the tombs of the great Italian dead in Santa Croce and visits Montaperti, illustrious for the first fratricidal struggle between Italians. He goes to Milan, where the aged and neglected Parini speaks despairing words about the conditions of the fatherland and the impossibility of liberating it. Since Jacopo feels that he is closely watched by the Cisalpine police, he continues on into Liguria with the intention of entering France. At Pietra in Liguria he meets another man who had emigrated after Campoformio and is leading a wretched life with his wife and young daughter. At Ventimiglia he proceeds up the valley of the Roia and meditates in the Alps on the varying omnipotence of human fates. But at Nice he has not the courage to go on to France, and he returns by way of the Monferrato hills. Soon he is in Ravenna at the tomb of Dante. Meanwhile, news reaches him that Teresa is married. He must return; it will satisfy him just to see her. After a brief visit to Venice to greet his mother for the last time, he is once more at the place of his grace and his unhappiness. In the night he writes a long letter to her whom he has worshipped in vain; in the morning he is found dead with a dagger piercing his heart.

Love is the dominant passion in this short novel, expressed with throbbing tenderness; and the more ardent the affection, the purer and more divine it becomes. But another great passion mingles with it: despair for the fatherland, betrayed and enslaved by the new masters. In his journey through Italy Jacopo sees the new government in all its most odious aspects. Justice is so hypocritical and inhuman that at Bologna two poor stealers of wood are condemned to death. The police are so intrusive as to violate the privacy of correspondence. The French-sympathizing educated classes are ashamed to read Italian books and decree the discontinuance of Latin studies. Now Jacopo is the legitimate heir of Parini and Alfieri: his letters are the heartiest affirmation of the Italian spirit at the moment that Italy was about to be absorbed by the power and arrogance of the French. Therefore, *Ortis* is a great book of faith, even though despair moans on every page. Mazzini the boy was carried away by it and learned it by heart, and much of his later eloquence derived from that oratorical and imaginative style.

The Lyrics

The really lyrical poetry of Foscolo, with the exception of his boyhood and adolescent output, does not fill many pages: twelve sonnets and two odes, which are among the most perfect in Italian literature. Almost all the sonnets were composed during the time that the novel was being developed, and they are filled with the same spirit. Thus in one of them, *Te nudrice alle Muse* [*Thou, nurse of the Muses*], he deplored the contemplated suppression of the Latin language. Several tell of his love for the woman of the novel. Among the most affectionate is the one written for the death of his brother Giovanni, who died by his own hand, and the one honoring his birthplace, Zacinto: *Nè più mai toccherò* [Nevermore shall I touch . . .], which is full of nostalgia for the distant homeland, laughing at the Hellenic myths. *Forse perchè,* the sonnet to evening, is deep in melancholy lyricism. *Solcata ho fronte . . .* [*Furrowed my brow . . .*], the one in which he paints his own portrait, quivers with the powerful individuality of the poet. An epigraphic conciseness that does not exclude impulsive sentiment, and the full spontaneity of image, are the characteristics of these admirable compositions.

In the ode *A Luigia Pallavicini caduta da cavallo sulla riviera di Sestri* [*To Luigia Pallavicini Thrown from Her Horse on the Riviera of Sestri*], the poet, in emotion-filled strophes, narrates the sorrow of the Cupids and echoes the desire for her presence felt in the elegant salons; it deplores her having taken up this utterly masculine sport and describes the horse as he rears and throws his mistress to the ground. Despite her envious lady friends, Luigia will return in beauty to fascinate and to charm. The animated picture of the plunging horse is the finest part of this ode in which the lack of animating passion is felt; it is the compliment that is felt. The other ode, *All'amica risanata* [*To a Friend, on Her Recovery*], written for Countess Antonietta Fagnani Arese after love had died but its remembrance still lingered, more poetical and almost frightening, seems to be far more profound and original. The prosaic details of the return to health are idealized into an equal number of mythological images until the poet reaches his climax: the apotheosis of the Fairest, La Bellissima; according to his idea, the ancient goddesses were women who, like the present subject, had been made divine by poets: here our poet feels and pours out his pride in being a poet, a poet born on Sappho's sea. It is an ode that reaches almost sacred height and atmosphere.

I Sepolcri [*Sepulchres*]

This is Foscolo's eternal poetic page. In September, 1806, the Napoleonic legislation dated 1804 at Saint-Cloud was extended to apply to Italy. It forebade burial of the dead in the churches or within the cities and prescribed burial in places far from the residential sections (a thing which to us today seems most just and natural, but which was violently opposed both then and later). In addition, to prevent deviation from truth, it was prescribed that epigraphs for the dead should be submitted first to a commission for approval. Foscolo, whose soul was adverse to everything savoring of French innovation, saw in these two laws things which probably were not there: an outrage to illusion, not so much to the illusion of life beyond the tomb, in which he did not believe, but to that soft and gentle illusion in which, with the nearness of the tombs, the survivor can live with the one who has died. He also saw a danger: that the few free spirits of the passing generation, because of the envy of the living, would be left without a name and without glory. The poem is developed from these two basic ideas. It is dedicated to Ippolito Pindemonte, as to one who shared the poet's aversion, not so much to these provisions as to the whole state of affairs. With it, as an inscription, is a law from the Twelve Tables, which recognized as holy the rights of the dead: as though the poet wished to confront the iconoclastic and equalitarian laws of the new government with the word of the wisest of the political peoples of antiquity.

It would be neither easy nor good to summarize the vehement poem, whose unity lies wholly in the fundamental sentiment that pervades it, far more than in a logical development or order. The importance to civilization of the tombs, which join the past to the present, is one of the basic concepts: in more concrete form, it says that only with its past can Italy create its future. Italy is eulogized in its greatest men of the last generation: Parini and Alfieri are extolled in lines which sing the glories of Santa Croce. The battles for the fatherland are symbolized in the admirably evoked battle of Marathon; while in the lament of Cassandra for the imminent ruin of Troy there is the lament of Foscolo the poet on the servitude of Italy, a lament of death and of hope. For the *Sepulchres* are the tombs but also the resurrection of the fatherland. It is a deeply Italian chant, published the year after Monti brought out his *Bardo*. It is significant that it does not mention Napoleon but recalls with sympathy the hated England and Nelson. The solemn, stately rhythm, the transition to the middle ideas, and a certain obscurity of expression which constrain the reader to meditate, are the extrinsic characteristics of the austere chant, which stands unique in its age and perhaps in the entire modern age.

The Tragedies

We have touched on the *Tieste* of the youthful Alfieri, a subject famous for the horror that it awakens and well known to ancient and modern tragic poets. In his full maturity, Foscolo wrote *Aiace* [*Ajax*], a subject already used by Sophocles but on an entirely different motif. The story turns on the competition between Ajax, son of Telamon, and Ulysses for possession of the arms of dead Achilles. The warriors want them to go to Ajax; Agamemnon and the kings favor Ulysses, for he has earned the arms with his stratagems. Ajax, strong in his rights and his pride, but slandered by Ulysses as a traitor for having married Tecmessa, an orphaned Trojan princess, is abased, and commits suicide, exhorting his partisans to harmony and to obedience to Agamemnon, the king chosen by the Fates. The figure of Calcante, the old priest, is splendid with his words of wisdom and goodness; only he succeeds in calming the raging hero. Tecmessa inspires pity when she is left, deserted by all and unloved even by Ajax. But the story is too naïve and complicated in development. Ajax (in whom Foscolo represented himself) is too uncertain as a character, too reserved; while Ulysses and Agamemnon are too undeveloped in their cunning and pride.

Ricciarda met with greater success than *Aiace*. Ricciarda and Guido, the children of two estranged brothers (Guelfo, Prince of Salerno, and Averardo), are in love. To prevent her marriage to Guido, Guelfo kills his own daughter Ricciarda, then takes his own life. Likewise Guido kills himself. The drama is violent rather than strong. The invectives voiced by noble Averardo against the dissensions of the Italians initiated the vogue of patriotic allusions which thereafter continued on the Italian stage.

Le Grazie [*The Graces*]

For many years Foscolo had nurtured the idea of expressing his aesthetic and moral principles in a poem uniting lyric and didactic qualities, following the example of the so-called Homeric hymns and other short poems of the Alexandrine age. Canova's Venus, a statue representing pure and true beauty, symbolized in the celestial Venus, furnished the occasion. Originally *Le Grazie* was a poem of one canto; then the material increased until it made three hymns. The first has Greece for its background where, around the shell of Venus rising from the sea, the Graces first appeared, coming to instill feelings of humanity in the still wild inhabitants: the hymn is entitled *Venere* [*Venus*]. The scene of the second hymn is near Florence, at Bellosguardo, where Foscolo resided. Here, before the altar of the Graces, he evokes three women he had loved or admired. The first of the beauties symbolizes music, the second, poetry, and the third, the dance. In this the pictorial part is interrupted by aesthetic digressions and by praise of ancient and Italian poets and judgments on them.

The hymn is called *Vesta,* the goddess of the hearth and of traditions, whom the poet wished to be venerated. In the third hymn it is related how Love, that is to say, the passions of violence, threatens the Graces; but Pallas (Wisdom) protects them with a mysterious veil (Modesty) which leaves beauty intact but curbs in others the sensual instincts. That veil, woven on the sacred island of Atlantis, is embroidered and adorned with images that portray and extol the most inward, modest, and humane virtues. *Pallade* [*Pallas*] is the name of the hymn, which ends with a remembrance of Signora Bignami, who had loved the poet so madly that she had attempted to kill herself for him in the hope that the Graces would send her every solace.

This then is the idea of the poem, which Foscolo never completed because of a lack of fire and inner passion. Some parts of it he published in his lifetime; the remainder was published after his death. No doubt many of the pages are perfect in form. Indeed, Foscolo never wrote anything more studied, or wrought with greater care and elegance. Perhaps never before did blank verse reveal such prodigies of pictorial writing and of harmony. But *Le Grazie* remains the work of an artist rather than of a poet.

Foscolo as Critic and Translator

We have mentioned Foscolo's version of Sterne's *Journey* in which the English humorist is rendered with great fidelity, although with a little too much savor of literature. Foscolo's great ambition, though, was to translate the *Iliad,* and the idea persisted even after Monti's version, which he appreciated highly. Foscolo's *Iliad* remains unfinished: it is faithful to the text, full of vigor, but colder and less limpid than Monti's splendid work.

Foscolo as a critic is much more interesting than Foscolo as a translator. With Foscolo, criticism ceases to be censure or eulogy for the first time. He tries to understand, and to discover behind the writer the man, who alone gives character to the work of the writer. To understand that man, it is necessary that he be reconstituted from the history, moral as well as political and external, of the age in which the writer took form. Thus Foscolo's criticism is transformed into history: not a history of events, but rather a history of ideas. Along this line he is a precursor of modern criticism and anticipates De Sanctis. The discourse (originally in French) *Dante Alighieri e il suo secolo* [*Dante Alighieri and his Century*], and the one of capital importance *Sul testo della Divina Commedia* [*On the Text of the Divina Commedia*]; the *Saggi sul Petrarca* [*Essays on Petrarca*]; the *Discorso storico sul testo del Decamerone* [*Historic Discourse on the Text of the Decameron*], are among Foscolo's most mature and significant critical writings. Even his *Lezioni di eloquenza* [*Lessons of Eloquence*], taught as a young man at Pavia, and especially the inaugural lecture mentioned above, inspired by the Alfierian concept of the independence and the function of literature, are still pleasing in their warmth and impetuosity. Literature should be the reconciler between the tyranny of the throne and the spirits of the multitudes impatient with the yoke.

Minor Writers

The Life and Works of Ippolito Pindemonte

In his time, the Marquis Ippolito Pindemonte was esteemed almost as highly as Vincenzo Monti, and much more than Foscolo. Born in 1753 in Verona into a rich patrician family, he traveled while still quite young, to Florence, Rome, Naples, Sicily, and Malta: he was one of the Knights of Malta or Knights Hospitalers. While making this journey he met many famous writers: Monti and Alfieri among them. After his return to Verona to the solitude of the villa to which he had withdrawn following a severe illness, he published *Poesie campestri* [*Rustic Poems*] and *Prose* [*Prose Writings*], which created a stir of delight among the sentimental. These works are almost all imitations or plagiarisms from English lyric poets — Pope, Collins, Gray, Young, Thomson, Burns. Later he undertook a second journey, this time towards the north: into Savoy, Switzerland, and to Paris where he saw Alfieri again, witnessed the beginning of the Revolution, and shared the common enthusiasm for liberty. Then he went to London, from there to Berlin, Vienna, and thence to Marseilles. There he published a rather unfortunate autobiographical and satirical novel, *Abaritte*. Back home, he wrote the *Epistole in versi* [*Letters in Verse*], in which he expressed his dismay at the news from France and his attachment to the Italian tradition. In 1804 there was a performance of his tragedy *Arminio:* a eulogy of the Germanic hero of whom Tacitus spoke — a subject previously treated by the great German poet Klopstock. In imitation of Klopstock, Pindemonte composed his "bardic" chants or choruses, which he imagined sung by the ancient warrior poets of Germany. It is probable that in the person of Arminius he represents Germany (and not Germany only) opposed to Napoleon. But the Imperial police, which only later on became very strict, did not prohibit the drama which, besides, was only moderately successful.

When Pindemonte heard about Foscolo's *I Sepolcri,* he was working on a poem about the cemeteries of Verona, relative to the burial ground established there by law and in which the dead were buried pell-mell with no honoring inscriptions. He stopped this composition and responded to Foscolo's dedication of the poem to him with an *Epistola* of the same title, in which he treats the young poet somewhat contemptuously and deplores his lack of belief in another life. He shows he had not penetrated the liberal and generous spirit of the poem. In his precocious old age Pindemonte wrote *Sermoni* [*Sermons*], a poetic genre dear to tired and complaining old men; a form of moralizing satire, and, at least in Pindemonte's case, lacking in any faith or enthusiasm. In reality Pindemonte is remembered today only for his version of the *Odyssey* which occupied him in the last twenty or twenty-five years of his life. This was highly praised by Foscolo and seemed more faithful to the original than the Monti's *Iliad,* but it was much colder and more "literary."

Ippolito Pindemonte died in 1828. As early as 1812 his brother Giovanni had preceded him to the tomb; this brother wrote several patriotic tragedies at the time of the Revolution and achieved great popularity with the one entitled *I Baccanali.*

Other Poets

Let us begin with some poets who, in a manner of speaking, enter into the lives of Foscolo and Monti. Angelo Anelli of Desenzano, professor in Milan of legal eloquence, holder of a chair which Foscolo desired, was, in his happy period, the prolific author of *opere buffe,* almost all published anonymously. Later he became one of the many malevolent critics of the time in a short poem in stanzas entitled *Le cronache di Pindi* [*Pindo's Chronicles*] in seven cantos, published in Milan from 1811 to 1818. It is a sort of burlesque history of Italian poetry, especially that of recent years. The allusions to Foscolo are frequent and ignoble; high praise is given to Monti; the burgeoning Romantic movement is loathed.

On the other hand, Francesco Gianni, a Roman tailor given to the art of improvisation, was ferociously opposed to Monti. He was one of the loudest trumpeters of the Revolution; Napoleon appointed him Imperial improviser. Every victory of his new god was celebrated in extemporary rhymes. After the restoration of 1815, he turned to religious poetry. Among his most notorious things was *Proteone allo specchio* [*Big Proteus in the Mirror*] against

Monti who in the *Mascheroniana* had labeled him "a mad demagogue." *L'Assedio di Genova* [*The Siege of Genoa*], *La battaglia di Marengo, La presa di Ulma,* [*The Capture of Ulm*], *La presa di Vienna, La battaglia di Jena, La battaglia di Friedland* are some of the many epical compositions of that improviser which did not seem unworthy of preservation.

Poets who are no longer read, yet form a fine garland around the two greater ones are given brief mention here. By the grace of the *Mascheroniana* which Monti composed on the occasion of his death, Lorenzo Mascheroni became famous. A native of Bergamo, he was gifted in mathematics, of which he was a professor in Pavia. There he wrote an *Epistola a Lesbia Cidonia,* the Arcadian name of the countess Paolina Secco Suardo Grismondi of Bergamo, in which he invites that noblewoman to come visit the museum of physics and natural history in Pavia. This supplies the poet with a reason for describing phenomena and wandering into the dogmas of science; that is to say, for expressing in poetic form concepts least amenable to poetic treatment. He resembles Parini in style. He wrote other poems on scientific themes: *La geometria, La trigonometria,* and so forth. He proposed to attempt the Latin hexameter in his unfortunate *Gli strumenti dei Martiri* [*The Instruments of the Martyrs*]. He died in 1800 at Paris, where he had been called for the compilation of a new metric decimal system.

Giovanni Fantoni of Fivizzano in the region of Lunigiana, a restless spirit, an ardent republican at the outbreak of the Revolution, Foscolo's companion in Genoa during the siege, and an exile in France, was, in more quiet times, elected president of the Academy of Fine Arts in Carrara. He died at the height of his powers in 1807. While still young he made himself famous with his three books of *Odi* in which he endeavored to reproduce the meters of Horace as Carducci did later with more felicity.

However, Fantoni preserved the rhymes of the strophes, which Carducci suppressed. For the most part his *Odi* are noble and breathe stoicism; some are in response to the dictates of a virile love of country.

Angelo Mazza (d. 1817) wrote poetry in Parma. Parma was the city of music, and it was around music, its beneficent effects, harmony, and on the Christian and Platonic ideas concerning it that Mazza composed his poems: several Hymns to Saint Cecilia, *L'aura armonica, La bellezza armonica ideale* [*Ideal Harmonic Beauty*], *La musica direttrice del costume*[*Music as a Shaper of Customs*], *La musica ministra della religione* [*Music in the Service of Religion*] and so forth. He did much imitating of English works. He was prolific, also, in religious and moral poetry, without any sympathy for the ideas of the times. As a poet he is obscure on account of his striving for novel imagery and intentional brevity of expression.

Bartolommeo Lorenzi of Verona (d. 1822) was, among other things, the author of a didactic poem on *La coltivazione dei monti* which was much to the liking of as austere a judge as Parini. Another didactic poet, Cesare Arici of Brescia, who died in 1836 after a life filled with honors, first from the French government, afterwards by the Austrian, was much esteemed by a less severe judge, Vincenzo Monti. As a youth he made a name for himself with the didactic poem *Gli ulivi* [*Olives*], followed later by *I coralli* [*Corals*], *Sirmione, Il camposanto di Brescia* [*The Brescia Cemetery*], and *L'origine delle fonti* [*The Origin of Springs*]; but his capital work is *La pastorizia* [*Stock Raising*]. He also started a poem on the capture of Jerusalem and translated all of Vergil. He is a poet easily inspired, animated by his own special romantic sadness.

Luigi Lamberti of Reggio (d. 1813) was a worthy follower of Parini. The Florentine Marquis Angiolo d'Elci (d. 1824) was the author of twelve *Satire* in *ottava rima:* quite elegant, quite learned, cold. On the contrary, the

Tuscan Filippo Pananti was a spontaneous writer who, after a life of journeys and adventures (on returning home from England he was captured and taken to Algiers on a pirate ship), died in Florence in 1837. He left *Epigrammi, Avventure e osservazioni sopra le coste di Barberia* [*Adventures and Remarks on the Barbary Coast*], lively prose writings of various sorts, and a poetic novel, partly satirical and partly comic, *Il Poeta del teatro* in which he, as the poet of the Royal Italian Theater in London, portrays the woes and the ridicule of that profession.

The age of moralizing had several writers of fables in verse which until a few years ago were read in school. Such a one was Luigi Fiacchi of Scarperia in Mugello, better known as Clasio (d. 1825); another was Lorenzo Pignotti of Figline (d. 1812), the author not only of fables and novellas, but also a short satirical poem *La treccia donata* [*The Gift of the Trees*] in imitation of Pope's *The Rape of the Lock* and a satire of the world of gallantry. But his chief work is *La Storia della Toscana avanti il cominciamento del gran Ducato* [*History of Tuscany Prior to the Grand Duchy*], a most elegant work but of doubtful veracity and little boldness.

A Dialectal Poet

A great popular poet of the epoch deserves special mention: Carlo Porta, the last and the greatest of a race of poets in the Milanese dialect, such as Maggi, Tanzi, and Balestrieri. The Milanese Porta spent his life as an employee: at his death, when barely forty-four years old (1821), he was general accountant for the state pawnshop. But bureaucracy did not dry up the splendid flow of the poet's talent. He made a name for himself with the *Desgrazi de Giovanin Bongee* [*Misfortunes of Johnnie Bongee*], who was a poor wretch, the jocular victim of the French regime. Following in its wake were, among other things, *Lament del Marchionn di gamb avert,* in which a man of the people relates the story of his unhappy marriage with great truth and passion; *El viagg de Fraa Condutt; La nomina del Cappellan; El Miserere,* all exhilarating, and at times, melancholy pictures of the poverty, degradation, avarice, and vulgarity of priests and monks; *Fraa Diodatt de Tolosa, Fraa Zenever,* mocking parodies of wonder tales; *Meneghin biroeu di ex monegh* [*Meneghino, Servant of that Monk*], which ends in an energetic protest of a Christian against the opportunistic and dissipated clergy; *La Preghiera* [*Prayer*], one of the numerous mockeries of the patrician class, especially the ladies, who made no distinction between religion and pride of caste. Several of Porta's poems carry us into the heart of the struggle between Classicists and Romantics; e.g., *El Romanticismo* and the *sestinas* of *Per el matrimoni del sur cont don Gabriell Verr con la sura contessina dona G. B.;* [*For the Wedding of Milord Count G. B. and Milady Countess Giustina Borromea*] *it goes without saying* that the poet sides with the Romantics. There is also extant a waggish paraphrase in Milanese dialect of the first canto of Dante's *Inferno* and of fragments of the second, third, fifth, seventh, eighth, and eleventh. Porta is a creator of types, a photographer (so far as an artist may be) of Milanese life, a powerful advocate of good sense against all literary and social untruths.

Dramatists

Among the poets of the first half of the nineteenth century, a separate group is made up of the quite mediocre dramatists. Francesco Avelloni of Verona was a prolific author of comedies and of dramas of striking effect, comparable in this quality to the German Kotzebue. The Bolognese noble Francesco Albergati Capacelli (d. 1804) was a more artistic playwright. He left behind him many volumes of comedies, far less spirited than Goldoni's with which they were supposed to compete. A fellow countryman and friend of his was Giuseppe Greppi (d. 1827), who wrote fewer but more refined comedies, which he called *Capricci teatrali.* The Roman Gherardo De Rossi (d. 1832), an archaeologist, historian, and journalist, published three volumes of lifeless comedies. Better than he was another Roman, Giovanni Giraud (d. 1834), who was perhaps the only true Goldonian of the comic dramatists of that age; his *L'Adionelli'imbarazzo* [*The Tutor in Trouble*] is still popular. Alberto Nota of Turin sought to ennoble Goldoni and often trod in the footsteps of Molière. He died at a ripe old age in 1847, leaving thirty comedies, none of which now stands the test of theatrical performance.

The Purists

Ideas about criticism made little progress in the nineteenth century. These were times for action rather than for study. In compensation, the old "Question of the Language" was revived. In the renewal of its purity two ends were sought: a reaction against the Frenchified and weakened language of the prose writers of the eighteenth century, and also an affirmation of the Italian spirit and nationality of the language. Count Gianfrancesco Galeani Napione (d. 1813) of Turin rose up against the French tendencies practiced and predicated by Cesarotti. His *Trattato dell'uso e dei pregi della lingua italiana* [*Treatise on the Use and the Virtues of the Italian Language*] in three books is especially interesting where, in the second book, he compares the French tongue with the Italian and teaches that the latter is richer than the former and can be as clear and universal. The purpose of the work is principally practical: to increase the use of Italian in the private and public life of Piedmont, where French still persisted as the language of society. By "Italian" the author means a noble national language, derived from all writers of all centuries.

Antonio Cesari (d. 1828), a priest of the Oratory of Verona, had a more limited conception of the "Italian" complex of the language. His basic idea, clearly expressed in a *Dissertazione sopra lo stato presente della lingua italiana* [*On the Present State of the Italian Language*] is that the language must return to the usage of the fourteenth century, for only in the writers of that time is there purity, strength, beauty, and richness. He personally carried out his theory in practice, writing his many works in the language and style of the fourteenth century. The more important of those works, as far as the history of literature is concerned, are *Le Grazie,* dialogues which demonstrate the beauties of the language of the fourteenth century, and the vast work in dialogue form, *Bellezze di Dante quanto a lingua, poesia ed eloquenza* [*Beauties of Dante in Language, Poetry and Eloquence*]. This would have been the first attempt at an aesthetic interpretation of the poem, if Cesari had been capable of going beyond the poet's words and reaching his soul. The good priest did publish many other works. He composed *Novelle* in the style of Sacchetti and of the *Novellino* and many Petrarchian and comic verses. Highly religious as he was, he left us many writings on sacred themes, like *La Vita di Gesù Cristo* [*Life of Christ*]. He also thought to prove the virtues of the Italian language with many translations of such works as the odes of Horace, the letters of Cicero, and the comedies of Terence. In 1806 he had the dictionary of the Academy della Crusca reprinted at Verona with the addition of many words that he and his collaborator Lombardi selected from the obscurist and often misunderstood, authors of "the good century." It was this that brought about Monti's spirited *Proposta.*

As a collaborator in the work of the *Proposta,* Monti had the help of Count Giulio Perticari of Pesar, who had married Monti's daughter Costanza. Perticari died in 1822 in the prime of life. The Count aided Monti in his studies, and two of his writings were included in the *Proposta.* While he accepts the principle of the reform of the language, Perticari denies that this must restrict itself to the fourteenth century alone and maintains that in the fourteenth century itself there was both dialect and language: the dialect was one thing, and the language was something else. Thus he renewed Dante's opinion, who in his own time saw a *lingua illustre* [noble language] flourishing in Tuscany, which was quite different from the local vernaculars. Drawing upon these fundamental ideas, he compiled the treatise *Degli scrittori del Trecento e dei loro imitatori* [*On the Fourteenth-Century Writers and their Imitators*]. And to show that Dante, in despising the Tuscan vernaculars, had not spoken out of hatred against Florence, he wrote the essay *Dell'amor patrio di Dante Alighieri e del libro intorno il volgare eloquio* [*Dante's Patriotism and his Book on the Vernacular*], after which came the *Difesa di Dante* [*Defence of Dante*]. All these writings were very learned and more modern in thought than their rather academic form would lead one to suspect.

Pietro Giordani of Piacenza may be classified as belonging to the purist school. He died in 1848, after a long life spent nobly in aid of every humanitarian cause. After the Restoration, the Austrian government never ceased its persecution of him. His status would be still higher if he had not composed a *Panegirico a Napoleone* (1807) in which adulation surpasses any hyperbole. Giordani was not a prolific writer, nor did he write anything that might be called a book. His work consists of eulogies (the one in honor of Canova is particularly fine), discourses on special occasions, and epigraphs, all written in a style so correct as to approach affectation. Many of his *Letters* are still in existence, in large part unpublished, or published in partial collections. He reveals himself as a man of great and especially artistic culture. However his literary judgments too often limit themselves to a study of form, and are those of a rhetorician rather than a critic. He was a great admirer of Monti and detested Foscolo. He has the considerable merit of having proclaimed to the world the greatness of young Leopardi, who, at least for many years, adored him.

Philosophers and Thinkers

In the last years of the eighteenth century and the beginning of the nineteenth century, the thought of the Encyclopedists had its last adherents in Italy. In Naples, Mario Pagano, one of the founders of the Parthenopean Republic in 1799 [as an ancient Greek colony, Naples was known as Parthenope] paid for his ideas of liberty on the scaffold. In a series of political and literary *Saggi* [*Essays*], he sought to apply the ill-comprehended ideas of Vico to modern history and to clarify them. In Milan, Melchiorre Gioia of Piacenza (d. 1829) stood out among other thinkers; he devoted himself principally to economic studies, which form the subject matter of many of his works. His *Nuovo Galateo,* a species of civic and moral catechism, enjoyed a great success. Giandomenico Romagnosi (d. 1835) of Salsomaggiore was a far more powerful thinker, highly esteemed by the French regime, which entrusted him with the compilation of the penal code. He was imprisoned and oppressed in many ways by the restored Austrian government, which deprived him of the right to teach and to practice publicly his profession of lawyer. *La Genesi del diritto penal* [*Genesis of Penal Law*]; *Introduzione allo studio del diritto pubblico* [*Introduction to the Study of Public Law*]; and the *Saggio su la costituzione di una monarchia nazionale rappresentative* [*Essay on the Constitution of a Representative National Monarchy*] are among his most important works. His ideas stem from Vico no less than from the French thinkers. His sense of reality was keen, as was his idea of the limitations on the exercise of liberty and equality. He preached a state that would safeguard, by force, the liberty of all. Among the economists, Giuseppe Pecchio of Milan has an honorable place. When the Italian movements of 1821 were broken up, he went to Switzerland as an exile, then to Spain, and later to England, where he lived a long time, and died in 1835. His *Storia dell'economia pubblica in Italia* is a small book that is very useful to anyone who wants a summary of the thought of the principal Italian economists. It was published before his death by Pietro Custodi in some fifty volumes. Pecchio is the author of a *Storia della letteratura inglese* and *La Vita di Ugo Foscolo,* whom he knew intimately.

Historians

With the exception of some fine archeologists, like the Roman Ennio Quirino Visconti (d. 1818), purely erudite men, such as the great learned men of the eighteenth century, are of lesser stature in the epoch that now concerns us. The times were not then propitious for the quiet of research, and men's minds were more given to argument than to knowledge. However the great events of that stormy age, and the thoughts which they excited in certain select minds, as well as the need to add luster to Italy's past just when it was on the point of becoming a French province, aroused a fair number of historians, among them some of great worth.

The *Commentari alla rivoluzione francese* by Lazzaro Papi of Lucca (d. 1834) are still read. Works by the Neapolitan Francesco Lomonaco, a professor of history at Pavia, are inspired by a great feeling for Italy: *Vite dei capitani illustri* [*The Lives of Illustrious Leaders*] and *Degli illustri letterati italiani* [*On Illustrious Italian Men of Letters*]; his *Discorsi letterari e filosofici* are filled with the new manner of thought. Lomonaco may have taken his own life. Today, the greatest historical temperament of that time is thought to be Vincenzo Cuoco (d. 1823) of

Civitacampomarano in Sannio (Samnium), a resident of Naples. He was imprisoned as a member of the government of the Parthenopean Republic in 1799 and thereafter a refugee in Milan. During the Italian republic and the first years of the Italian kingdom he was director of the *Giornale italiano,* the most effective organ of Italian resistance to the French encroachments. At last he exercised high functions under the king of Naples, Joachim Murat, to whom he proposed a wise reform of the scholastic regulations. He had participated in the Neapolitan revolution and had been a witness to it, his *Saggio storico sulla rivoluzione di Napoli* is an authoritative book on the subject. The author maintains that that revolution could not but fail because it was imported from outside, was not the spontaneous consequence of the conscience of the Neapolitans, and did not correspond to their needs and customs. It is the application of one of Vico's concepts to a practical case: history does not come before its time and does not occur until it is ready. His allegorical and didactic novel, *Platone in Italia* is less interesting. In its basic theme and its development it is reminiscent of *Le voyage du jeune Anacharsis en Grèce,* a famous novel of the eighteenth century, by Jean Jacques de Barthélemy. In the *Plato,* the Greek philosopher is imagined making a journey to southern Italy (Magna Graecia, Calabria, Puglia, Samnium) accompanied by a young man, Cleobulus, who was hungry for learning. It is a learned evocation of the Italian-Greek world in the form of letters interspersed with long speeches of philosophers such as Plato and Archita of Taranto (fl. fourth century B.C.) who discuss the more important moral, civil, and political themes, not omitting allusions to persons and events of the author's own time.

The Neapolitan Pietro Colletta was a contemporary of Cuoco. Filled with enthusiasm for the new ideas, he fought in defence of the Parthenopean Republic. When it fell, he was imprisoned but miraculously escaped death. King Joseph Bonaparte, and after him, King Joachim Murat, held him in great esteem and entrusted him with rather delicate military missions to quell the risings of the many rebels against the new kingdom. Later he was director of the office of bridges and roads (Highways Department, Civil Engineering) and finally Director of Military Engineers. With the restoration of the house of the Bourbons in Naples, he was exiled to Trieste and to Brünn; in time he was allowed to exchange this exile for the more agreeable one of Florence. There, after enjoying the friendship of the many great men who flocked to that city from every part of Italy, he died in 1831.

Colletta's chief work is the *Storia del Regno di Napoli,* which covered the years 1734 to 1825 in ten books. This may well be the most eloquent and magnanimous historical work in Italian literature. The fourth and fifth books, in which the story of the Parthenopean Republic and its bloody suppression is told, are the most dramatic parts of the work. The sympathies of Colletta are for the French, especially for King Joachim, who, in truth, was Italian in everything but name and who imposed daring reforms, such as the abolition of fiefs, the partition of communal lands, and wise laws in every field of the administration. But more than anything else, Colletta endeavored, with his history, to vindicate the Neapolitan people from the offensive concept of them that was still current in Italy. The work is written in a concise, picturesque, profound style, reminiscent of the manner of Tacitus.

A lesser author but one who was more widely read, Carlo Botta (d. 1837) of San Benigno Canavese in Piedmont, was a doctor of medicine, but he was born for letters. He was constantly on the side of the French, although he did not always share their ideas. Even after the fall of Napoleon, he received honors in France, such as the chancellorship of the University of Rouen. His *Storia della guerra della independenze degli Stati Uniti* [*History of the American War of Independence*] was the first of his works to make him famous (1809), inspired as it was with ideas of liberty and humanity. Later he could write, with considerable objectivity, the *Storia d'Italia,* which encompassed the years 1789 to 1814. The favorite thesis of the author is that, for Italy, the Revolution represented a disturbance and a regression. His principal historical work is the more thoughtful *Storia d'Italia continuata da quella del Guicciardini* [*History of Italy Continued from that of Guicciardini*], from 1534 to 1789. In it is great affection for Italian traditions, above all for the Venetian republic, as well as hatred of the Papacy as a temporal power; he extols every noble undertaking, even if unsuccessful. Botta is a magnificently oratorical writer. Today, however, many of his archaic forms and constructions are hard to bear, for, being the purist that he was, he was a great student of the old Italian language. His first historical work was awarded a prize by the Academy della Crusca.

Literary history also received attention at the beginning of the century but with less erudition and more spirit and philosophy than in the preceding century. Among others, Count Ferdinando Arrivabene of Mantua (d. 1834) is still read; his *Secolo di Dante* [*Century of Dante*] is one of the first attempts to interpret Dante in relation to his times. Also remembered is Francesco Salfi of Cosenza, who was a power in Milan, especially during the French occupation. Then he was director of a demagogic journal, *Il Termometro politico* [*The Political Thermometer*]. He wrote such patriotic things as blank verse on the killing of De Bassville, and a tragedy, *La Virginia bresciana* [*Virginia of Brescia*]. He was in Naples later, and after the departure of King Joachim Murat, he was exiled to France where he died in 1832. Pierre Louis Ginguené used material supplied to him by an Italian, Giralomo Tiraboschi, to write in French an agreeable history of Italian literature to the end of the sixteenth century. Salfi continued it, also in French, down through the seventeenth century, and his book even now is perhaps the richest in views on that literary century.

Romanticism

It was in Germany more than anywhere else that the battles between Classicists and Romanticists were fought; that is, the struggle between stubborn rationalism and the new philosophy of the spirit or renewed religiousness, and, in the really literary field, between the scholastic tradition and national traditions, between the stranglehold of rules and individual liberty of inspiration. There, Romanticism was clearly defined by the Schlegel brothers, Wilhelm and Friedrich. Post-Napoleonic Germany also produced illustrious poets of the new school, such as Burger, Novalis, Tieck, Werner, Lenau, Körner, Uhland (in case some do not wish to consider Schiller and Goethe Romanticists). Like the Schlegels, these writers were known directly or indirectly in Italy, where English authors of the Romantic Age were no less read, and probably more so, especially Sir Walter Scott and Lord Byron. Despite the battles waged by Madame de Staël in favor of the new school, Classicism, as though native to the soil, held out longer in France than elsewhere. A conscious, informed, and vast Romantic production began there only after 1820. A few years earlier the debate between Classicists and Romanticists was already brisk in Italy and particularly in Milan. A periodical founded in that city with a name more indicative of pacific than of polemical intentions, the *Conciliatore* (1818–1819), spread the new ideas combatted by other periodicals, principally by the *Biblioteca italiana,* and, more temperately, by the *Antologia* of Florence. The theorists of Romanticism, most of them contributors to the *Conciliatore,* were Giovanni Berchet, Silvio Pellico,

Ludovico di Breme, Pietro Borsieri, Pietro Maroncelli, Ermes Visconti, Giovanni Torti, and some lesser writers, to say nothing of Manzoni, and, in his own way, Porta too. In truth the treatment of the principles of Romanticism was much less profound in Italy than in Germany, and later, in France. It would not be difficult to demonstrate that Romantic criticism in Italy was the direct continuation of that criticism of Classicism that had begun in the late eighteenth century, although German thought had much influence upon it, as did the principles expressed by Mme. de Staël in *De l'Allemagne*. The documents or, as they would be called today, the "proclamations" of Italian Romanticism may be considered to be the *Lettera semiseria di Grisostomo sul Cacciatore feroce e sulla Eleonora di G. A. Bürger,* 1816 [*The Serio-comic Letter of Chrysostom on the Fierce Hunter and on the* Eleonora *of G. A. Bürger*] written by Berchet to a hypothetical son; *Le Avventure letterarie di un giovine,* 1816 [*Literary Adventures Of A Young Man* or, *Advice Of A Gentleman To Divers Writers*] by Pietro Borsieri; *Idee elementari sulla poesia romantica,* 1818 [*Elementary Ideas on Romantic Poetry*], by Ermes Visconti; and the four *Sermoni sulla Poesia,* 1818 by Giovanni Torti. Further on we shall touch on the critical writings of Manzoni.

Principally and practically, the reform instituted by the Italian Romanticists may be reduced to these points: to know foreign literatures together with the classics (as Staël suggested in *Biblioteca italiana*) ; to popularize literature, or at least to diffuse it through the middle classes, who are the nation – hence hatred of any academic form and tradition; to treat subjects in harmony with the effective currents of the ideas of the time, religious or political; to exclude mythology, which had played such an important role in the apparatus of classical poetry and was a facile expedient for nonpoets. It was on this last point that the struggle grew acrimonious. Monti rose to the defence of mythology in the *Sermone* mentioned above. Besides, the ideas of the Romanticists concerning the innovations to be adopted in individual artistic creations were not very clear, save those of Manzoni concerning the reform of tragedy. In general, lyricism was praised or practiced as a *sine qua non* of artistic creation. Consequently the *ballads* or *romances* (short, often epico-lyric poems) which had been so successful in Germany were also favorably hailed in Italy. The Romantic poets had a liking for the short poetic line, lively rhythms, rapid strophes, and expressions of violent emotion.

But this summary outline of the Romantic movement in Italy would be too incomplete if we failed to speak of its most attractive feature, even though it is one having little connection with aesthetics: the passionate cult of patriotism. These lovers of freedom in art were champions of their nation's liberty; many of them ended up in prison or in exile. Classicism stood for reaction; Romanticism meant Italian spirit and Italian feelings. From the ranks of the Romanticists came the most dedicated patriotic poets of the Risorgimento while the Romantic movement coincided with the whole vast and varied national political literature, which stirred up religious, philosophical, social, and historical problems that even now have not lost all their interest.

Giacomo Leopardi

His Life

Before going on to discuss particular writers of the Romantic era, we must sketch the figure of a poet who deplored Romanticism and yet did not belong in the ranks of the Classicists, and almost alone, persisted in a philosophy that the Neo-Christianity of the times had abandoned: Giacomo Leopardi.

The life of Leopardi is the story of a heroic soul imprisoned in a poor, sick body, surrounded by narrow-minded people poor in spirit. It is the story of an enthusiastic lover of life, intense life, for whom it would forever be impossible to live that life. Perpetual ill health and lack of money were his external enemies. He bore his most formidable foe within himself: the keenness of his intelligence, with which he dissipated every illusion that rose before him, and his inexhaustible imaginative faculty and exquisite sensitivity, which forced him to pursue all those illusions. He was born in 1798 in Recanati, a small city of the Marches: the "primitive native village" *natio borgo selvaggio,* which caused him much suffering, although it was there in the affection of his brother Carlo and his sister Paolina that he found the only real consolations of his life. Neither his father, Count Monaldo, a reactionary, nor his mother, a Marquise Antici, the stern administrator of a shrunken patrimony, were capable of understanding the boy. Giacomo taught himself in his father's library: he learned Latin, Greek, Hebrew, French, and English, all between the ages of ten and seventeen years. This intense application ruined his health; he himself contributed to the wasting of that youth which ever after he considered the only flower of life. In that solitude he may have made himself a man of great learning, but he felt himself to be a poet.

Giordani came to know him. He eulogized him to his fellow countrymen, and tried in vain to make him resigned to what Leopardi felt was his prisoner's fate at home in Recanati. The prisoner freed himself for the first time, after his father's refusal made him think of suicide. He then undertook a wretched series of journeys toward glory, toward life, from which unfailingly he returned to his prison, under duress of necessities and of his illnesses.

First he went to Rome, in 1822, and could have entered upon the career of prelacy, but he did not feel at home there. In Rome nothing interested him save the tomb of Tasso, bare at that time, in Sant'Onofrio; the city appeared to him to be too big for undersized men. Among famous personages there, he met Niebuhr, the historian and ambassador of the king of Prussia to the Holy See, who became enthusiastic over the philological attainments of the young man and would have liked to take him to Germany. Leopardi returned to Recanati. He went to Bologna, welcomed there by his friend Giordani, then to Milan and back again to Bologna. He did some work for the Milanese book dealer Stella, who had undertaken an edition of the Italian classics and asked Leopardi for a commentary on Petrarch and an Italian anthology.

He went to Florence in 1827, where he met Manzoni, whose *Promessi Sposi* had recently been published; the following year he found himself in Pisa, in whose mild climate he felt renewed life; but the year after he was back in Recanati once more. In Florence again, he thought that at last he was loved by a woman, Signora Fanny Targioni Tozzetti, until the illusion of love faded away, as the illusion of glory had done. In Florence he met other celebrated men: Capponi, Vieusseux, Gioberti, Niccolini, and Mamiani, who liked him and pitied him; he met Tommaseo: their detestation was mutual. Among those optimists, those believers in progress and the perfectibility and future felicity of mankind, the sceptical pessimist found himself more solitary than ever.

He felt an affinity of spirit with Colletta, the historian, and he entered into a brotherly friendship with another Neapolitan, Antonio Ranieri, who wanted him to go with him to Naples. He lived in Naples for five years, his mind growing ever more embittered, his health more than ever deteriorating. He died of dropsy of the heart in 1837, the year of the cholera epidemic. Ranieri had his mortal remains interred in the church of San Vitale, in Fuorigrotta, on the road which goes to Pozzuoli. His old and ever faithful friend Pietro Giordani composed an epitaph for the monument.

Leopardi's Poetical Work

Leopardi became a poet rather early in life, although his work did not attain its definitive form very quickly. A *cantica* on *L'Appressamento della Morte* [*The Approach of Death*] in five cantos, in tercets, composed when he was eighteen, is the first of his poems worthy of note. An angel sent by Mary announces to the youth that his death is near, and to console him, shows him the vanity and the unhappiness of what men extol most highly: love, riches, knowledge, military glory, supreme political power — all this in a series of visions in the manner of Petrarch's *Trionfi* — until at last the youth sees the joys of paradise. But he mourns the necessity of dying so very early, of renouncing glory and poetry to which he had felt that he was called, and he prays that God will help him at the supreme moment. This last part is extremely moving. There are other passages that reveal the poet, such as the telling of the loves of Ugo and Parisina. The imitation of Dante is manifest. The following year he wrote *Primo Amore,* an elegy in which, in accents of ineffable truth and sorrow, he tells of the departure of the beloved, who had not even been aware of him (a Gertrude Cassi Lazzari, his cousin). In 1818, Leopardi appeared before the public for the first time, with two *canzoni,* which at the time caused astonishment and still have the power to stir the emotions: *All'Italia* and *Sopra il monumento di Dante.*

The first is a lament on the decadence of Italy, an Italy deceived by the Napoleonic domination still living on in memory. It is also a presage that the Italians will rise up to fight for themselves. It ends with the passionate evocation of Simonides, eulogizing the Greeks fallen at Thermopylae. The second canto stresses still more the recent tyranny of France and recalls the Italian soldiers who fell during the Russian campaign. The informing theme is the exaltation of that which belongs to Italy alone: Italy's past, and the necessity, incumbent on living Italians, of once again being worthy of their dead. But patriotic poetry remains merely episodic in Leopardi's work. He withdrew very quickly into himself, listening only to the voices of his sad heart. Then the poems were born which he later published under the title of *Idilli* [*Idylls*]: *L'Infinito,* which tells in a few verses of the poet's ecstasy and ravishment in the sense of the All; *Alla luna* [*To the Moon*]; *Il Sogno* [*The Dream*], about the apparition to the poet, at dawn, of a cherished girl who had died; *La vita solitaria* [*The Life of Solitude*] of which the finest part repeats the theme of *L'Infinito; La sera del dì di festa* [*The Evening of the Feast Day*], a tragic comparison between the peace of the night and the torment of the poet, who knows he is unloved; *Il passero solitario* [*The Solitary Sparrow*]. These are stifled laments, indefinite aspirations, feelings beyond words, and expressed in a most limpid and musical language.

Thereafter the poetry of Leopardi fed on thought and expressed progressively the main points of his philosophy, of his heroic and yet pessimistic interpretation of life. The *canzone Ad Angelo Mai* to a very learned cardinal and bibliophile who, in 1820, discovered the lost books of Cicero's *De Republica* in the Vatican, is an evoking of the intensely alive age of the Renaissance which, for Leopardi, begins with Dante and ends tragically with Tasso. The poem ends with the conclusion that henceforth the world of noble illusions and generous sentiments is dead: Alfieri sought vainly to restore it, and now reason and mediocrity are triumphant. The *canzone Nelle nozze della sorella Paolina* [*On the Wedding of his Sister Pauline*] — which incidentally did not occur — is a statement of the power of love, a power which can be heroic, and an admonition to women to bring up children who can rise above the meanness of the times. Another, *A un vincitore nel pallone* [*To a Winner in the Ball Game*] eulogizes the strong life and the Hellenic games, which prepared the young for the battles for freedom. In the *Bruto minore* [*Marcus Junius Brutus the Younger*] the slayer of Caesar, who committed suicide when defeated in battle at Philippi, the poet pictures the last of the men of antiquity, the hero who discovers the vanity of virtue, who doubts the existence of the gods, who feels himself oppressed by the evil force of Destiny, yet stands in the way of that force, begs no mercy, and does away with himself, scorning the laments over his fate voiced by the survivors, scorning glory. In the words of the Roman hero Leopardi expresses his now stoical attitude. Among the various concepts one may distinguish an old one, which has new force here: man is alone in the world; Nature is unaware of him; and the ends of the Universe are unknown. In the canzone *Alla Primavera o della favole antiche* [*To Spring, or On Ancient Fables*] the same thought is expressed, this time in the form of a lament: for the ancients, the world was full of beings who consoled or guided man; now the world is terribly empty. In the *Ultimo canto di Saffo* [*Sappho's Last Song*], in which fragments are interwoven here and there from the great poetess' verse, the author does not portray only himself, sublime soul in a contemptible body, but also the moaning of the soul which is answered only by the indifference and cruelty of things. The *Inno ai Patriarchi* honors the first men who lived in the state and the illusions of Nature, before the rule of perverse Reason. In the poems of this period, the *canzone Alla sua Donna* is like a parenthesis. In it, the poet seeks to define, and leaves in its divine indefiniteness, the pure image of the ideal and heavenly *donna* that shines in his imagination and moves his heart. It is one of the most truly poetical pages, most filled with a sense of the divine, ever written by the poet of the ineffable. The lines *Al*

Conte Carlo Pepoli (1826) conclude this period; here the poet considers the substantial uselessness of all human travails and resolves to yield no more to the seduction of poetry but instead to seek the bitter truth.

Most of the *Operette morali* had been written by this time. But in poets, poetry never dies. In the mild tranquility of Pisa, Leopardi again felt lyrical intoxication and expressed his new state of being in the short, nimble Metastasian strophes, unknown to his usual grave meter, of the *Risorgimento* (1828). And, still in Pisa, and in that same year, he called back from times long past the sorrowful pure image of a girl, loved and vanished, in one of the tenderest and most evocative of his lyrics, *A Silvia.* A year later, during his last stay in Recanati, he recalled in the *Ricordanze* [*Souvenirs*] the imaginings, passions, and dreams of adolescence, and wept for Nerina who was no longer there: perhaps the same girl as Sylvia.

Now reflection and imagination were being coupled in some gnomic, or sententious, lyrics, in which the poet rises spontaneously from the appearance of things to the principles of his philosophy: *La quiete dopo la tempesta* [*Stillness after the Storm*] concludes with the maxim that joy is only the cessation of sorrow; *Il sabato del villaggio* [*The Village Saturday*] teaches that the expectation of joy is finer and more substantial than joy itself or, rather, that pleasure lies only in hope and imagination; *Sopra un bassorilievo (On a Bas-relief)* and *Sopra il ritratto di una bella donna scolpito nel monumento sepolcrale della medesima* [*On the Portrait of a Beautiful Woman Sculptured on Her Tombstone*] are considerations upon a theme frequent even in the early years of Leopardi's musings and imaginings: the sadness in the death of young beings. But *Il tramonto della Luna* [*Moonset*], composed in Naples perhaps a year before his death, is pure poetry: a lament on youth, which returns no more, and a realization of the cruelty of Nature, which leaves the desires of the young in the aged.

Before these last lyrics, Leopardi had composed the *Canto notturno di un pastore errante nell'Asia,* 1830 [*Night Song of a Wandering Shepherd in Asia*], in which the shepherd asks the lone star for an answer to the whys that never will have an answer: why life? why death? why sorrow? It is the song of the mystery of the universe. In his love for Fanny Targioni Tozzetti he had composed *Il pensiero dominante* [*The Dominant Thought*] and *Amore e Morte* [*Love and Death*], meditative lyrics which deeply probe and luminously express the melancholy and sanctifying intoxication of love; and *Consalvo,* the story of a young lover who dies happy, because in death his beloved Elvira, pitying him, kisses him — a heart-rending love poem. When he becomes aware that the love is all on his side, he writes the short admonition *A se stesso* [*To Himself*] to despair and to scorn. Also *Aspasia,* in which the poet, still wanting the woman he loved, still recalling the moments of his worship, sings — or thinks he sings — in pleasure at his release.

In the *Palinodia,* written about 1835 to Marquis Gino Capponi, the poet pretends to portray his pessimistic principles. He pretends to praise the theory of progress, but he is unfamiliar with the art and joy of jesting. For the same reason, the piece that he wrote in tercets in Naples, *I nuovi credenti* [*The New Believers*], is unsuccessful in its treatment of the many who had repudiated the negative philosophy of the preceding generation and had turned to Christianity. However, he did not publish this poem. Nor was he very felicitous in a short narrative poem in eight cantos in *ottava rima,* composed in the last years of his life and not published until 1846, *I paralipomeni della Batracomiomachia* [*Paraleipomena of the Batrachomyomachy* (futile, ridiculous controversy)]. Here Leopardi, pretending that he is continuing the poem attributed to Homer on the war between the Frogs and the Rats (which he had translated several times), seizes the opportunity to express the dogmas of his sensistic philosophy and allegorizes the unsuccessful Neapolitan insurrection of 1820 to obtain the constitution: in the rats he depicts the liberals; in the frogs, the conservatives; and in the crabs coming to the aid of the frogs, the Austrians. The author divides his derision among all three, with perhaps a little more for the rats than for the others. His pessimism did not allow him to have any serious interest in the fight for the Risorgimento.

His vision of life was becoming more and more tragic; he expressed it in the last and longest of his cantos, *La ginestra o il fiore del deserto* [*The Broom Plant, or the Flower of the Desert*], published posthumously and perhaps never finished. It is a contemplation of Vesuvius the Destroyer, of the starry sky, of the nothingness of man with respect to the forces of Nature, of the infinity of the worlds. It is a teaching to men of love through consciousness of their common misfortune. It is a bitter invective against the "proud and foolish" century and a statement of the philosophic credo of Illuminism, which by then was almost completely abandoned, but which the author still considered the only credo for a man seeking truth. It had the value of a gospel for him, wherefore the poem quotes a verse of the third chapter of the Gospel of Saint John: ". . . and men loved darkness, rather than light."

Such is a summary account of the Leopardian lyric poetry. It is remarkable for its inwardness and passion, for its never labored but spontaneous originality — which is characteristic of truly poetical individualities — for its admirably clear and precise expression, at least in his mature works, an expression able to awaken the most shadowy evocations.

Operette Morali

In the *Operette morali,* most of which were written in 1824, in the period when he thought he would write no more poetry, Leopardi translated the sentiments expressed in his poems into concepts or, rather, into poetical images.

Many of them are dialogues; others are fiction of one kind or another, somewhat akin to the usage of the Greek, Lucian, or of French philosophical literature of the eighteenth century, especially that of Voltaire. According to one interpretation, interesting but perhaps too systematic, the *Operette* constitute a whole and have significance and importance within that whole. They express the progress of the negative thought of Leopardi, also that which is vital in that negativeness.

They are divided into three groups of six *Operette* each. The first group contains the dialogues *Di Ercole e di Atlante* [*Hercules and Atlas*] and *Della Moda e della Morte* [*On Fashion and Death*]; the fantasy *Proposta di premi fatta dall'Academia dei Sillografi* [*Proposal of Awards Made by the Academy of Syllographers*]; the dialogues *Di un lettore di umanità e di Sallustio* [*On a Reader of Humanities and of Sallust*], *Di un Folletto e di uno Gnomo* [*About an Elf and a Gnome*], and *Di Malambruno e di Farfarello* [*Concerning M. and F.*]. These first *Operette* are concerned mostly with the emptiness and mechanicalness of modern life, of civilized life, deprived of any heartfelt illusion and stripped of all value. The second group contains the dialogues *Della Nature e di un'Anima* [*On Nature and a Soul*]; *Della Terra e della Luna* [*Concerning the Earth and the Moon*]; *Di un Fisico e di un Metafisico* [*On a Physicist and a Metaphysician*]; *Di Torquato Tasso e del suo Genio famigliare, Della Natura e di un Islandese* [*About Torquato Tasso and his Family Genius, Nature and an Icelander*]; and the fantasy *La Scomessa di Prometeo* [*Prometheus' Wager*]. These *Operette* go more deeply into Leopardi's philosophy. In them he derides the concept that man is the ruler of the world. He teaches that Nature fulfills her mysterious laws of death and reproduction without any concern for mankind, that the least unhappy life is the life most filled with sensations, the life richest in imagination. Tedium, that is to say pure consciousness of life, without content and without purpose, is more serious than any sorrow.

The *Operette* of the third group have as their goal teaching what happiness is possible and reasonable for mankind. It consists of the renunciation of glory, regarding the substance of human affairs with calm and tranquility, not fearing death which is extinction and not pain or sorrow, risking or attempting dangers in order to lull our boredom and tedium, and losing ourselves in the life of the physical world. The writings of this group are: the discourse *Il Parini, ovvero della gloria* [*Parini, or, On Glory*]; the dialogue *Di Federico Ruysch e delle sue mummie* [*On Federico Ruysch and his Mummies*]; the *Detti memorabili di Filippo Ottonieri* [*Memorable Sayings of Filippo Ottonieri*] — Ottonieri is none other than Leopardi; the dialogue *Di Cristoforo Colombo e di Pietro Gutierrez;* the *Elogio degli uccelli* [*Eulogy of the Birds*] filled with ardent lyrical joy; *Cantico del gallo silvestre* [*Canticle of the Wild Cock*], a tragic elegy.

La Storia del genere umano [*The History of the Human Race*], which opens the *Operette,* and the dialogue *Di Timandro e di Eleandro,* which closes it, correct whatever is despairing in the Leopardian philosophy, appealing no longer to reason but to effective reality and to sentiment, which for Leopardi weighs far more heavily than reason. In the body of the *Operette,* life is *seen*; in these two, life is *lived. La Storia del genere umano* ends with a eulogy to love: love is a phantasma, but it is enough to give the fullness and beauty of life to the elect, the chosen souls; the others do not feel sorrow. The dialogue *Di Timandro e di Eleandro* is inspired by the very human virtue of pity.

In the later *Operette, Copernico* (1827), the dialogues *Di Plotino e di Porfirio* [*On Plotinus and Porphyry*], *Di un venditore di almanacchi e di un passeggere* [*About a Seller of Almanacs and a Passerby*], *Di Tristan e di un amic* [*On Tristan and a Friend*], all belonging to the year

1832, the main points of the preceding *Operette* reappear and are examined more deeply. Thus *Copernico,* a very spirited piece, is aimed against the vainglory of man who considered himself king of the world and the earth the center of the universe; the dialogue of Plotinus and Porphyry is the justification of suicide in the light of reason, and its condemnation according to human sentiment. The pseudo-fragment of *Stratone di Lampsaco* is included with the *Operette*; it is a strange fantasy of the author concerning the eternity of matter and the way the world will end.

In Leopardi's estimation, the *Operette morali* must have ranked as equal to or better than the *Canti*: in reality they form the best commentary on the poems and, to a degree they are also poetry, although the imagination and emotion are purposely restrained in a prose that may seem cold and academic but is in reality a marvel of precision and strength.

Other Writings of Leopardi

Leopardi wrote a series of one hundred and eleven *Pensieri* [*Thoughts*] which, for the most part, are the essence of his bitter experience of men. A philologist from his earliest youth, and admired as such, while still very young he composed a *Saggio sugli errori popolari degli antichi* [*Essay on the Popular Errors of the Ancients*] and many writings on classical authors, such as the discourse *Della fama avuta da Orazio presso gli antichi* [*The Success of Horace Among the Ancients*] and another, *Sopra Mosco* [*On Moschus*]. He was very interested in the writers of the Greek and Latin decline. He did many translations: such things as the *Batracomiomachia* of the pseudo-Homer, mentioned above, the *Titanomachia* of Hesiod, the second book of the *Aeneid* and the first of the *Odyssey,* and in his mature years and with the intent of helping his readers morally, the manual of Epictetus, the Stoic philosopher of apathy and courage. When just a boy he pretended that he had found *Due odi di Anacreonte* [*Two Odes of Anacreon*] in the Greek text, and *Inno a Nettuno* [*Hymn to Neptune*] of which he gave only the Italian version: learned men believed him. Later on he reproduced the style of the fourteenth century so well in the *Martirio dei Santi padri del monte Sinai* [*Martyrdom of the Holy Fathers of Mount Sinai*] that his "version" was thought to have originated in that century. Leopardi left a quantity of letters which are of more interest for understanding his life and his mind than the time in which he lived. In 1898, the year of the centenary of his birth, there was published from manuscripts preserved in Naples, the vast collection of notes, thoughts and reflections of every kind which he brought together in what he called *Zibaldone dei miei pensieri* [*Miscellany of my Thoughts*] and which his editors called *Pensieri di varia letteratura e filosofia.* Their pith and essence, however, were already contained in the *Canti* and the *Operette morali.*

Alessandro Manzoni

His Life

Considered outwardly, Manzoni's life is one of the least agitated and least romantic of lives. He was born in Milan in 1785 to Giulia Beccaria, the daughter of Cesare Beccaria, and it must be supposed that something of the interest in and worship of justice, which made Cesare Beccaria such a noble figure, was transmitted to his grandson, and also a great deal of his indolent character. Alessandro's father, Pietro, was on bad terms with Giulia, who was for a long time the object of the admiration and friendship of Carlo Imbonati, whom Alessandro regarded with the affection and the reverence due to a father. After time spent in religious schools, he went to Paris, for his worldly education, in accordance with the custom of nobles. His mother was awaiting him there. Manzoni remained in Paris for five years, during which time he became well acquainted with the sceptical and humanitarian philosophy of the eighteenth century, which was still dominant there and which left indelible traces in his thought. Among the famous salons which he frequented was that of M. and Mme. Cabanis (Pierre Jean Georges Cabanis carried sensism to its ultimate consequences in his *Traité des Rapports du physique et du moral de l'homme*). He knew another sensist philosopher, Count Antoine Louis Claude Destutt de Tracy. But he formed an intimate friendship with Claude Fauriel, a historiographer of the Middle Ages, and very prominent among scholars of the language and literature of that period. In Paris he received the visit of Foscolo, who before long was to honor him with a note in *I sepolcri*.

In 1808 he married Henriette Blondel, the daughter of a Geneva banker, and a Protestant. In order to enter a Catholic family Henriette adopted the Catholic religion, and Alessandro, an indifferent Catholic, returned to his bride's new religion, stimulated thereto by the conversation of such churchmen as Degola and Tosi, and by his reading of the great French apologists of Catholicism: Pascal, Massillon, Bossuet. His conversion remained the capital fact of the inner and artistic life of Manzoni. For him, religion was a stern moral law, far more than a mere observance of rites (from which it is possible to deduce that there flowed into his religiosity some of those currents of purer Chistianity called Jansenism). In 1810 Manzoni took up residence in Milan, but he spent more time in his villa of Brusuglio than in the city.

From approximately 1815 to 1830, he wrote his most important works. After the first edition in 1827 of *I Promessi Sposi* [*The Betrothed*] he went to Florence to improve his knowledge of the Tuscan tongue, and he returned there several times thereafter. After the second edition of the novel (1840), Manzoni lived only for himself, his studies, and his religion. His first wife having died in 1833, in 1837 he married Teresa Borri, Stampa's widow. Rosmini was the great friend and guide of his last years. Victor Emanuel II made him president of the Lombard Institute and granted him a considerable pension; the economic affairs of the writer had been deteriorating. In 1860 he was elected senator, and he went to Turin to vote in favor of proclaiming Rome the capital of Italy, notwithstanding the opposition of close friends and of his son-in-law Massimo d'Azeglio. A year before his death (1873), he was made an honorary citizen of Rome.

For many years Manzoni was in ill health and suffered from nervous disorders. His was a contemplative rather than an active spirit, shy of crowds, shy of honors. Although his love for the cause of Italy was keen and he considered it the cause of justice, he took little part in the political troubles. He loved the countryside and took a great interest in agriculture. He was a man of strong passions, but he had the strength to hold them in and curb them. He was a man of deep, sure culture and vast erudition; he knew English literature well, French even better. He always looked back nostalgically on his years in Paris.

Youthful Poetical Writings

Manzoni was not a prolific writer, but he was a precocious one. At fifteen he composed a little poem in tercets in four cantos, following in the steps of Monti whom he always admired: *Il trionfo della libertà,* filled with the equalitarian ideas of the time. In 1803 he wrote an idyll, *Adda,* rich in mythological imaginings, in which the river Adda invites Monti to come enjoy her most secret depths. More significant is the canzone in blank verse, like the preceding, *In morte di Carlo Imbonati* [*On the Death of Carlo Imbonati*], dedicated to his mother Giulia (1806). Here we have the spirituality of Parini and Alfieri. In a dream, the revered spirit of Carlo Imbonati appears to the young man, deplores the vanity and falseness of the life of the noble classes, and exhorts him to persevere on the austere path of life on which he has set out. And when the youth asks him how to become an original poet, he answers with counsels that aim at forming the moral man first, to preserve the dignity of the mind and to respect truth.

The following year, on the occasion of Fauriel's translation into French prose of the idyllic poem *Parthénaïs* by the Dane, Baggesen, Manzoni composed the rather obscure *A Parteneide* in blank verse, in which there is glorification of a very pure feminine image. He was inspired to write *Urania* (1809) by a desire to extol the good that poetry confers on mortals by inspiring them with the most humane virtues, and to affirm that without the Graces, that is, without art, poetical inspiration is insufficient. The poem is named after one of the muses; its theme is a poetical contest in which Pindar, who has not yet sacrificed to the Graces, is outdone by Corinna, who has their help. It is an exquisite thing in the classical style. In 1814 Manzoni composed a *canzone* of joy over the fall of the French regime and of hopes placed on the provisional government; hopes which were later frustrated by the Congress of Paris. On the appearance of the *Lettera semiseria di Grisostomo* [*Semi-serious Letter of Chrysostom*] in 1816, he took the side of the Romanticists with a humorous *canzone, L'ira di Apollo* [*The Wrath of Apollo*]. Neither of these two compositions are characteristic of him. Besides, Manzoni excluded all of the poems mentioned so far from the edition of his works that he prepared, and probably he did so not for artistic reasons alone.

After the Conversion

For Manzoni, his return to the faith marked a new literary program and initiated his fairly short but intense literary activity; not that his heart was heedless of the great events occurring in his country and in the world. After the return of Italy to the domination of Austria and the Bourbons (when the former king of Naples Joachim Murat planned to found a Kingdom of Italy and in March of 1815 issued a proclamation from Rimini in which he called the Italian peoples to independence), Manzoni wrote a *canzone* in the Petrarchian manner, which he left half done, much as the enterprise was left half done and then ended badly. When in 1821 the Piedmontese revolution aimed at the conquest of Lombardy by means of war against Austria and it was expected that the Piedmontese forces would cross the Ticino, Manzoni composed the noble ode *Marzo 1821,* which is a song of faith in the union and the resurgence of Italy. But the unhappy outcome of that undertaking did not allow the publication of the chant; later on, after the "Five Days" of Milan in 1848, he added the last two strophes. On May 5, 1821, Napoleon died at Saint Helena, and Manzoni, who had followed the many vicissitudes of the Corsican with passionate interest, erupted in the ode *Il cinque maggio* [*The Fifth of May*], a superb commemoration of the greatness and tragedy of the Man of Destiny raised up by God and before whose tremendous work the judgment of mortals wavers uncertainly.

In all these lyrics religious feeling is predominant, but it finds its fullest expression in the *Inni sacri* [*Sacred Hymns*], composed between 1812 and 1822. There are five of them: *La Resurrezione, Il nome di Maria, Il Natale, La Passione, La Pentecoste.* There were to have been twelve, one for each great solemnity of the Church. In lines and strophes full of agitation, with a forcefulness sometimes reminiscent of the Bible but with a completely classical severity of form and solidity of construction, the poet does not so much celebrate the Church rite or the sacred story, but rather extols their human meaning. *La Passione* is tragic, *La Resurrezione,* full of emotion, while *Il nome di Maria* is delicate. *Il Natale* is too weak. *La Pentecoste* is superb: it is one of the most superb things in Italian poetry, especially in its second part. It is the prayer of a disappointed and weary humanity which again has need of faith.

The Tragedies

The principal poetical works to which Manzoni dedicated himself in the first years following his return to Catholicism were his tragedies. The first, *Il Conte di Carmagnola,* published in 1820, is dedicated to Fauriel. In the Preface, the author, on the authority especially of Wilhelm von Schlegel, defends drama lacking both the unities of time and place, of which *Carmagnola* is an example. He shows that the illusion of reality does not suffer any loss without those unities, and that the unities are purely arbitrary. He also provides reasons for the introduction of the chorus into the tragedy in which the voice of the author himself is heard expressing the moral of the drama. The five-act tragedy is written in noble yet restrained poetical language. The hero is Bussone, Count of Carmagnola, a famous captain, a soldier of fortune or *condottiere* of the early fifteenth century who served first in the pay of Filippo Maria Visconti, Duke of Milan and was the builder of his power. When he was offended by the Duke, he offered his services to the Venetian Republic, inflicting serious losses on the Milanese in a long war. Maclodio was the chief battle of that war. But the captain showed an overwhelming generosity towards the conquered, who after all were his former comrades-in-arms. Because of his temporizing after the victory and some unfortunate actions of his officers, Carmagnola was suspected of treachery to the Republic; he was recalled on the pretext of asking his advice and decapitated. The action of Manzoni's tragedy fills the years between the appointment of Carmagnola as commander of the Venetian army down to his execution (1426–1432). His is the dominant character in the play; the author (from the historical notes which follow the Preface) believes him to be innocent and the victim only of his pride and imprudence in the face of the jealous and cunning authority of the Venetian government.* He makes a simple and powerful figure, who sometimes recalls Goethe's Count of Egmont, or Schiller's Wallenstein. There are many scenes rich in psychological movement and dramatic contrasts: for example, the argument among the soldiers of fortune of the Milanese army, in camp near Maclodio, the defence of the count in his appearance before the somber Venetian senate, and the final farewell to his wife and daughter. The drama is lacking in plot, love episodes, and all those means, or expedients, which make up the success of a theatrical piece. The classical critics revolted. Manzoni wrote a long letter in French to one of them, Chauvet, which is a masterpiece of acute criticism. In it he touches upon the ultimate reasons of poetry which, for the author, can be nothing but the development and the probing of truth, just as it is given by fate and by reality. The chorus of the second act won great popularity, as did the battle of Maclodio, which reveals the generous intent of the drama, and the censure and regret for the wars between Italians and Italians. Such sentiments were very opportune in the first decades of the nineteenth century when to Manzoni, as to Foscolo and Mazzini also, the municipal and regional spirit appeared to be the greatest obstacle to the liberation and the resurrection of the fatherland.

Adelchi was no more successful. It was published in 1822 and dedicated to his adored wife. The action arises from the defeat of the Lombards by the Franks and embraces and occupies the space of about two years (772–774). It treats the repudiation by Charlemagne of his wife Ermengarda, a daughter of Desiderius; the war between the Frankish king and the Lombard king with his son Adelchi (Adalgis), heir to the throne; the treachery of the

* Studies on Francesco Bussone, Count of Carmagnola, have instead shown, almost completely that he was a "traitor." Cf. N. Zingarelli *L'Ottocento* Vallardi: Milano, 1949), p. 275.

Lombard dukes; the arrival in Charlemagne's camp of Martino from Ravenna, who comes to show him a way across the Alps which he had despaired of crossing; the rout of the Lombard army at Le Chiuse; the death of Ermengarda in the monastery of San Salvatore in Brescia; the fall of Pavia and surrender of Verona through the treason of Guntigi, another Lombard chief; the entry of Charlemagne into this city; the imprisonment of Desiderius; and the heroic and Christian death, in his presence, of his son Adelchi. These are the highlights of the vast tale, which again, except for the death of Adelchi, follows the sequence of historical events. Desiderius is violent, Charles astute; Adelchi is noble to the highest degree; in him the poet concentrated all his own Christian humanitarianism. Adelchi is fighting for a cause that he knows is hopeless; he is a hero come before his time, like Schiller's Don Carlos, and therein lies all the pathos that he diffuses around him. Ermengarda is ardent in her true but scorned love. She worships that Charles who has sent her back to her father, and even in the cloister she cannot silence her love. She dies of bitterness when she learns that Charles is taking another woman with him. The scene of her death throes in the fourth act provides some of the most pure and moving pages of Italian literature. There are also minor characters of great interest, like the traitor Svarto; pages of a new poetry, like the deacon Martino's narration of his miraculous journey across the Alps, all filled with the mysterious feeling of the high mountains. The two choruses of this tragedy are Manzoni's perfect lyrics. One of them closes the third act with passages of unique epic power. It tells of the invasion of the Franks and the hopes of the Italian peoples to regain their liberty through these foreigners, but the poet warns them to understand and to despair. This chorus brings the drama into the political currents of the time. One might call this the reflection into the past of an event all too present in the consciousness of contemporaries. Another Frank had crossed the mountains and promised liberty, and the people of Italy had been more enslaved than before; now they must act on their own behalf and have hope only in themselves. The second chorus, for the death of Ermengarda, is the lament for that unhappy victim of her own hidden and unbridled passion, and her offering made to God as an expiation for the many sins of her ancestors, the oppressors. Manzoni's religious lyricism here reaches its supreme heights.

I Promessi Sposi [*The Betrothed*]

Manzoni's masterpiece was begun in 1821 and finished in 1823; it appeared for the first time in 1827. In that same year, the author made a journey to Tuscany in order to master the living Tuscan language, which he considered the Italian speech par excellence. Then he set about the linguistic revision of the *Promessi Sposi,* in whose first edition there were many unseemly and dialectal expressions. The corrected work, in its definitive form, appeared quite late, between 1840 and 1842. Of late years there has been some republishing of the primitive version of the *Promessi Sposi* (or *Sposi Promessi*), which is quite different, even in the story, from the novel as we now have it. Among the more important divergences are those concerning the nun of Monza and the death of Don Rodrigo. The comparison between the two versions is informative in showing how the more refined and aesthetic critical sense of the author suppressed in the definitive edition whatever was not necessary to the action of the story, and aimed at effectiveness rather than artistic verity.

I Promessi Sposi bears the subtitle *Storia milanese del secolo XVII scoperta e rifatta da A. Manzoni* [*Milanese Story of the Seventeenth Century Discovered and Revised by A. Manzoni*]. In order to create an illusion of reality in his narrative (such expedients were much used by novelists of the time), he alleges having found his story in an anonymous manuscript of the seventeenth century couched in the pompous and unbearable style of that age (of which a hypothetical sample is given at the beginning of the Preface) and having rewritten the interesting narrative in the style now in current use.

In the years from 1628 to 1630, in a Lombardy subjected to the rash and hypocritical Spanish government, the novel finds the materials for its narration. Renzo (Lorenzo), a silk spinner, and Lucia are the two young commoners from a town on the shore of Lake Como (the anonymous author was so very cautious and prudent that Manzoni finds very few place names!). Although already betrothed, they cannot become man and wife because of the perverse obstinacy of a country squire, Don Rodrigo, and the culpable weakness of Don Abbondio, the curate. A saintly friar, Father Cristoforo, has undertaken to protect the young pair, but in vain. They are forced to flee from their little town. Lucia finds hospitality in a convent in Monza, where she is entrusted to the care of Mother Gertrude, a power in the convent and outside as well. Carrying a letter from Father Cristoforo, Renzo travels to Milan, where another ecclesiastic is expected to find him an occupation. Don Rodrigo does not give up, however: with the help of a ruffian, whose name is not revealed by the anonymous writer (and who therefore is called *L'Innominato* [The Unnamed], he succeeds in abducting Lucia from her asylum. In the castle of L'Innominato, the innocent girl awakens the pity and remorse of the lord, who is more fierce than evil. Pushed by an obscure remorse to pay a visit to the Cardinal Federico Borromeo, who was that day making a pastoral visit in the village near the castle, L'Innominato is converted to a life of piety and virtue. The Cardinal places Lucia in the home of a lady in Milan, where she is safe from any aggression. Don Rodrigo is the laughing stock of his associates, and the best he can do is to see that Father Cristoforo has to leave his monastery. Meanwhile Renzo has passed, and is still passing, through a number of misfortunes. He had reached Milan on an unlucky day when the people were attacking the bakers' shops because of lack of bread. He is involved in the attempt to assault the house of the deputy in charge of provisions, the man whom the people claimed kept the price of bread high against the wishes of the Great Chancellor. He helps the carriage of that same Chancellor who had come to save the deputy. He becomes a hothead and talks in public about justice and, in a public house, refuses to give name and surname to the host, as required by law. He is arrested, but escapes from the law officers and, after a difficult journey, he crosses the river Adda to a town in the province of Bergamo where he has a cousin. Bergamo was a Venetian territory, and there Renzo was safe from the Spanish authorities. A suit is instituted against him in which he is accused of nothing less than the crime of *lèse majesté* and of little less than plotting against Spain in favor of France, or little less. So the young people are more than ever separated, and with little or no hope of ever again coming together. But man proposes and God disposes: war breaks out in Lombardy for the succession of Casale, a territory claimed by the French, the Emperor, and the Duke of Savoy. Then the Lansquenets invade Italy and spread ruin and terror everywhere. As a probable result of that invasion, a pestilence breaks out. The plague devastates Milan and all Lombardy; it abolishes all laws and lawsuits. Renzo, who has survived it and is immune, can enter Milan in search of Lucia. Finally, he finds her in the lazaretto and convalescent. In the lazaretto he comes upon Father Cristoforo who will die there by the charity of Christ and in the lazaretto Renzo sees Don Rodrigo dying on a cot. However, during the night she had spent in the castle of L'Innominato, Lucia had vowed to renounce marrying Renzo if the Virgin would return her to her mother. This is the last serious difficulty, but Father Cristoforo absolves the girl from her promise. When the plague is over, and when Don Abbondio is sure that Don Rodrigo is quite dead, the two young people are finally married and settle down in the little town in the province of Bergamo where Renzo had found a second homeland and a better living.

The Art and Spirit of *I Promessi Sposi*

The novel belongs to the historical genre which was then, and later, in great favor. Its great events are historical: the lack of food, the war, the plague. Some of the characters are historic; that is, they really existed, such as Cardinal Borromeo, the Grand Chancellor Ferrer, L'Innominato (a certain Bernardino Visconti), the Nun or Lady of Monza (Virginia de Leyva). The story develops in a most natural way, without any complication or far-fetched expedient. During the writing of the novel, the author wrote to Fauriel that he wanted to keep anything with a flavor of *esprit romanesque* out of the work, and in truth the sense of reality is at all times present in the work. Indeed, sometimes reality changes into historicism; Manzoni was accused of having given too much space to historical investigation and documentation, as where he talks about the origin of the pestilence. But even there he was applying the fundamental canon of his art: to seek and respect the truth. Truth is especially to be found in the portrayal of the characters: they are all alive with a life of their own, and there are so many, with their own unforgettable physiognomy. Perhaps Don Abbondio is the most successful portrait. On the other hand, the figure of the protagonist, Renzo, was not very well individualized. An extreme spontaneity is one of the outstanding merits of the language of the *Promessi Sposi*. It marks the end of the pompous or academic language that was still the general rule. Here, at last, is the meeting, the coincidence, of the written and spoken language, and if sometimes that style might seem a little too modest and analytic, it nevertheless continued to be the typical style of Italian prose.

As for its intrinsic significance, the story is prevailingly inspired by a lofty and consoling religious idea: God is the hidden actor in the story of human beings and even the scourges sent by Him have their reason for existence in a superior moral order. To accept the divine will, even when it seems to take the form of the violence of man, is perhaps the ultimate teaching of Manzoni. The *Promessi Sposi,* therefore, seemed to some a book less than suitable in a time of struggles for the reconstitution of the fatherland, a time when resignation might not seem the virtue most required. But it is well to observe that the pure, austere religiousness of Manzoni is itself a high law of justice and a standard of heroic life. Like the purest Christians, from Dante to Pascal, he demands religiousness that is opposition to evil and not that which compromises with all troubles and iniquities. Therefore, next to Father Cristoforo and Federico Borromeo, he placed Don Abbondio, the monastery of Monza, the provincial father, and the ecclesiastics in name only. He never, in the serenity of his descriptive art, conceals the emotion of his conscience wounded by the unworthy ministers of the Gospel. One thing is sure, Manzoni is an authentic Christian. With a deep and pessimistic vision he analyzes what are, or seem to be, the greatest of human values: justice, learning, wisdom, and the art of administering and governing – they are all vanities, or iniquities. Man's only reality is sorrow and error.

In Manzoni, it is never the sentimental note that is powerful, but rather the humane (which dominates in the description of the plague, of which some of the episodes bring a sob to the throat). At the same time, the satirical and humoristic vein is copious. Just recall the figure of Doctor Azzeca-garbugli (i.e., Dr. Pettifogger), that of "my uncle the Count," of Don Ferrante, of Donna Prassede, and the scene of the feast in Don Rodrigo's house and that of Renzo's arrest. In the Christian Manzoni, there remained no small amount of the spirit of the ironic writers of illuminism who were his teachers when he was young. But scepticism in him became goodness and humanity. *I Promessi Sposi* is one of the most cheering and consoling of books to be found in modern literature. Except for a few academicians, its contemporaries welcomed the novel with exceptional warmth, and today's readers esteem it still more highly than its contemporaries.

Historical and Critical Writings

Besides having the soul of a poet, Manzoni had the temperament of a thinker, and he sometimes busied himself with historical, religious, literary, or aesthetic questions. The Genevan historian, Sismondi, in Chapter CXXVII of his *History of the Italian Republics,* had attributed the corruption of Italy to the Catholic Church. Manzoni replied with the *Morale Cattolica,* upholding the thesis that the happiness of the inhabitants would be in the carrying out of the law of the Gospels as the Fathers and the preachers have constantly interpreted it. His researches into the age of the Lombards, for information useful in writing *Adelchi,* inspired Manzoni to compose a very learned *Discorso sopra alcuni punti della storia longobardica in Italia* [*Some Points of Lombard History in Italy*] in which he demonstrates, contrary to many historians, that the Lombards were not aiming at unifying Italy, but, indeed, at the total extinction of the Latin name. The *Storia della colonna infame* [*Story of the Infamous Column*], published as an appendix to the 1842 edition of *I Promessi Sposi,* is a rehabilitation of some unfortunates condemned to death in the seventeenth century as propagators of the plague. The house of one of them was torn down and a column erected there so that the fate of the supposed criminal might deter others; it is more a juridical than a historical work. The *Parallelo tra la rivoluzione francese del 1789 e la rivoluzione italiana del 1859* was published posthumously and is of little worth.

Various other writings of Manzoni are tied to the Romanticist reform, such as the already mentioned Preface to *Carmagnola* and the letter to Chauvet. In 1823, in a letter to Cesare d'Azeglio, Manzoni actuated especially by religious reasons came out against the old classical expedient of mythology and formulated the principle that literature must choose the useful as its purpose, the true as its subject, and the interesting as its means. Concerning, or rather, in opposition to the mixed genres combining history and poetry, in 1845 he wrote the discourse *Del romanzo storico* [*The Historical Novel*]. His worship of the true, of reality, would not let him tolerate the alteration that the poetical work naturally effects in the historical. His dialogue in 1850, *Dell'invenzione,* inspired by Rosminian and Platonic ideas, is a piece of research on the origin of the idea of the beautiful.

Like Monti, Manzoni gave much attention to the problem of the language. However, in contrast to Monti, who drew on writers, Manzoni thought that the Italian language should follow the usages of the language as spoken by the educated Florentine classes. Thus those Tuscan idioms which so delighted certain Manzonians came to be excluded from the vocabulary. He left several writings on the language question, of which the most important are a close study of Dante's *De Vulgari Eloquentia,* which upholds, or seems to uphold, a thesis contrary to that of Manzoni; and a *Relazione al ministro Broglio sull'unità della lingua e sui mezzi per diffonderla.* [*Report to Minister Broglio on the Unity of the Language and Means to Spread It*].

Novelists

Innumerable novelists, representing the most diverse trends, flourished around the author of *I Promessi Sposi;* mostly, however, they favored the historical novel. Such a one was Giambattista Bazzoni of Novara, author of the *Castello di Trezzo,* a novel filled with fearful ghostly evocations, and *Falco della Rupe* [*Hawk of the Cliff*], whose protagonist, Gian Giacomo dei Medici, somewhat resembles L'Innominato. Another is Achille Mauri, who closely follows Manzoni in his *Caterina di Broni,* a story of the sufferings of an innocent foundling. There are also Lorenzo Ercoliani, whose *I Valvassori Bresciani* [*The Brescian Vavassors*] was considered very interesting for its well-developed plot and its dramatic themes; Carlo Varese, whom some called "the Italian Walter Scott," author of *Sibilla Odaleta;* and Giuseppe Torell, the bitter and sceptical author of *Ruperto d'Isola.* The Pisan Giovanni Rosini, a literary soul, in *La Monaca di Monza* continued and amplified with great sufficiency the famous episode of *I Promessi Sposi.* Nor were sentimental novelists lacking. *Angiola Maria* by the Milanese Giulio Carcano enjoyed high repute. This author contributed more to Italian letters, however, with his translations of the principal tragedies of Shakespeare, although his translations are not among the most faithful. In the sentimental category also belongs Niccolò Tommaseo's *Fede e Bellezza* [*Faith and Beauty*] a novel combining the sensual element with the mystical. In reality the most-read novelists of Manzoni's age were Grossi, D'Azeglio, and Guerrazzi.

Tommaso Grossi (d. 1853), of Bellano, by profession a notary, a great friend of Porta and of Manzoni, began by writing poems in the Milanese dialect. *La Prineide,* in Milanese, which evoked the grave crime of the Austrian-inclined patrician class, the killing of Prina the last minister of the Italic Kingdom, was composed for a visit which Emperor Francesco I was to make to Milan in 1816. It caused the author some unpleasantnesses, which dissuaded him from trying any more satirical poetry. In the vernacular, he also wrote the moving sestinas on the death of Porta and the ultrasentimental and ultraromantic novella in *ottava rima La Fuggitiva* (translated later from the Milanese into Italian) . He is the author of a story of unhappy loves, *Ildegonda,* which was preparatory to the poem in fifteen cantos *I Lombardi alla prima Crociata* [*The Lombards in the First Crusade*], 1826. The latter was a work of much pretension, it tried to be more historical, more religious, and closer to reality than the *Gerusalemme Liberata.* In reality it is a vast sentimental novel with heroical accessories. The historical novel *Marco Visconti,* published in 1834, is more successful; its action takes place in Lombardy in the fourteenth century. It has many moving episodes, depicts a marvelous and fanciful world and contains several lyrics which have remained quite popular. It is made up of the same material as the novellas in verse form, to which Grossi returned with his *Ulrico e Lida.*

Massimo d'Azeglio (d. 1866), of Turin, played no small part in the movements for the Italian Risorgimento. He fought in 1848 and was presiding officer of the Council of Ministers in 1849. He gives an account of his life in a virile book, *I miei ricordi* [*My Recollections*]. After politics, his great enthusiasms were painting, especially landscapes, and literature. He wrote a very popular historical novel, *Ettore Fieramosca o La Sfida di Barletta* [*Hector Fieramosca, or, The Challenge of Barletta*] in 1833. As a basis he used a challenge sent by thirteen Italian knights at Barletta to a like number of French knights in the early sixteen century, (wth victory favoring the Italian side). In this he interwove the story of a protagonist who was an unhappy lover that committed suicide and included famous people of the times, among them Duke Valentino. The Manzonian influence is evident. His other novel, *Niccolò dei Lapi o i Palleschi e i Piagnoni* [*Niccolò dei Lapi, or, The Palleschis and the Piagnonis*] was less successful.

But the novelist who really set his public aflame was Francesco Domenico Guerrazzi (d. 1873) of Leghorn. He was an ardent patriot who suffered imprisonment and exile. On the flight of the grand duke in 1848, he became dictator of Tuscany. When the former government was restored, he was exiled to Corsica, but after 1860 he was active in public life, combating the conservative party. He was a very prolific writer. His principal novels are: *L'Assedio di Firenze* [*The Siege of Florence*], *La Battaglia di Benevento, Beatrice Cenci,* and *Pasquale Paoli.* A master of language, he was capable of pages of great virtuosity as were few others; yet he remained a man of letters and rhetorical declaimer. His constant attitude is one of strain and exertion, and the characteristic of his writing is riotous prolixity. He enjoyed describing striking scenes, dreadful and monstrous actions, and his interpretation of life was a pessimistic one. He was a great admirer of Byron, and this is present in his novels, as Lesage and Sterne are present in his satirical or humorous writings, such as *L'Asino* [*The Donkey*], *Il Buco nel muro* [*The Hole in the Wall*], and, praised above the others, *La Serpicina* [*Little Snake*].

Other Writers and Poets

After Manzoni, perhaps the most popular writer of the time was Silvio Pellico. Born at Saluzzo in 1789, he spent his early years in France; but the reading of *I Sepolcri* aroused his enthusiasm for Italian poetry and for Italy. Thereupon he settled in Milan, serving as preceptor in aristocratic families, becoming a close friend of Foscolo. In Milan he wrote the tragedy *Francesca da Rimini* (1815); the drama, modeled on Alfieri, enjoyed an immense success. The romantic delicacy of the love story of the two protagonists, and some apostrophes to Italy were attuned to the tastes of the new times. Pellico was soon numbered in the ranks of the Romanticists. We have already mentioned his collaboration with Ludovico di Breme and Pietro Borsieri on the *Conciliatore,* in which he specialized in foreign poetry and more particularly the theater, spreading those opinions on dramatic reforms which Manzoni later was to apply to his tragedies. On the urging of Pietro Maroncelli, he became a member of the *Carboneria* (the clandestine patriotic *Carbonarist* movement, the "Charcoal Burners") and assisted in preparing an uprising which was scheduled to break out in Piedmont. When this was discovered by the authorities, he was arrested (1820), and after a trial in which neither threats nor favors would make him reveal his associates, he, Maroncelli, and the actor Antonio Canova were condemned to death, but the sentence was commuted to fifteen years at hard labor. Pellico was sent to the prison of the Spielberg castle in Bohemia, where he spent nine horrible years of material and moral suffering. In his solitude and abandonment he found his only solace in the religion of his early years, to which he returned fervently and forever. He was freed, or rather pardoned, in 1830, and he returned to the bosom of his family in Turin.

Two years later, his book *Le mie Prigioni* [*My Prison*] was published. It is a simple, true account of the years he spent in prison, from his first arrest until his final liberation from the prisons in Milan, in Venice, to that in Spielberg. No hatred of his oppressors is voiced; no revelation, nor allusion, to the causes of his trial; no criticism of the system of violence of which he had been the victim. Instead, we find an attitude of goodness and of forbearance toward all, and the constant eulogy, expressed or implied, of the Christian idea and morality. But by its very mildness, and by the spirit of resignation which pervades it, the story is unconsciously an effective accusation against the government of oppressors. It was said that this little book hurt the Austrian cause more than a lost battle would have. In 1834 his *Doveri degli Uomini* [*Duties of Men*], was published and had almost as wide a circle of readers as *Le mie Prigioni.* It is a sermon on moral and civic virtues, subordinated to that Christian imperative that prohibits rebellion and imposes obedience. Actually Silvio Pellico was a vanquished man now. Becoming an intimate friend of the Barolo family, which was opposed to any liberal ideas, Pellico became more and more detached from the political and literary life of the nation. Wrapped up in religious practices, he died in 1854.

The preceding are Pellico's more significant but by no means his only works, for he was a prolific writer although a somewhat careless one. For a long time his ambition was to attain the highest place, after Alfieri, among Italian tragic writers, perhaps even to give Italy tragedy in accord with the ideas of the Romanticists. In addition to the *Francesca,* his tragedies are numerous. One was written before his imprisonment, *Eufemio da Messina;* others in the first years of his incarceration: *Ester d'Engaddi, Iginia d'Asti, Leoniero da Dertona*; after his liberation: *Gismonda da Mendrisio, Erodiade* (perhaps the best), *Tommaso Moro. Boezio* [*Boethius*], published posthumously, was certainly the closest to the ideal of the Romantic tragedy. Pellico was more apt in numerous *Cantiche,* tales in blank verse against a medieval background of the poet's own imagination. Here his natural elegiac and melancholy vein found the form best fitted to it. Of these, *Tancreda, Raffaella, Ildegarde,* and *I Saluzzesi* are the most moving. He also wrote many minor lyric poems, mostly of a religious nature.

The Milanese Giovanni Berchet, was of an entirely different temperament. He has already been mentioned among the forerunners of the Italian Romanticist movement, especially for his *Lettera semiseria di Crisostomo.*

He was a government employee under the French regime, and under the Austrians he was official German translator. In 1820, the year of the arrest of Pellico and other conspirators, he fled, taking refuge first in Switzerland, then in Paris, later in England. He returned to Milan in 1848, the year of great new hopes, and when these failed, he emigrated to Turin and to Tuscany. He died in Turin in 1851, being then a representative in the Sub-Alpine Parliament.

Berchet's poetry is largely inspired by the historical and political conditions of his time. His first little original poem was *I Profughi d'Epiro* (1824). A small part of Epirus, formerly a dominion of Venice, then oppressed by Ali Pasha, finally had been ceded to Turkey by the English. Many of the wretched inhabitants preferred exile to the horrors of Turkish rule. The event aroused European indignation. In England Foscolo wrote the story of the vile contract which, however, was not published until after his death. In his poem Berchet imagines that an exile tells an Englishman the whole story of the infamous cession: there is much vehemence and eloquence. Later he composed various *romanze* on themes interwoven into contemporary Italian history. The background of *Clarina* is the Piedmontese revolution of 1821, first favored, then deserted by Carlo Alberto, who is then subjected to torrents of violent imprecations. *Il Romito del Cenisio* [*The Hermit of Mont Cenis*] is a lament on the captivity of Pellico. *Il Rimorso* is the remorse of an Italian woman who has married a German, and so on. The poet breaks away from the history of his times, but only in appearance, in *Le Fantasie,* which are visions in an exile's dream of the different events of the Lombard League: the Oath of Pontida, the battle of Legnano, and the flight of Barbarossa. *Le Fantasie* is more full of life than any of Berchet's works. Later, in 1830, on the outbreak of revolts in Modena and Bologna, he wrote the ode *All'Armi* [*To Arms*], one of the strongest of Italian patriotic lyrics. It should be added that like many Romanticists he was an enthusiast over foreign literatures Berchet translated, among others, Gray's *Bard,* two romances of Bürger, and many old Spanish romances.

The *Ballate* [*Ballads*] of the Venetian Luigi Carrer (d. 1850) have some analogies with the romances of Berchet, save that he liked imaginative tales of the conventional Middle Ages. *L'Anello di sette Gemme* [*The Seven-Jewelled Ring*] is a beautiful book in which he describes the history and customs of Venice poetically. He wrote a *Biografia di Ugo Foscolo,* and an essay, *Saggio sulla vita e le opere del Goldoni,* both very praiseworthy works.

Gabriele Rossetti is one of the most noted of Italian patriotic poets. Born at Vasto on the Adriatic in Abruzzi, he spent his youth as a lawyer in Naples. When the Bourbon king was forced to give a constitution, which he withdrew as soon as he was able, Rossetti chanted liberty in a famous hymn. With the loss of constitutional liberties, Rossetti fled to Malta and later to England, where he died in 1854. *Iddio e l'Uomo, Il Veggente in solitudine,* and *L'Arpa evangelica* [*God and Man, The Seer in Solitude,* [*The Evangelic Harp*] are the titles of the collections of his patriotic poems, with frequent recurrence of the apocalyptic theme of the imminent justice of God upon the oppressors of Italy and especially on the Pontificate, for Rossetti inherited a strong hatred of the priesthood in civilian affairs from the historical and political Neapolitan tradition. He also conceived of the *Divina Commedia* as an essentially anti-Catholic poem, a thesis which he developed in *Lo Spirito papale nella Divina Commedia* [*The Papal Spirit in the Divine Comedy*] and in the *Commento analitico* [*Analytical Commentary*] on that work. His son Dante Gabriele was born in England: he was an admirer and imitator as in *The Blessed Damozel,* of the *Vita Nuova* of Dante, and a noteworthy painter.

Another Neapolitan, Alessandro Poerio, himself the son of a patriot who suffered in the imprisonments of 1799, wrote chants of fervent love of country and of hope in the destinies of Italy. Alessandro was exiled in 1815 and again in 1821; in 1835 he was permitted to return to Naples, but he left the city again in 1848 to defend Venice. Wounded at Mestre, he died a few days later. Another poet died in defence of the glorious and short-lived Roman Republic of 1849, at the age of twenty-one: Goffredo Mameli of Genova, author of the famous hymn "Fratelli d'Italia," set to music by Novaro and by Verdi. Mazzini, while he was triumvir of the Roman Republic, wrote winged words on the death of the young patriot. In its time *L'Esule* [*The Exile*] enjoyed a certain fame. Published in London in 1827, it was a polymetric poem in fifteen cantos by Pietro Giannone, a patriot of Modena and ardent disciple of Mazzini.

Giovanni Battista Niccolini was also a poet of the fatherland. Born at I Bagni di San Giuliano near Pisa, in his early years he was friend and confidant of Foscolo, who portrayed him as Lorenzo Alderani, the bosom friend of Jacopo Ortis, and he remained faithful to his friend's ideas for the rest of his life. He distrusted the Papacy at a time when all Italy was pinning its hopes on Pio IX. He became professor of eloquence at the Academy of Fine Arts in Florence and died in that city in 1861. His life's greatest passion was the tragic theater. He began with classical subjects, such as *Polissena,* awarded a prize by the Crusca Academy in a competition held in 1810; then followed *Ino e Temisto* [*Wives of Athamas, King of Boeotia*]; and *Edipo* (an imitation of Sophocles *Oedipus at Colonus*). Sometimes he translated directly, as he did the *Seven against Thebes* and *Agamemnon* of Aeschylus. Thus continuing the classical manner and the spirit of Alfieri, he passed on to medieval subjects, as Foscolo had done in his *Ricciarda,* and composed *Matilde* (an imitation of John Home's *Douglas*), *Antonio Foscarini, Lodovico Sforza, Rosmunda d'Inghilterra,* and an imitation and correction of Shelley's tragedy, *Beatrice Cenci.* More significant are *Il Nabucco* (which in the guise of the powerful king of Babylon, portrays Napoleon), *Giovanni da Procida* in 1834, and *Arnaldo da Brescia* in 1843. Around the legendary figure of Giovanni da Procida, the inciter of the Sicilian Vespers of 1282, the poet gathers all his spirit of insurrection against foreign arrogance; in Arnaldo da Brescia, the restorer of the Roman republic, all his aversion to the temporal Papacy. Recently the patriotic poetry of Niccolini, the *Canzoniere civile,* was published; its tone is rather more rhetorical than impassioned. Niccolini placed great hopes on Victor Emanuel. A youthful poem, *La Pietà,* and several literary discourses, of which the more important discuss the nature of tragedy, complete Niccolini's output. He was more a poet by the strength of his will than a poet of genius, he is a poet who no longer says anything to our souls.

Giuseppe Giusti

Giuseppe Giusti (d. 1850) occupies a place all to himself in the history of the poetry of the Romantic age. He was born at Monsummano in 1809. He studied law unwillingly. He traveled for his health and for diversion, and in Milan he came to know Manzoni well. He took an active part in the 1848 Tuscan uprisings, representing in opposition to Guerrazzi the moderate party. Thus it later was easy to abuse him as a reactionary, or worse. He served in the Tuscan National Assembly as the representative from Borgo a Buggiano. The poems of Giusti were learned by heart by the fathers of succeeding generations, and not merely for their quick spontaneity and originality. Except for a few sentimental lyrical poems, some full of delicate emotion, (for example, *Ad una Giovinetta),* Giusti's poems are almost all written with satirical intent. The most popular ones have a political basis, for example, *Dies irae,* a song of joy on the death of Franz I of Austria; *La Incoron-*

azione, in which the Italian princes who took part in the coronation ceremony of Ferdinand I in Milan are treated disparagingly; *Lo Stivale* [*The Boot*], a sort of history *con brio* of the Italian peninsula concluding with the necessity of its unity and independence; *La Terra dei Morti* [*Land of the Dead*], a eulogy of the great *living* Italians, written against Lamartine who had described Italy with that circumlocution; *Il Brindisi di Girella* [*Turncoat's Toast*], put in the mouth of one of the many who changed their jackets with changes in the (political) weather, and which appeared especially applicable to the famous French minister, Talleyrand. Other poems might be called social satires, such as *La Vestizione* (ceremony of taking the ecclesiastical habit) against the conferring of honors on unworthy people; *Il Re Travicello* [*King Log*], inspired by a well-known fable of Aesop; *La Scritta* [*The Contract in Writing*], on weddings between the old nobility and the plutocracy; *Gl'Immobili e i Semoventi* [*The Immovables and the Self-Propelling*], concerning the old and the new systems of education, the former detestable in its creation of mummies, the latter hateful in its production of machines; *Il Papato di Prete Pero* [*The Pontificate of Father Pero*] — perhaps Pio IX, who became pope the year afterward but turned out *not* to be what Giusti had in mind — a humoristic depicting of what a truly spiritual pope should be; *Gingillino* [*The Dawdler*], a masterpiece of the poetry in this manner, the story of the cowardly and selfish youth of one who would later get rich in public office. Other poems of Giusti can not be put into either of these two categories, such as the emotional stanzas of *Sant'Ambrogio* [Ambrose, patron saint of Milan] inspired by hatred of the Germans and by a humanity still stronger than that hate. Others are sprightly tales, like *Il Sortilegio* [*The Charm*], or pages of just good humor, like *L'Amor pacifico* [*Peaceful Love*]. Giusti's satirical poetry is outstanding for its immediate inspiration which finds and renews the most varied and emotion-causing meters. Frequent allusions to persons and events too peculiar to his own environment sometimes make him an obscure poet, as does also an abuse of dialectal expressions. Giusti's *Lettere* were long admired.

Because of a certain affinity of spirit, his contemporary, Antonio Guadagnoli of Arezzo (d. 1858), may be mentioned here. He was the author of very popular bantering poems not lacking in wit or knowledge of life. More worthy of mention is the Roman poet Giuseppe Gioacchino Belli (d. 1863), who, in his innumerable dialectal sonnets, pictured most happily the customs of the people and the absurdities and selfishness of the noble classes and the clergy.

Other Historians and Writers

The ardent enthusiasm of the Romantic age was broadly human, especially in France and England. There flourished, with the poets, a new manner of historians who looked on the vicissitudes of the past and the drama of collective life with the passion of poets. New writers wrote with equal warmth on the most diverse subjects: these were genial men, if not men of genius. Among Italian historians, Gino Capponi (d. 1876) is to be remembered. A great Florentine gentleman, he participated actively in the political life of Tuscany, becoming president of the provisional government in 1848. He did much to promote culture in the region. He collaborated with Vieusseux and others in the founding of the *Antologia* (1821: a periodical suppressed by the Grand Duke in 1832). One of the most originally conceived of Italian historical works is his *Storia della Repubblica di Firenze* from the origin of the Commune down to 1530.

In Lombardy, Cesare Cantú wrote on historical and other subjects. Born at Brivio, he was very old when he died in 1895 at Milan, where he was director of the State

Archives. His *Storia Universale,* a vast and animated compilation, is the work that brought him fame. But his minor historical works are more interesting: such as *La Storia dei Cento Anni* [*A Hundred Years of History*] from 1750 to 1850; and the monographs, *Il Monti e l'eta sua* [*Monti and his Age*], and *La Lombardia al tempo di Parini* [*Lombardy in Parini's Time*]. Cantú was a nonliberal, even reactionary spirit. When he was young, he wrote a novel, *Margherita Pusterla,* which in its time was very popular.

Different motives actuated Carlo Cattaneo of Milan. He was a leading spirit in the "Five Days" of the Milanese insurrection, and he opposed the intervention of Carlo Alberto. When exiled, he became professor of philosophy at the *liceo* (secondary school) in Lugano and died in that city in 1869. In politics he was a constant advocate of the "federalist" program. In his opinion, the New Italy should be a union of republics in which the local laws and traditions would be respected. This made adversaries for him even among republicans. He was a prolific writer on history and statistics, as in *Notizie naturali e civili su la Lombardia;* he wrote on literature, with an interesting comparison of Schiller's *Don Carlos* with the *Filippo* of Alfieri; and on penal law and philosophy — all with sure learning and new viewpoints. For his philosophic essays he may be considered the promoter of the positivist philosophy in Italy. One of his most widely read and discussed writings was the story of the "Five Days," that is, *Dell'Insurrezione di Milano del 1848 e della successiva guerra* [*The Milanese Insurrection of 1848 and the Subsequent War*].

The Milanese Carlo Tenca (d. 1883) was another writer of the time on diverse subjects. During the "Five Days," he was director of the organ of the provisional government, *Ventidue Marzo* (March 22). Then he founded the *Crepuscolo* [*Twilight*], to which the best Italian literary and political writers contributed. Among his most interesting articles are several on Italian authors. A still more prolific contemporary, Cesare Correnti (d. 1888), represented during the insurrection the element disposed to accept the intervention of the king of Sardinia. Like Cattaneo, he also narrated the events in which he played a part. For ten years he wrote the patriotic almanac *Il Nipote del Vesta-verde.* His various essays are innumerable, and among them are some good translations from foreign poets.

Like Cattaneo, Giuseppe Ferrari (d. 1876) of Milan was a federalist. He was a fervent disciple of Vico and published an edition of his works, with many notes. His own chief works were *La Filosofia della Rivoluzione; La Storia delle Rivoluzioni d'Italia,* which he first wrote in French; *Corso sugli Scrittori Politici* [*Course on Political Writers*], from the Middle Ages down to the revolution; and *Opuscoli vari di Storia e di Letteratura* [*Diverse Pamphlets on History and Literature*], originally in French, which contain some profound pages on Machiavelli, Foscolo, and Italian popular poetry. He had a paradoxical mind, but it was rich in intuitions. It was his thought, contrary to that of Mazzini, that the resurgence of Italy lay in acceptance of the thought and politics of France, which represents enduring revolution.

Niccolò Tommaseo, of Sebenico in Dalmatia, wrote with learning equal to his great mind on many and diverse fields. He died in Florence in 1874 after a very active life spent in furthering the national culture and the Italian cause (for which he suffered exile in France and on Corfu). His dictionaries, *Dizionario dei sinonimi* and *Dizionario estetico,* and his notably poetic commentary on the *Divina Commedia,* are perhaps the best-known of his many works. But he wrote on everything: politics, education, religion, and also wrote poetry (rather more vigorous than beautiful), and even a novel, *Fede e Bellezza,* mentioned above. A caustic spirit and a sense of hatred, or perhaps envy, of writers who were great but not to his liking, made him often express unfair judgments, such as those on Alfieri, Foscolo, and Leopardi.

Political Writers

It is time for my readers to have at least some idea of the more properly political writers who, in the first half of the century, discussed or debated the national problem whether from historical or philosophical viewpoints. This is a large and glorious group, out of which we can select only a few names. Most of these writers come down in a straight line from Alfieri, whose Italian spirit and, sometimes, aversion to France they have made their own. The first condition for winning independence, for liberty, was to achieve consciousness as a people. It was essential that the Italians should feel the greatness of their own past in order to build the future.

Among the first of the Alfierians must be mentioned Santorre di Santarosa of Turin, who was the soul of the Piedmontese revolution of 1821. After its failure, he emigrated to England and, later, to Greece, where he died for the liberty of that nation at Sfacteria, in 1825. The *Speranze degli Italiani* [*Hopes of the Italians*], written by this noble fighter for liberty, was published posthumously.

Santarosa's friend Cesare Balbo (d. 1853), also of Turin, was a soldier and a diplomat. In 1821 he had hopes that the prince would grant the constitution; in 1848 he was president of the Council of Ministers and resigned after Novara (where Carlo Alberto was defeated March 23, 1849). In the years prior to his public life, he devoted himself to historical studies, which for him meant knowledge of the Italian soul and the mission of Italy through the centuries. Out of those meditations resulted the two volumes of the *Storia d'Italia* from the time of the Lombard invasion; the *Vita di Dante,* 1839, which is one of the books of most fervent and reasoned homage to that first of the

Italians; and the *Sommario della Storia d'Italia,* 1846, which is a book of ideas rather than of information in which an overwhelmingly sympathetic vision of the Church did not allow the author to make an equable estimate of the other elements of Italian civilization. Two years earlier *Le Speranze d'Italia* had been published and had been a national event. For the first time the Italian problem was dealt with publicly and concretely, and with superior efficacity, discussion was raised above conspiracy. Therein lay the importance of the book, rather than in the theses of the author, of which the favorite one was that Italy should aim at spontaneously obtaining freedom and autonomy from Austria in recompense for aid which Italy would give her in the war against Turkey, an undertaking that interested European and Christian civilization.

Another great Torinese was the Abbé Vincenzo Gioberti, whose lofty philosophical speculation never lost sight of the national problem; on the contrary, it was like the presupposition to is solution. An exile in Paris in 1833, then in Brussels where he taught in an institute and found time and faith to compose his most fervent works, he hastened to Turin in 1848, where he was elected president of the Chamber, then Minister of Education in the Collegno cabinet. After Novara, Victor Emanuel wanted him to come back into government. His hostile attitude toward Mazzini made him hated by the republicans, while his liberal ideas were unacceptable to the clericals. He died in Paris in 1852 at the age of fifty-five years. Gioberti's literary production coincides almost entirely with the period of his exile. *Il Primato morale e civile degli Italiana* [*The Moral and Civic Primacy of the Italians*], published in 1843, was the work that made him suddenly famous. It is a eulogy of Italy in her past and her present as the nation which Providence has chosen as teacher and guide for the return of Europe to the life of the spirit. For the author, the welfare and safety of Italy lies in a federation of the various states under the leadership of the Papacy, the most Italian and the most universal of the powers. But the clergy did not respond to the call of Gioberti, who wanted it to be a living part of the moral and political revival of the nation. The Jesuits opposed him, and against them Gioberti wrote *Il Gesuita Moderna* (1847), and then *Apologia del Gesuita Moderna* (1848). *Il Rinnovamento civile dell'Italia* [*Civic Revival of Italy*] was a work of the year preceding his death. It is an examination of the events of 1848–1849, which concludes with the necessity of Italy's unification under the scepter of the house of Savoy in contrast to the federal idea expressed in his preceding works. In a field quite apart from politics, the treatise *Del Bello* [*On Beauty*] is closely connected to the idealistic philosophy of Gioberti, which he expounds in various works: *La Protologia* [*First Science*], *Introduzione allo studio della filosofia,* and *La Teorica del sovrannaturale* [*Theoretics of the Supernatural*]. Critics now recognize that he occupies one of the most eminent places in contemporory thought.

Terenzio Mamiani della Rovere of Pesaro was exiled after the risings in Romagna in 1831, then recalled and made a minister by Pio IX in 1860 with Cavour. As Minister of Education, he was author of *Inni Sacri* [*Sacred Hymns*] in blank verse, in the manner of the so-called Homeric hymns and also of many philosophic writings, among them the *Rinnovamento della filosofia antica italiana* (1934) which is an honoring of Italian thought and culture in contrast with foreign thought and culture.

Giuseppe Mazzani

The most inspired and eloquent political writer of the time, and the one who most aroused the national conscience, was Giuseppe Mazzini. Born in Genoa in 1805, his austerely religious mother contributed much to the high sense of morality and the mystical tendencies of her son. A passion for poetry and literature captured the adolescent boy, but his passion for Italy was even stronger. Having become affiliated with the *Carboneria,* he was arrested and taken to jail in Savona; later he fled to Corsica. His acquaintance with French politics persuaded him more than ever of the necessity for Italy to act independently in her own behalf. He had left the *Carbonari* as being too sympathetic toward France, and he founded the *Giovine Italia* [*Young Italy*], a society of ardent patriots. Their publication, a call to battle bearing the same name, was disseminated over the entire peninsula in the most diverse and ingenious way. Everywhere in Italy the *Congreghe* [confraternities] were forming. In Piedmont the new conspirators were discovered and many of them shot; Jacopo Ruffini, an intimate friend of Mazzini, killed himself. Mazzini was in Marseilles where he attempted an expedition to Savoy, which failed miserably. Condemned to death by the king of Savoy, he spent several years in Switzerland, watched unceasingly by the then international Austrian police. In 1837 he escaped to London where he suffered extreme poverty and dejection but soon recovered his spirits. He wrote for English papers and founded the *Apostolato popolare.* From London he fomented various Italian revolutionary movements: one in Bologna in 1843; another led by the Bandiera brothers in 1844 (he sought in vain to dissuade the rash young men from their attempt, but they were captured and shot at Cosenza in that year); and another in Rimini in 1845. Often he succeeded in slipping back into Italy. In 1848 he was in Milan where he founded the *Italia del Popolo.* In 1849 in Rome, he was a triumvir, with Armellini and Saffi, of the glorious republic defended by Garibaldi and killed by French arms. Then he again sought shelter in England and continued to foment conspiracies, such as the wretched one that brought the "martyrs of Belfiore" to their trials in Mantua and to the scaffold (1851–1853). In 1853 he penetrated into Milan to encourage an insurrection which also failed, and in 1857 he was again in Italy and fanned risings in Genoa, Leghorn, and Naples. Though the conspiracies expressed the heroism of the Italian spirit, and continued failure of such efforts proved that another way should be tried, the way advocated by Balbo, Gioberti, and D'Azeglio: open affirmation of the rights of Italy, and unification of the national sympathies around a strong state, such as Piedmont. Thus it was that some Mazzinians abandoned their master. Founded in 1857, the National Society took the place of the *Congreghe*. Its founder was Giuseppe La Farina, of Messina, not the least of the historians. Cavour secretly approved. All this led to the successful war of 1859, Garibaldi's expedition in 1860, and to the annexations. Mazzini clung to his unitary republican ideas. As a man who prized sacrifice above success, he was left more and more alone, and surrounded by forgetfulness and calumny. As a representative from Messina in 1865, his election was voided by the parliament. Henceforth official Italy looked upon him as a dangerous enemy. In 1870, on his last return to Italy, he was arrested at Gaeta. He died in Pisa in 1872 and was buried in the cemetery of Staglieno at Genoa.

Mazzini was the object of unwavering loves and of ungenerous hatreds. Today he stands above parties. His policies may even be held impractical, but it is impossible not to admire his unyielding moral conception; his faith in the innate heroism of the multitudes; his religion of sacrifice; his objective of an Italy, above all, spiritually great and for the third time mistress of the world's civilization; his understanding of every most delicate problem of the spirit; and his religiousness. Mazzini's writings are couched in a poetical prose, all afire with enthusiasm. They are mostly long articles, published in the periodicals of which he was a collaborator or director. Others were published after his death, such as the *Note autobiografiche,* which are so interesting in their telling the story of his soul, its objectives, its enthusiasms, and its disappointments. In his youth he was an enthusiastic reader of literature, and he left noteworthy essays: *Dell'amor patrio di Dante* [*Dante's Love of Country*], where Foscolo's ideas about that poet reecho; *Della Fatalità come Elemento drammatico* [*Fatality as Dramatic Element*], in which he preludes a new type of tragedy no longer generated by Destiny or by Chance, but by Providence; *Parallelo fra Byron e Goethe;* and *La Filosofia della Musica.* Of his political writings, which are much more numerous, let us mention the *Lettera di un Italiano a Carlo Alberto di Savoia* (1831); *Lo Statuto della Giovine Italia* [*Regulations of the Young Italy society*]. Also some articles fundamental for an understanding of Mazzini's thought are *Dell'unità italiana* (1833); *Lettera ai Siciliani* [*Letter to the Sicilians*], on the revolution in Palermo in 1848; the *Lettera al Ministro francese,* in defence of the Roman republic; the *Ammonimento ai giovani d'Italia* [*Warning to the Young Men of Italy*] in 1859, after the disappointment of the Treaty of Villafranca; *Italia e Roma,* the *Questione morale; Agli Italiani* [*To the Italians*], the program of the last journal founded by him; *Roma del Popolo;* and the essay on the *Rivoluzione francese.* In the little book *I doveri dell'uomo* [The Rights of Man] addressed to the workers, he concluded all his sermonizing against materialism and individualism, which he considered the greatest enemies of progress and human dignity, and also his views on the necessity of sacrifice. Collected after his death, Mazzini's innumerable *Lettere* document his extremely rich spiritual and sensitive nature.

Other writings and other writers lead us back to Mazzini. Carlo Bini of Leghorn (d. 1842) was one of

Mazzini's intimates, a contributor to the *Indicatore Livornese,* and the author of a strangely sad and ironic book, *Manoscritto di un Prigionero* [*Manuscript of a Prisoner*]. Count Felice Orsini of Meldola in Romagna, a member of Giovine Italia, fought in defence of Venice in 1848 and of Rome in 1849. He was imprisoned in Mantua in 1854, but soon escaped to England. He plotted against Napoleon III because he had not given aid to Italy, but his attempt at assassination on January 14, 1858, failed, and the Count was guillotined soon after. A pious priest, monsignor Luigi Martini, who accompanied almost all of "the martyrs of Belfiore" to the scaffold, narrated the last days of those ardent Mazzinians in a simple, moving book to which he gave the title *Confortatorio;* this was the name of the cell of the fortress in which the condemned men prepared for death. The lives of earlier martyrs was nobly narrated by Atto Vannucci of Pistoia (d. 1883) in his book *I Martiri della Libertà Italiana dal 1794 al 1848.*

The Second Half of the Nineteenth Century

General Characteristics

In the second half of the century, literature continued to have a prevalently national spirit, down to the establishment of the kingdom. But there already rose, together with it, another literature that would ultimately win the upper hand with its social, religious, or philosophical tendencies of the most varied and contradictory nature. In it, French literary influences are visible: passionate, turbulent romanticism, and later, the Parnassian school, which stood for the exalting of pure beauty over the sentimentalism and negligence of the Romanticists. The tendency, of French and Russian origin, toward realism and later, the spiritual and mystic reaction to it were also visible.

Lyricists

Giovanni Prati, who was born at Dasindo in Giudicarie and died at Rome in 1884, was conspicuous among the poets. He was very prolific. Many of his lyrics are on patriotic themes, such as one to Ferdinand II in 1850 and another on the anniversary of the battle of Curtatone in 1851. More important are some of his bold, warm lyrics in which he affected Manzonian meters, such as *Uomo* [*Man*]; *Donna* [*Woman*]; and *Igea* [*Hygeia*]. Some of his poetry is introspective and melancholic, such as the beautiful *Psiche* sonnets. His romantic poems were widely read, such as *Edmenegarda,* a sad love story; and *Ariberto,* which has the war of 1859 for its background and whose objective was a eulogy of Italy in arms and the house of Savoy, to which Prati was always devoted. If musicality of verse and abundance of images were enough to make a poet, Prati would have been a poet.

Aleardo Aleardi (d. 1878), of Verona, was less prolific, but more delicate than Prati. In his poetry, the elegiac note prevails. Poems that speak of pure and unhappy loves, recollections of childhood, old stories of glory and sorrow, such as the *Lettere a Maria* and *Monte Circello,* are perhaps his best things.

Arnaldo Fusinato (d. 1868) of Schio wrote poems in a minor key. His narrative poem on the siege and surrender of Venice in 1848 was once very popular, and some of his jocose lyrics, and a poem in *ottava rima, Lo Studente di Padova,* were no less popular.

Luigi Mercantini (d. Palermo, 1872) of Ripatransone continued the tradition of the patriotic poets of the preceding generation. He wrote many lyric poems inspired by the sorrows and the hopes of Italy (many were inspired by the Greek islands, where he spent some time in exile after the disasters of 1849) and a small poem in eight cantos on *Tito Speri,* the martyr of Belfiore. Long popular was his chant *La Spigolatrice di Sapri* [*The Gleaner of Sapri*] which relates to the unfortunate expedition of Pisacane and his Three Hundred to Calabria. His impetuous and magnanimous *Inno di Garibaldi,* composed in 1859, became a national song. A hymn of war for the campaign of 1866 was composed by the Piemontese Angelo Brofferio of Castelnuovo, who died in that very year. But his satirical comedies and poems, adverse to Cavour's policies, were more popular; many of them were written in dialect. One of the last patriotic poets, Domenico Mauro (d. 1873), should not be forgotten. Born in San Demetrio Corone in Calabria, he emigrated to Turin and was a representative in the first parliament. In his fervent songs of love for the fatherland and some religious compositions, he followed the Manzonian *Hymns* with fair success. Francesco Dall'Ongaro, of Treviso (d. Naples, 1873) was an unusual national poet in the formerly very popular *Stornelli* [*Ditties*].

A coterie of poets, who liked to be called *scapigliati* ["dishevelled,": bohemians], flourished in northern Italy from about 1860 to 1870 and had some important representatives. Among them were Emilio Praga (d. 1875) of Milan, a painter and poet, who was in much of his verse an imitator of Heine and Baudelaire: Arrigo Boito of Padua (d. 1918), an outstanding musician, composer of the operas *Mefistofele* and *Nerone,* an uncommon poet in the fable of *Re Orso* [*King Bear*], and in other tales; and Vittorio Betteloni of Verona (d. 1910), who differs from the others in his accent of realism, which often debases his poetry to the level of plodding prose.

Another group of poets centered around Carducci in Bologna. Among the foremost were Enrico Panzacchi (d. 1904) of Bologna, whose fairly numerous volumes of literary and artistic criticism are more noteworthy than his poetry; Olindo Guerrini (d. 1916), better known under the pseudonym of Lorenzo Stecchetti, a native of Ravenna. His *Postuma* (because the verses of this collection are supposed to be written by a young man who has died of phthisis), *Polemica, Nuova Polemica,* and more recent, the *Rime di Argia Sbolenfi,* are his collected poems. Great realism which, especially in the later books, descends to pornography, an easy and slipshod versification, and at times a plebeian and vigorous satirical accent against politicians and evil political usages made Stecchetti one of the most popular poets of his age. Giovanni Marradi (d. 1922) of Leghorn was a singer full of rhythm and easy imagery. His last book of poems is *Rapsodia garibaldina,* which is the one read in schools and in reading rooms. Severino Ferrari (d. 1905) of Molinella was a poet of delicate sentiment and carefully studied form; he was, perhaps, more an archaeologist of poetry than a poet.

Southern Italy also brought forth, if not a school, a poetical center with its own characteristics. The philosophizing poet Vincenzo Padula was foremost. Sicily produced a warm evocator of the wars of the Risorgiments in Eliodoro Lombardi; and an ardent social poet in Giuseppe Aurelio Costanzo of Siracusa (d. 1913). Aurelio's best thing is *Gli Eroi della Soffitta* [*The Heroes of the Garret*] in four cantos, a eulogy and a lament for the great hopes and dreams of young men fated to perish obscurely or tragically in a humdrum existence. Others of his verses irradiate melancholy affection, such as the sonnets to his mother, *A mia madre Maria.*

Giosuè Carducci (F. F.)

Writing within a prevailingly Romanticist or Manzonian generation, the figure of Giosuè Carducci was that of a restorer of the classical tradition. His style and language, as though reverting to the somewhat solemn modes of Foscolo, departed from the "spoken" character of Manzonian prose and recovered a native literary flavor. Drawn more from the wellspring of writers than from the ordinary popular language, they raised even the speech of the people to the special tone of the more distinctly literary tradition. In so doing, there was no contriving or willful capriciousness, because such was the spontaneous tendency of the poet.

Furthermore, a large part of Carducci's poetry touched on themes which seemed to depart from the atmosphere of the Romantic nineteenth century. It carried human nostalgia back, not towards the Middle Ages, but towards Hellenism and the Roman spirit. Nonetheless Carducci was a poet, and poetry is incompatible with polemical schemes and principles. While on the one hand he was in accord with the Classicists of the pre-Manzonian and pre-Romantic tradition, on the other hand he brought to his poetry and even to his prose the affections and the ways and the forms of a more intense Romanticism.

As always happens with true poets, he had at one and the same time the visage of tradition and that of innovation. D'Annunzio and Pascoli later were to take their treatment of the poetic image from his example, and from him D'Annunzio derived the form of his prose phraseology, although directing it to other ends.

Carducci was born on July 27, 1835 in Val di Castello, a hamlet of Pietrasanta in Versilia, Lunigiana (near Viareggio), to Dr. Michele and his wife Ildegonda Celli. His father was among those affected by the great patriotic aspirations that resulted in the Italian Risorgimento, and because of his ideas he had been confined for a year in Volterra.

In 1838 young Giosuè followed his father to Bólgheri, a hamlet of Castagneto in the Maremma region. It was in that place that the world of his affections and imagination was formed. We might say that the nostalgic foundation of Carducci's poetry, that which nourished the melancholy of his great odes came from this experience directly, because in poetry it brought him recollections of that land, and also indirectly, because the first movement of his meditations upon the "enormous mystery of the universe," upon the change of forms in the immutability of life, was always joined to an image of that sunny and funereal land which was an illustrious burial place of the Etruscans and revealed some of their abandoned ruins. Thereafter, in whatever place he happened to be, he always silently compared the landscape with that of the Maremma in which he spent his childhood.

From Alfieri he received his first images of poetry and his first civic affections, and it was with Alfieri's tragedies that his mother taught him to read. The emotional force of the Carduccian style, in its best virtues and also in its defects, would sometimes seem the natural result of such teaching. He learned Latin from his father, and it was by that path that the heroic myths of classical antiquity entered his mind. Homer and Vergil attracted him far more than Manzoni, whom his father, a "fervent Manzonian," never succeeded in making him truly like. He read Roman history and was passionately drawn to the French Revolution.

In 1848, the year when the movement for independence seemed close to victory and then was miserably disappointed, Dr. Michele, opposed by the reactionaries and even struck by peasants, was obliged to abandon that inhospitable country and move, first to Laiatico and later to Florence. The boy went to finish his studies in the humanities and rhetoric with the padres of the *Scuole Pie* [religious schools] and stayed there until 1852. His teacher of rhetoric was Father Geremia Barsottini, to whom the poet rendered homage for his prose translation of all the odes of Horace and to whom he always remained devoted.

These studies revealed to him the greatness of poetry. In awaiting Italian unification, his feeling drew from the liberalism of his father and his favorite authors, such as Mazzini and Foscolo. Because of the privations of his impoverished home, the mind of the adolescent was tempered in lofty passions including the supreme passion of poetry, and there too was formed that difficult, disdainful character which often made difficulties for him in social encounters.

When he had completed his secondary education, he went for a year to Celle on Monte Amiata, following his father's peregrinations, but towards the end of 1853 he won a competition for a resident scholarship in the Normal School of Pisa. In 1856 he received his doctor's degree and the degree for teaching.

In that year, with his friends Gargani, Targioni and Chiarini, he founded the literary society of the *Amici Pedanti* [Pedantic Friends]. This was an anti-Romantic and pagan movement, which quickly aroused violent arguments, as may be seen in the writing which Carducci published in December, *Giunta alla derrata.* Meanwhile, in October, he had begun teaching rhetoric in the secondary school of San Miniato al Tedesco.

In July, 1857, the first book of poems by Giosuè Carducci appeared, the *Rime.* It contained twenty-five sonnets, twelve cantos, and three lyrics entitled *Saggi di un canto alle Muse* [*Essays of a Song to the Muses*]. The poet had repudiated any poems which testified to a romantic immediacy, and here he soberly published what best represented him. He was still far from his great poetry, but already, in certain places, the particular accent of the poet was discernible, that accent which was to sound purer and higher in the *Rime Nuove* and in the *Odi Barbare.*

In that same year, he was the winner in a competition for the chair of Greek in the secondary school of Arezzo, but his appointment was not approved by the grandducal government. Thereupon he went to Florence, where he existed in dignified poverty by giving some lessons. Meanwhile, he was studying and reading.

In November of that year his brother Dante took his own life, casting the darkest sorrow into the heart of Carducci, who penned heartbroken lines to his dead brother. And a new misfortune struck the poet the following year, the death of his father; he found now himself the head of the ruined family. In August of 1858, he took his mother and his brother Walfredo to a very poor house in the Borg'Ognisanti section of Florence and set to work to earn a living by giving private lessons and editing the texts of the Bibliotechina Diamante of the publisher Gaspare Barbèra. In March, 1859, he married young Elvira Menicucci.

On April 27 of that year, the union of Tuscany to Italy became a fact; times were changing, and the free spirits of the Risorgimento felt that their hour had struck.

Toward the end of the year the poet went to take the chair of Greek in the secondary school of Pistoia and remained there until November, 1860. Terenzio Mamiani, the minister of education, appointed him to the chair of Italian eloquence in the University of Bologna. On the 27th of that month, the poet gave his inaugural lecture. At first he felt uncomfortable; he felt the conflict between his own poetry and the obligations of philology. But while he fortified his knowledge of the classics at Bologna, he also turned his attention to the poetry and prose of other nations.

The political life of Italy, only just emerging from the great travail of the Risorgimento, was pressing everywhere and urgently with all its passions. Many hopes seemed to be disappointed, because the highest-minded men always found that everything that was accomplished was inferior to their great dream. Hence, criticism and discontentment were born.

Carducci had been a monarchist, and now, after the tragic event of Aspromonte in Calabria (where Garibaldi was wounded and captured by government troops, August 29, 1862), he felt himself a republican. For a man of Carducci's stature, however, being a monarchist or a republican did not mean shutting oneself up within a party; it meant rather having a feeling for whichever party might seem best fitted to further the development of Italy. Faithful to this important truth, in his riper years Carducci could look toward the monarchy with new sympathy without being unfaithful to his principles.

So now Carducci was a republican, and an impatient one. His nature was too impetuous for him to realize what a great effort the men coming after the heroic period were making to weld a unity so recently achieved. He felt too much urgency, and his language was impregnated with that sense of urgency, losing expressive force in proportion to its increase in violence; just as when a man falls prey to rage, his voice changes to strangled, inarticulate sound. Many of his poems of this period bear in their lines the aggressive impetuosity which he could not give vent to in political action.

Then, under the pseudonym of Enotrio Romano, he wrote his polemical poems, those which would be called *Giambi* [*Iambi*], the name which one of his books of collected poems later bore. In 1863 he wrote his famous *Inno a Satana* [*Hymn to Satan*].

In 1868 the volume *Levia Gravia* appeared; then in 1871 the volume of *Poesie,* which, in addition to the preceding collections, contained the *Giambi ed Epodi* and is divided into three parts: *Decennali* (1860–1870); *Levia Gravia* (1857–1860); and the *Nuove Poesie* (1872).

Having suffered so many trials, the poet finally freed himself of that sort of fieriness which sometimes kept him from being poetical. By now, more than one of the poems that were to form the *Rime Nuove* (Eng. tr., 1916, *New Rhymes*), in which is found the best of Carducci's art, had been composed. In 1873 the poet began the *Odi barbare,* of which the first series appeared in July, 1877.

With the *Odi barbare* the poet intended to depart from the old meters: "I hate the outworn poetry," he wrote. This was a momentary hate, but it is certain that he felt an urge for new melodic forms, which would give to the Italian language the swirls and spirals of the ancient meters: the hexameter and the pentameter, the Alcaic, the Asclepiad and the Sapphic. The result was an amplification of his own melodic ability. Even when Carducci turned back to the usual meters of Italian poetry, he bore the musical experience that he had acquired in the *Odi barbare* and reached a more inward and original melodiousness.

From 1881 Carducci's fame, especially with the younger generation, grew stronger and more assured. It was helped by new literary periodicals, such as the *Fanfulla della Domenica,* the *Cronaca Bizantina,* and the *Domenica Letteraria.* His poems were awaited by his followers with an anticipation of beauty that was never disappointed. His words as a teacher and a great Italian brought light to their minds and encouraged them.

The *Nuove Odi barbare* appeared in 1882, and in that year he delivered his famous speech "On the Death of Giuseppe Garibaldi," a full-voiced oration in which, with epical accent, the legend of the hero in the years to come is foretold. In 1883 the sonnets of the *Ça ira* appeared. Then in 1887 the *Rime Nuove,* followed in 1889 by the third series of *Odi barbare.*

The last volume of Carducci's poetry, *Rime e Ritmi,* appeared in 1899. Then the poet collected all his poetic work from 1850 to 1900, and in farewell set the famous lines:

Fior tricolor,
Tramontano le stelle in mezzo al mare
E si spengono i canti entro il mio core.

[Three-colored flower,
The stars set in the sea
And in my heart the songs die away.]

He had written them one joyous evening, with other *stornelli* [ditties] in the office of the *Cronaca Bizantina* in Rome. He detached them and included them with a different meaning in that collection.

The last years of his life were sad. Illness had already set in by 1885. Then in 1899 hemiplegia deprived him of the use of one hand and made speech difficult. Nevertheless, he kept on working, but in 1904 he had to resign from teaching. He had been made a senator in 1890, and the Italian Parliament decreed him a pension. The poet answered: "Who am I that a national pension should be given me? What have I done, except love the fatherland, this poor and great and lovely Italy, even when I seemed most provoked with her! I have done this and nothing more. But it is little." In 1906 he was awarded the Nobel Prize in literature, but that prize came to a man exhausted and almost destroyed by illness. On February 16, 1907, Giosuè Carducci died in his modest house in Bologna.

In various ways the critics have indicated certain ideal stages in the development of Carducci's poetry, grouping the various compositions according to their spontaneous affinity. This is a matter of chronological, not inward phases. In this study we shall make use of this expedient, arranging the various moods of inspiration in groupings which best serve interpretation of that poetry.

A first stage is the landscape: the vision of nature; yet in which human history is present, for there is no fragment of earth where the memory of man is not alive. But the poet's mind clings closer to the vision of nature than to the appeal of human history, or to a need to retire into himself and to resolve the landscape into an inner meditation. The heights to which this Carduccian poetry of the elementary landscape can reach are shown in the verses of *San Martino* or of *Mezzogiorno alpino.* (I say "elementary" to distinguish it from the landscape on which the imprint of human history is stronger than nature.)

In *San Martino,* that rough land, that sea howling and lashed to whiteness under the mistral, and the mist, the odor of the wine, the first crackling under the spit, and the hunter who whistles and watches the migration of the flights of birds black as "exiled thoughts," make up in sharp focus, a simple town, which has the same the enchantment of a *fata morgana* (of a mirage) .

Even more inward is *Mezzogiorno alpino* [*Alpine Noontime*], which was written on August 27, 1895, at Courmayeur. The silence of "the great circle of the Alps" is expressed with solemn quietness in eight lines, in which even the rhyme of the fourth and the last lines, accented and broken off, contribute to the creation of a new musicality as a prelude to more modern styles:

Nel gran cerchio de l'alpi, su'l granito
Squallido e scialbo, su' ghiacciai candenti,
Regna sereno intenso ed infinito
Nel suo grande silenzio il mezzodi.

Pini ed abeti senza aura di venti
Si drizzano nel sol che gli penètra,
Sola garrisce in picciol suon di cetra
L'acqua che tenue tra i sassi fluì.

[In that great circle of the Alps, on the granite
Bleak and pale, above shining glaciers,
Intense and infinite in its great silence
Serenely reigns midday.

Pines and firs in the still air
Stand in the sun which pierces them,
Only the water with faint sound of lyre
Murmurs softly as between the stones its flows.]

But sometimes landscapes are partly real, partly of desire, as in a sonnet from *Iuvenilia:*

Candidi soli e riso di tramonti
Mormoreggiar di selve brune a' venti
Con sussurio de fredde acque cadenti
Giú per li verdi tramiti de' monti . . .

[Bright suns and laughter of sunsets,
Murmuring of dark woods in the winds,
With whispering of icy waters falling
Down, beside green pathways in the mountains . . .]

In these landscapes of desire ("and bright moonlight which whitens the silent paths"), there is often a thought of woman ("And the cherished appearance of my lady"), and sometimes recollections of history, but not such that taking them unto himself the poet creates a personal, almost autobiographical lyric, as he does at other times.

In *Mattutino e Notturno* [*Matinal and Nocturne*], thought of a woman is linked with a landscape: in the morning purified by rain, the poet's thought wings back to a woman "like the trill of an ascending lark": in the moonlit night, "he admires the moon glimpsed from the lone hillocks . . ." The same is true also in *Sol e Amore* [*Sun and Love*]; *Primavera classica* [*Classical Spring*]; *Autunno romantico,* and so on.

Vendette della Luna [*Moon's Revenge*] is a lunar landscape seen above a moon-white girl, and in it are visual touches of rare lightness, "a green night of April," and a sweet and gentle ending:

Com'uom che va sotto la luna estiva
Tra verdi susurranti alberi al piano
Che in fantastica luce arde la riva
Presso e lontano,

Ed ei sente un desio d'ignoti amori
Una lenta dolcezza al cuor gravare,
E perdersi vorria tra muti albori
E dilaguare.

[As one who to the plain goes through green trees
Rustling beneath the summer moon
Which bathes in wond'rous light the shore,
Both near and far,

And feels desire of unknown loves
Etch slow a sweetness on his heart,
And gladly mid the silent trees would lose himself
And vanish.]

Then there is the *Notte di Maggio* [*May Night*], a Petrarchan sonnet, elegant in its purely melodic play of rhymes and echoes: *notte, stelle, onde, verde, colli, luna.* It is a nostalgic landscape, but one where the remembrance is something still fleeting and tenuous: "Alas! how much of my early youth I saw again at the top of the shining hills." There is something of a diffused, pale moonlight in the lines. For no matter how Carducci vituperated the moon, and in spite of lines like "I hate your stupid round face" *(Classicismo e Romanticism),* the moon is still an essential part of much of his poetry.

La Madre is landscape, and one of the finest in Carducci. The sight of the sculptured group in which Adriano Cecioni had shaped a mother and her child, creates in the poet's mind a landscape over which questioning and hopes arise concerning the "pious justice of work." The dawn saw this woman who is now tossing her little one in the air: "watched her as with rapid bare feet she passed through the dewy odor of the hay" (where one must admire that dexterous juxtaposition, that *callida junctura* of the *roridi odori* "dewy odors" still more daring than the "green silence" which was so much discussed). The landscape takes sharper focus in the luminous lines that follow. "As she bent her broad back at noon over the blond furrows, the elms white with dust heard her humming defiance of the raucous crickets on the hillocks."

At another time, this landscape will be that of *Il Bove* [*The Ox*] where all the images that depict the "pious ox" create around him the broad atmosphere of the countryside, that *divin del piano silenzio verde* [divine silence of the green plain], which is one of the boldest and most charming expressions of the poet.

Even the ideal image of a poet will, for Carducci, resolve itself into a landscape, as in the sonnet *Virgilio*. An extended melody evokes lyrical reminiscences of Vergil: the "compassionate moon," which over the "parched fields" "diffuses the impending summer coolness," the river bank, the "hidden nightingale," and the vast serenity. Here Carducci has composed a landscape in words which will close with a line taken from Vergil, and before Carducci, was translated by Tasso: *Tale il tuo verso a me, divin poeta.* [So is thy verse to me, divine poet].

In this poetry of landscapes, not yet affected by the inspiration of history, the sonnet *Momento epico* has a place. The epos rises to the poet's mind from the vision of "rich Bologna," passing on to "epic Ferrara," and in his heart "once more the sun kindles the immortal fantasies" — a sonnet of grave and powerful beauty. Here too is the place of the pathos of the sonnet *Santa Maria degli Angeli* in which the poet invokes Fra Francesco as an image of that landscape. Also the poem *Fiesole:*

Su le mura, dal rotto etrusco sasso,
La lucertola figge la pupilla,
E un bosco di cipressi a i venti lasso
Ulula, e il vespro solitario brilla.

[On the walls, from the crumbled Etruscan rock,
the lizard stares,
And a weary wood of cypresses wails in the wind,
and the lonely evening shines].

Courmayeur is a vast landscape in which the view suggests this introspective movement. "The soul strays in slow wandering, coming from its regretted memories, and reaches eternal hopes."

This sense of landscape will touch still more tenuous, ghostly, and dreamlike forms, as in *Visione,* which ends: "Without memories, without sorrow, yet like an island, green, afar, in a pale serenity."

The vignette, or sketch, also has some relation to landscape; for example, those lines which Carducci himself named *Vignetta,* in which he sketches a girl in a "tender forest," and in that sketch entitled *Egle*. Sometimes the landscape is a recollection, as in the beautiful hexameters of *Un Sera in San Pietro* [*An Evening in Saint Peter's*].

Although dominated by his sense of landscape, the poet voiced an invective against "old Nature" in *Idillio di Maggio*. "Oh, how shabby is this masquerade of roses and violets! This vaulted sky, how closed! How wan thou art, O Sun!" But it is a pose; the first impulse of Carducci's heart is to cling to Mother Earth, not to the old but to eternal Nature.

Whereas in this first stage of the Carduccian lyric, the landscape, external nature, prevails over the inward affections of the poet and over history made by men. In the second stage the poet contemplates his own heart, his own joys and sorrows, and questions himself, binding those feelings to the landscape and at times attaining the highest nostalgia.

Levia Gravia, the book in which there is already more apt gracefulness of images and rhythms than in his polemical poems, opens with the "Farewell" which, as it announces "the new hymns," sings:

> Addio, serena etate,
> Che di forme e di suoni il cor s'appaga;
> O primavera de la vita, addio!
> Ad altri le beate
> Visioni e la gloria, e a l'ombra vaga
> De' boschetti posare appresso il rio
> E co 'l queto desio
> Far di sé specchio queto al mondo intero:
> Noi per aspro sentiero
> Amore e odio incalza austero e pio,
> A noi fra i tormentati or convien ire
> Tesoreggiando le vendette e l'ire.
>
> [Farewell, serene age
> Which appeases the heart with forms and sounds,
> O springtime of life, farewell!
> For others the blessed visions,
> And the glory and, in the pleasant shade
> Of woods to rest at water's edge
> And, moved by calm desire,
> To serve as quiet mirror of all the world:
> We must needs tread the rough harsh path,
> By love and hate pursued, stern and devout,
> Our lot 'tis now to mingle with tormented men,
> Treasuring the vengeance and the wraths.]

The fact is that that "springtime of life" in the poetry of Carducci is an ideal time that acts as a "quiet mirror of all the world." It is a moment which he is going to find in every epoch of his life: in the of *Juvenilia* and *Giambi* [Iambuses] as well in that of *Rime nuove* and of *Odi barbare.*

One of the first and clearest examples of this introspective poetry is the *Ripresa* [Resumption] between Books I and II of *Giambi ed Epodi: Avanti! avanti!* [Forward!] of October, 1872. Here attention to word and rhythm is greater than in previous compositions. The invocation to glory, with that withdrawal of the poet within himself, has with a certain expressive ease the marks of high poetry: the words to Mameli are intimately pure.

The lines to the author of *Il Mago* are part of this introspective poetry: "O Severino [Ferrari], the dwelling of thy songs, the haunt of thy dreams, I know it well." The sonnet *Francesco Petrarca,* in *Levia Gravia,* is an idyllic desire of the world to raise an altar to the poet of Laura "in the green darkness of the woods," "with a nightingale singing 'mid the fronds."

Then there are the poems which might be called "songs of Maremma nostalgia. Such a nostalgic song is *Colli Toscani* [*Tuscan Hills*]. Another is fittingly called *Nostalgia* and contains these rough, unforgettable lines:

Dove raro ombreggia il bosco
Le maligne crete, e al pian
Di rei sugheri irto e fosco
I cavalli errando van,

Là in Maremma ove fiorio
La mia triste primavera,
Là rivola il pensier mio
Con i tuoni e la bufera.

[Where the scarce woods shade
The evil clays, and on the plain

Bristling and dark with cork oaks
The horses go awandering,

There in Maremma, where flowered
The sad springtime of my youth,
There on the wings of the gale
With the thunder flies my thought.]

The poem entitled *Davanti San Guido* [*Before San Guido*] is famous, almost popular. As he rides by on the train, the poet sees again the great cypress-lined road that leads from San Guido to Bólgheri, where he had spent his childhood. The beloved earth calls to him, and everything thereabouts has a part in the life and griefs of the poet, who had learned the myths of the past there, and had dreamed of the future. Even the dead call to him, and in his memory his grandmother Lucia appears, she who was sleeping in "the lonely cemetery up there." Even the cypress trees speak to him as though they had divined his hidden sorrow: "You can tell your human sadness and your grief to the oaks and to us." They recall to him the vital sense of holy Nature; they bring to mind the cherished illusions of the countryside. "And eternal Pan, who goes on the solitary heights at that hour and on the lonely plains, alone, will sink the discord of thy cares, O mortal, in the divine harmony."

In *Traversando la Maremma Toscana* [*Crossing the Tuscan Maremma*], the poet finds a promise of peace in the land of his childhood: "Oh, that which I loved, that which I dreamed, was all in vain; and always I ran and never reached the end; and tomorrow I shall fall. But from afar your hills say, peace, to the heart, with their dissolving mists and the green plain laughing in the morning rains."

The *Idillio maremmano* [*Maremma Idyll*], another song of pungent nostalgia, is also famous and rightly committed to memory. It is a poem in which the poet compares his literary life with that of the people who work the Maremma land, as he saw in childhood: "Oh how cold thereafter was my life, how obscure and disagreeable it has been!" He says it would have been better to remain there in the fields, to be a peasant of the Maremma, to marry blond Maria, and to forget himself in labor: "Better to forget, while working, without inquiring, this huge mystery of the universe." Here the nostalgia for the Maremma gives rise to a deep meditation and a discouragement with life. And who will forget the gentle sweetness of that *Sogno d'estate* [*Dream of Summer*] from the *Odi barbare?* "I dreamt, quiet things of my childhood dreamt."

With this poetry of evocative themes can be included *Tedio invernale* [*Winter Boredom*]; *Maggiolata* [*May Song*]; and even *Dipartita* [*Departure*]; *Disperata* [*Song of Despair*]; *Serenata* [*Evening Song*]; and *Mattinata* [*Morning Song*], where the poet reveals in himself a sort of popular vein of ancient knowledge. Here is where almost all Carducci's love poetry should be placed, whether as in *Ruit hora* [*Time is Fleeting*] where he is singing of wine and love to Lidia in the "yearned-for green solitude"; or as in the sorrowful lines of *Alla Stazione in una Mattina d'Autunno* [*At the Railroad Station on an Autumn Morning*], by which he sketches the feeling of the season and the monstrous life of the train: "Oh what a fall of leaves, icy, mute, heavy, upon the soul!" The same kind of poetry is found in the *Elegia del monte Spluga* [*Elegy to Mount Spluga:* Swiss, Splügen], a love elegy of the mature poet; and in that winged song for the birthday of M.G. entitled *Sabato santo* [*Holy Saturday*]: "the bells are singing with waves and flights of sounds from the cities on hillocks distantly green."

There are songs of domestic sorrow, the verses for his dead brother and his dead son. In *Funere mersit acerbo,* he entrusts his brother Dante, a suicide, with his little son who bore the same name and who is dead too: "It is my little boy who is knocking on your lonely door. . . ." In *Pianto antico* [*Ancient Lament*], the most felicitous poem that Carducci ever wrote in short lines, a serene sorrow makes him compare the green pomegranate tree, which is flowering again, with the little boy who stretched out toward that tree *la pargoletta mano* [his little hand] and now is dead, and never again will flower.

At another time he may meditate on death. He does so in *Colloqui con gli alberi* [*Conversations with Trees*], which in places recalls one of Zanelli's poems that Carducci greatly admired, *Egoismo e Carità* [*Selfishness and Charity*]. He no longer admires the "thoughtful oak" or craves the "unprolific laurel"; now he loves the vine: ". . . compassionate of me, thou ripenest the wise forgetfulness of life." But he honors the fir most: "he, between four planks, a simple coffin, finally closes the obscure tumults and the vain desiring of my thought." And in *Nevicata* [*Snowfall*] he pronounces a gentle chant of farewell to the world: "Soon, O dear ones, soon – be calm, unconquered heart – down into the silence I shall go, in the shade I shall rest."

Another stage is that of the civil poetry, from which, in celebrating heroes and memorable deeds, he passes on to the calm contemplation of history, to the epos.

The first style of Carducci's civil or political poetry is more a fine oration from the platform than a form of lyric poetry, but little by little it is purified, losing the violence of the direct polemic. In *Juvenilia* a fierce hymn *Alla Libertà rileggendo le opere di Vittorio Alfieri* [*To Liberty, On Rereading the Works of Vittorio Alfieri*] is found, and one day he would exclaim: "Would that I had lived to exterminate tyrants, with you, Rome and Athens. . . ." And he develops a long ode *Agli Italiani* [*To the Italians*] to remind them of the great examples, and he sings a hymn *Alla Croce di Savoia* [*To the Cross of Savoy*]. He invokes Victor Emanuel, "a new Marius" for the redemption of

Italy. He sings of Garibaldi, and he evokes the battles of the liberation: Montebello, Palestro, and so on. He sings *Sicilia e Rivoluzione*. Then in the second book of *Levia Gravia,* he chants *Per la Proclamazione del Regno d'Italia* [*For the Proclamation of the Kingdom of Italy*]; and *In Morte di G. B. Niccolini* [*On the Death of G. B. Niccolini*]; *Roma o morte; Dopo Aspromonte* [*After Aspromonte*]; *Carnevale; Per la Rivoluzione di Grecia* [*The Greek Revolution*]; *Per il Trasporto delle Reliquie di Ugo Foscolo in Santa Croce* [*Transfer of the Remains of Ugo Foscolo to Santa Croce*]; all political and heroic poems.

From Pieve Santo Stefano, on August 23, 1867, he sent out the violent and nostalgic quatrains *Agli Amici della Valle Tiberina* [*To Our Friends of the Tiber Valley*] where the landscape with its memories runs to the *fatal prora d'Enea* [the fated prow of Aeneas]. And there is the polemical shout "Death to the tyrants" and the violent close: "And flames instead of water to unworthy Rome, to the cowardly Capitol, I will send."

For January 19, 1868, he readied the poem *Per Eduardo Corrazzini,* who died of wounds received in the Roman campaign of 1867. A violent invective against the Pope closes these burning lines. Then, for November 30, 1868, he composed the epode *Per Giuseppe Monti e Gaetano Tognetti,* martyrs to Italian efforts to claim Rome, a poem in which, among other things, as a contrast to the violent words spoken against Pope Pius IX occur the fine quatrains on the Messiah which end thus: "The little ones smiled their profound sky-blue smile at the humble prophet; He weeping caressed their blond curls with pure and slender hand." The poem *In morte di Giovanni Cairoli* [*On the Death of Giovanni Cairoli*] is dated January, 1870, and begins in the style of the musical ariosa: "O Villagloria, from Crèmera, when the moon mantles the hills . . ." (Villa Glóri was a vineyard outside the Porta del Popolo of

Rome where, on October 23, 1867, Enrico and Giovanni Cairoli and sixty-eight comrades heroically resisted the papal troops in desperate battle).

As was remarked above, Carducci often wrote violent polemics rather than poetry, but already in the lines *A certi Censori* [*To Certain Censors*], which bear the date December 19, 1871, he was transmuting his activity as a political poet into beautiful strophes: "When I ascend the mountain of the centuries sad-faced and alone, like falcons the strophes rise and flutter around my brow." Then the strophes assume the substance of mythical nymphs:

Al passar de le aerëe fanciulle
Fremon per tutti i campi
L'ossa de' morti, e i tumoli a le culle
Mandan saluti e lampi.

[As the airy maidens pass,
In all the fields
The bones of the dead quiver, and the tombs to the cradles
Send greetings and lightnings.

Therefore he can say to them: "Fight against every evil power, against all tyrants."

Closer to poetry and often completely poetical are the praises of artists, poets, and saints: *Niccolò Pisano, Carlo Goldoni, Dante, Petrarca, Ariosto,* and other Italian poets, as well as Homer [*Omero*], *Virgilio,* and even *Jaufré Rudel* in the famous *novenari* (verse lines of nine syllables), which relate the romantic love and the romantic death of the troubadour, and even *Martino Lutero* [*Martin Luther*], in a sonnet which closes with a lofty, so very human, prayer: "Yet, looking behind him, he sighed: Lord, call me to Thee: weary am I; pray I cannot without cursing." We can even include *San Giorgio di Donatello* [*Donatello's Statue of Saint George*], a poem in which the voice of the prophet is heard: "Worthy, Saint George (oh that I might see it with these weary eyes), that a conquering people of heroes under arms should pass before you in review." Finally, the sonnet to Giuseppe Mazzini, of February, 1872, has lines of high poetry: "And a dead people formed ranks behind him. Ancient exile, to a sky mild and stern raise now thy countenance that never smiled, 'Thou alone,' thinking, 'O ideal, art true.' "

The ode to Victor Hugo is beautiful and songlike: "From the mountains smiling in the morning sun, descends the epic of Homer, which like a divine river peopled with swans goes flowing across the green Asian plain." And the expectancy of the close is clear and wholesome in that ode: "Sing to the new progeny, O divine old man, the age-old song of the Latin people; sing to the expectant world: 'Justice and Liberty.' "

There are lyrics inspired by a deed or by a historical figure, such as *La Sacra di Enrico Quinto* [*The Consecration of Henry V*]; with the pace of a romantic ballad, full of skulls and bones, it is a hearty thing. So too are *La Leggenda di Teodorico,* which is even more delightful, and *Nina Nanna di Carlo V* [*The Lullaby of Charles V*].

As the years passed, the praises grew purer and more calmly expressed. The poet reached the time of the odes entitled *Alla Regina d'Italia* [*To the Queen of Italy*], *Il Liuto e la Lira* [*The Lute and the Lyre*], *A Giuseppe Garibaldi, Scoglio di Quarto* [the little port from which Garibaldi and his Thousand set forth on the conquest of Sicily, May 6, 1860], *Saluto Italico, Per la Morte di Eugenio Napoleone, Alla Vittoria* [*To Victory*], *Sirmione* [birthplace of Quintus Valerius Catullus], *Miramar* [Adriatic castle near Trieste, from which Maximilian departed to become Emperor of Mexico]. In these poems, every image transfigures the vehemence of his passion. The sonnets of the *Ça ira* are violent and explosive, but beautiful just the same and harmonious with great self-possession.

Then come the odes of serene, historical contemplation, which were to culminate in the epos, the stupendous preface to which is the inspired ode *Ad Alessandro d'Ancona* with its strophe of lyrical pride: "Slothful terrors of the Middle Ages, black progeny of barbarism and mystery, pale swarms, away! The sun is rising, and Homer sings."

Already in *Juvenilia,* songs of love, landscapes, nostalgia, there is the call to Greece, to "free human genius," to "Mother Rome," to "thou, enigmatic Rome of our people," and the poets also sings hymns to Phoebus Apollo and Diana Trivia. Then he composed in great strophes the passion for the Roman spirit which he nourished within his bosom. "And everything in the world which is civilized, great, august, it is Roman still," he sang in the ode bearing the title *Nell'annuale della Fondazione di Roma* [*On the Anniversary of the Founding of Rome*]. And in the ode entitled *Roma,* he said: "I do not come to thee curious about little things: Who looks for butterflies under the Arch of Titus?" But he gave a still more austere, almost religious feeling of the Roman spirit in the ode *Dinanzi alle terme di Caracalla* [*Before the Baths of Caracalla*] with that severe landscape: "Between the Celio and the Aventine the clouds run darkly: the wind blows damp from the dreary plain: in the background stand the Alban Hills, white with snow." He describes the place in solemn, awe-struck lines, and in contrast to the present time which those Baths recall. He also invokes Fever, calling on that goddess to repulse "the new men" and "their trifling affairs; this horror is religious: here sleeps the goddess Rome." Here the Roman spirit is represented as a sacred sentiment in the form of high melancholy.

Indeed, this religious emotion that arose when he looked at history was to inspire the Carducci of maturity and old age. A limpid strength, softened by a calm melancholy, generated the poet's new odes, such as the one entitled *Furi alla Certosa di Bologna* [*Outside the Monastery of Bologna*]: "Here at the foot of the hill sleep the Umbrian forebears who first, with sound of axes, broke thy sacred silences, O Appennine: sleep the Etruscans descended with the horn [*lituus*], with the spear, with eyes fixed aloft on the green mysterious slopes, and the great, ruddy, red-haired Celts running to wash away the slaughter in the cold Alpine waters which they hailed as Reno, and the noble race of Rome, and the long-haired Lombard, who was last to camp on the wooded peaks."

There are praises of a people, or of a district, such as the odes *Piemonte, Cadore, Alla città di Ferrara, Bicocca San Giacomo, Le due Torri* [*The Two Towers*], *La Moglie del Gigante* [*The Giants's Wife*], *Davanti il castel vecchio di Verona* [*Before the Old Castle of Verona*], *A una Bottiglia di Valtellina del 1848* [*A Bottle of 1848 Vintage Valtellina*]. In each of these poems there are passages of high beauty; for example, the opening of *Piemonte,* which begins like a majestic dance, or the beginning of the second part of the ode to Ferrara: "O pensive land fading out to sea in the lowering sullen air, between gray sands and motionless pools of water, now shaded only by a few oaks, where rarely the wild boar roots," and so on.

L'Antica Poesia Toscana [*Ancient Tuscan Poetry*] or *I Poeti di Parte Bianca* [*The Poets of the White Faction of Dante's Florence*] bring us again to historical evocations. The lines that begin: *Era un giorno di festa e luglio ardea* ["It was a holiday and July was waxing hot"], take us back to the joy of seeing again in imagination an old, old story.

La Canzone di Legnano, epically serene and sorrowful, sketches in whole hendecasyllables almost without syntactical breaks, the victory of the Lombard over Barbarossa, and the figure of Alberto di Giussano stands out in masculine greatness: "And his voice like thunder in May."

Among the newest and most inward historical odes of Carducci — and among the most beautiful of modern poetry — are the odes entitled *Sui Campi di Marengo* [*On the Fields of Marengo*], *Faida di Commune* [*A Communal Feud*], and *Il Comune rustico* [*The Rustic Commune*]. The first of these has fitted the Alexandrine verse, which in Italian poetry almost always has a facile and slovenly musicality, to a sustained and elegant rhythm which permits strophes such as the one which depicts the emperor:

Solo, a piedi, nel mezzo del campo, al corridore
Suo presso, riguardava nel ciel l'imperatore:
Passavano le stelle su'l grigio capo; nera
Dietro garria co'l vento l'imperial bandiera."

[Standing alone in mid-field, hard by his passageway,
The emperor was looking up at the heavens:
The stars passed above his gray head;
Black behind him the imperial banner fluttered in the wind].

In *Faida di Comune,* history takes concrete shape in lyrical poetry without any residue. It is all infused with an ineffable love for that Tuscan landscape which played such an important role in the heart of Giosuè Carducci. There are the fertile hillocks where

. . . lieti
Ne l'april svarian gli ulivi!
Bacchian li uomini le rame,
Le fanciulle fan corona,
E di canti la collina
E di canti il pian risona,
Mentre pregni d'abbondanza
Ispumeggian i frantoi
Scricchiolando.

[. . . joyous
In April the olive trees in their changes!
The men knock the olives from the branches
as the girls form a circle,
and with songs, the hill
With songs the plain resounds,
While, rich in abundance,
The olive-crushers foam,
Creaking.]

There are also the rough stubble of the fields, all silvery with frost," the "languid olive groves," and the "stripped grapevines." Together with the historical incident which brought the Pisans and the Lucchese face to face, there is the airy and storied feeling of an ancient legend:

Bel castello è Avane, e corte
Fu de i re d'Italia un giorno.
Vi si sente a mezza notte
Pe' querceti un suon di corno.
Vi si sente a mezza notte
La real caccia stormire,
Dietro ad una lepre nera
Un caval nero annitrire.

[Avane is a fine castle,
And once upon a time it was the court of the Italian kings.
At midnight there, a sound of horns
Is heard through the oak groves;
There, is heard at midnight
The royal hunt thundering by,
Hard after a black hare,
And a black horse neighing.]

The *Comune rustico* is a landscape out of ancient history, sketched with a purity of images and of language that induce in the heart that Olympian melancholy which constitutes the effect of the loftiest poetry. "And the red heifers on the meadow/Beheld the little senate passing by,/As the light of noon shone down upon the fir trees." This last line tells the meaning of that sun at highpoint in the heavens which shines on the fields and stills the air of high noon. Carducci rarely reached such an intense and hidden understanding in the music of his verse.

It might be said that the ultimate stage of Carducci's poetry gathers together all these motifs into a cosmic vision in which objective history, landscape, and memories arrange themselves so as to express the high meaning of life, the supreme melancholy of living. In such moments Carducci, reaching a new serenity, feels "the Hellenic life flowing tranquilly in his veins." His poetry might be compared to the serene Hebe whom he extols in a landscape, like the one which surrounds "the gentle daughter of Jesse, all enwrapped in golden sparks," and she "contemplates, ethereal," villas, fields, rivers, harvests, and "the snows radiant upon the Alps," and smiles amid the clouds "at the flowering dawns of May, at the sad sunsets of November."

Examples of this Carduccian poetry are to be found in all the volumes of Carducci, without regard to chronological consideration. The stages of Carducci's poetry, which have been seen in landscape, in subjective, as well as nostalgic moments, in civil praise and political celebration and in history, and finally, in moments more complex and yet spontaneous in which all the others are mingled and fused, are ideal stages and therefore belong to any period of the poet.

In this last stage, the *Canto dell 'Amore* should also be included, although it has passages in which eloquence forces the lyrical quality somewhat. Here a historical recollection sets fire to his imagination: the Paolina fortress, which once stood in the very place from which the poet now is contemplating the valley, was destroyed by the people in September, 1860 — it was a symbol of tyranny. But now the poet, overcome by the beauty of springtime, raises his eyes above the human struggles and feels the song of love rising within him: ". . . but like sapphire I feel every thought of mine shining." Now he no longer cares about the priests and the tyrants whom he detested; he would become reconciled with the pope: "Open up the Vatican. I want to embrace him who is his own old prisoner. Come, I drink a toast to liberty. Citizen Mastai [Count Giovanni Mastai Feretti, Pope Pius IX], drink a glass!" And the whole composition is just a bit intoxicated with this last glass of wine so that sometimes it seems just too plebeian, but it is wholesome, and even amusing in certain benign sarcasms. There are unhackneyed lines of real poetical worth: "Do madonnas still walk the rose-colored pathway of these mountains? The madonnas seen by Perugino descending in the pure sunsets of April, with their arms opened in adoration over the child with such gentle divinity?"

In una Chiesa Gotica [*In a Gothic Church*] expresses a sentiment of pagan life (while he has amorous Lydia sitting beside him) against the Semitic god. It is the same impulse that would inspire him to pen the invective against the Galilean with the red locks. Now, however, the Carduccian form has lost the quite physical vehemence of certain epodes, and here, as in the ode *Alle Fonti del Clitunno* [*The Sources of the Clitumnus*], his protest against Christianity has the tone of poetry. But poets' songs are fleeting, universal sentiments; it was not much later that Carducci was to welcome even Christian poetry, and in the *Chiesa di Polenta* [a church of the eighth century], which is one of the great odes of *Rime e Ritmi,* he would feel the religious fascination of the Ave Maria.

The ode *Alle Fonti del Clitunno* is famous, and justly so: the initial landscape in itself would suffice to make it so, with its stern energy and its verdant freshness; here the reminiscence of the classical images naturally brightens into a genuine sensation.

Next to these odes should be placed the *Primavere elleniche* [*Hellenic Springs*] to which Carducci gave such an eminent position in his work; *La Moglie del Gigante* [*The Wife of the Giant*]; or *I due Titani,* which is more mature in feeling and in form, and in which Prometheus and Atlas curse the tyrant Jove in a sort of new hymn to Satan.

Su l'Adda [*On the River Adda*] is mainly love poetry; nevertheless, the presence of Lydia does not destroy the voice of history that the landscape evokes in the poet's heart; in vain he has exclaimed: "Adieu, history of man."

In *Presso l'Urna di P. B. Shelley* [*Close by Shelley's Grave*], however, the loving woman stands before the poet as a cherished being to whom he addresses a serene yet sorrowful discourse: "Lalage, I know what dream wells up from the bottom of thy heart." The presence of the woman infuses the words of the poet with tenderness: "The present hour is in vain; it but strikes and flees; only in the past is beauty, only in death is truth."

The thought of death inspired in him the powerful couplets with the title of *Mors:*

Quando a le nostre case la diva severa discende,
da lungi il rombo de la volante s'ode,
e l'ombra de l'ala che gelida gelida avanza
diffonde intorno lugubre silenzïo.
Sotto la veniente ripiegano gli uomini il capo,
ma i sen feminei rompono in aneliti.
Tale de gli alti boschi, se luglio il turbine addensa,
non corre un fremito per le virenti cime:
immobili quasi per brivido gli alberi stanno,
e solo il rivo roco s'ode gemere

[When to our abodes the stern goddess descends,
From afar is heard the roar of her flight,
And the shadow of the wing that advances coldly, coldly,
Spreads all about a mournful silence.
Beneath the goddess who comes, men lower their heads,
But feminine breasts burst into sobs.
So from the high woods, if July condenses the whirling
storm,
Not a quiver runs along the verdant peaks:
Motionless as though gripped by horror stand the trees,
No sound is heard but the moaning of the stream.]

In the verses *All 'Aurora* [*To the Dawn*], he fuses in a new melody the ancient myth of Aurora and her daily birth upon the world of today. He tells of her beauty and the bondage of those whom she awakens. He lifts the heart to a lofty new religious myth: "Carry me," he says, "Aurora, on thy steed of flame! Into the fields of stars, carry me, whence I may see the earth, all smiling once again in thy rosy light."

A deep melancholy converts the words of the ode entitled *Nella Piazza di San Petronio* into the purest of sounds; for example, he describes a sunset: "It is the soft sweet hour when the sun about to die hails thy towers and thy temple, holy Petronius." In that sunset, it seems as though the sun "reawakens the soul of the centuries . . . and a sad desire through the stern air awakens, a desire of red Mays, of hot, fragrant evenings, when the pagan women danced in the square, and the consuls were returning with defeated kings."

In *Su Monte Mario* [*On Mount Marius*], there is a sorrowful and pagan vision of a dying world. The poet says, "Pour out, atop the luminous hill, pour, friends, the blond wine, and let the sun be refracted in it. Smile, lovely women: tomorrow we shall die." Rarely has his poetry reached the heights of these following lines:

Addio, tu madre del pensier mio breve,
terra, e de l'alma fuggitiva! quanta
d'intorno al sole aggirerai perenne
gloria e dolore!
fin che ristretta sotto l'equatore
dietro i richiami del calor fuggente
l'estenuata prole abbia una sola
femina, un uomo,
che ritti in mezzo a' ruderi de' monti,
tra i morti boschi, lividi, con gli occhi
vitrei te veggan su l'immane ghiaccia,
sole, calare.

[Adieu, earth, thou mother of my brief thought
And of my fugitive soul!
How much glory, and sorrow,
Wilt thou whirl around the everlasting sun,
Until, forced beneath the equator
In search of waning warmth,
thy exhausted progeny shall number
One woman only, one man,
Who standing among the ruins of the mountains,
amid the dead woods, livid and with glassy eyes
Shall over the vast cruel ice see thee,
Sun, set!]

The power of this vision that pictures the ultimate catastrophe of the world has few equals in modern European poetry.

But against this sadness of the death of the earth, Carducci could set the joyous song of love: "Everything passes and nothing can die." That prodigious *Canto di Marzo* [*March Song*], transcribes even more clearly the sentiment previously expressed in the *Canto d'Amore*. Here the art of Carducci is in its moment of grace, and this March, this spring, without any symbolical meaning, becomes naturally the myth of the eternal change and renewal of the world. Here are the enchanting lines on "the forest which puts on its first throbs," or those which describe how "... the shadow of the clouds passes in splashes over the green as the sun pales and brightens," or the others which paint a vivid country scene: "Here comes the rush of rain and the grumble of thunder; the calf pokes its head out of the wet cowshed, the hen, shaking her wings, makes a din, deep in the orchard the cuckoo sighs, and on the threshing floor the children jump."

Such was the poetry of Giosuè Carducci. Beside it must be set the best part and the spirit of the Carduccian prose, which fills several volumes: *Discorsi storici e letterari* [*Historical and Literary Lectures*], which include *Lo Studio di Bologna, Dello Svolgimento della letteratura nazionale* [*Development of the National Literature*], *L'Opera di Dante* [*The Works of Dante*], *Per la Morte di Giuseppe Garibaldi,* and writings on Vergil, Petrarch, Boccaccio, and so on; *Archeologica Poetica,* essays on Petrarch, Matteo Frescobaldi, and on the Italian popular lyric of the thirteenth and fourteenth centuries; *Studi letterari,* on the poems and varying fortune of Dante, and on music and poetry in the fourteenth century, and so forth; *Cavalleria e Umanesimo* [*Chivalry and Humanism*], in which are found, among others, an essay on poetry and Italy in the Fourth Crusade, and a long essay on Poliziano; *Studi su L. Ariosto e T. Tasso; Melica e Lirica del Settecento* [*Melic and Lyrical Poetry in the Eighteenth Century*]; *Il Parini Maggiore* [*The Greater Works of Parini*]; and *Il Parini minore.* There are also various essays in the volumes *Primi Saggi, Studi Saggi e Discorsi, Bozzetti e Scherme* [*Sketches and Polemics*], *Poesia e Storia, Confessioni e Battaglie,* as well as in *Ceneri e faville* [*Ashes and Sparks*]. The poet also personally chose and brought together in one volume his most representative prose writings.

In so many pages of prose, what really strikes the reader is the poetical power of the style, though supported in part by ideas that he drew from the culture of his time and even from *De Sanctis,* the criticism of Carducci is above all useful for an understanding of the strength of his own style. That does not mean that the Carduccian studies of literary history do not have great importance. There is in them the soundness and the experience of a man of taste, and the authority of a man who felt poetry and who also wrote it. His remarks on the structure of a canto, of an expression, and of a poetical line serve to explain the essence of a poet: even the use of the schemata of the literary genres is redeemed in him by the way he groups them historically to grasp affinities, influences, and sources. From all his prose works it is possible to extract a Carduccian history of Italian literature; but, nevertheless, the real interest of Carducci's prose is not in the value of the criticism and history.

Carducci's prose always has a tendency to become poetry. And he worked on it as one would poetry: attentive within each phrase to the music in the accents, pauses, and contractions of the diphthongs; attentive to the creation of an imaginative and decorative substance around each idea, imparting to the very impetus of an invective the grave mischievous composure which redeems its passion. It is necessary to say that in prose polemics Carducci preserved a sense of limit, which, on the contrary, he seemed to lose in certain overly vigorous verses. Truly, the poetical prose of which Leopardi had spoken in connection with the *Operette Morali* is here displayed in full bloom.

The language that Carducci draws from the noblest literary tradition is enlivened by the new warmth with which he infuses the words, especially because of the poetical tendency that impregnates their rhythm and imagery; for example, the beginning of the five lectures on the development of the national literature (*Dello svolgimento della letteratura nazionale*) where he describes the men at the start of the year one thousand, and his pages on the *ottava rima* of Lodovico Ariosto, or the prose *Eterno femminino regale,* or the polemic for *Ça ira.*

Carducci's literary expression always seeks a poetic aura; and this is the great novelty of the prose of his time.

Other Poets

Carducci had one of his most famous polemics with Mario Rapisardi (d. 1912) of Catani. Rapisardi was a singer of man, free from all that he considered social and religious prejudices, especially in *Lucifero* and in *Giobbe* [*Job*], the singer of the fatal unhappiness of man. Both poems are very long. The *Atlantide,* a work of his last years, was a satirical allegory against men, and political, social, and literary tendencies which he hated or did not understand. Perhaps his best works are various poetic collections, such as the *Ricordanze* [*Souvenirs*], the *Poesie religiose* (with a religiousness which is the cult of the ideal), and *Giustizia* [*Justice*]. Rapisardi is a poet of sincere human spirit but of an impetuous vein. All too often he falls into the rhetorical, the declamatory, and the conventional. He translated poets who were dear to his rebellious heart. Lucretius *De rerum natura,* Shelley's *Prometheus Unbound.* He translated Catullus and, with barbarous strophes and, with little sympathy, the *Odes* of Horace.

Arthur Graf of Athens (d. 1913 at Turin) was a diligent and talented explorer of literary history: *Attraverso il Cinquecento* [*Through the Sixteenth Century*], and *Foscolo, Manzoni e Leopardi.* He also studied medieval myths in *Miti, leggende e superstizioni del Medio evo.* He was the author of a badly expressed psychological novel, *Il Riscatto* [*Ransom, or Redemption*] but he was primarily a poet. The eternity of grief, the vain search for happiness, the inanity of the sweetest illusions, the impenetrability of the mystery of Being, the eulogy of man rebelling against Fate, or accepting it without lowering himself — these are the favorite themes of his numerous lyric poems. They are written in a noble form that is sometimes a little academic, and at other times somewhat prosaic. *Medusa, Dopo il Tramonto* [*After Sunset*], *Le Danaidi* (the fifty daughters of Danaüs), *Morgana, I Poemetti,* and *Le Rime della Selva* [*Forest Poems*], which shows the most personal attitude of the poet, are the titles of his collections, which are regaining favor with a discriminating public.

Giacomo Zanella (d. 1888) of Chiampo near Vicenza, a priest, was more famous. The success of his poems was not due solely to their merit. He wrote of science and faith with great dignity of form rather than with warmth of inspiration. Especially noted among his poems is *Sopra una Conchiglia fossile* [*On a Fossil Shell*], which is an imaginative history of the earth and of humanity, and an indication of the higher destinies which await the latter. No less beautiful are *Microscopio e Telescopio,* the *Taglio dell'istmo di Suez* [*The Suez Canal*], *Egoismo e Carità* [*Selfishness and Charity*]. *La Veglia* [*The Watch*] is intimate and inward. The poem in blank verse *Milton e Galileo* is solemnly religious.

Dramatic Poetry

In the period that concerns us here, dramatic poetry was far inferior to lyric poetry, and it is impossible to record the name of a single true poet among all the dramatists. Paolo Giacometti (d. 1882) of Novi Ligue was the author of dramas of passion in verse and prose, such as *La Colpa vendica la Colpa* [*Two Wrongs Make a Right:* literally, *Guilt Avenges Guilt*] and *Torquato Tasso.* His *La Morte civile* [*Civil Death*] is still played. Leopoldo Marenco of Ceva (son of Carlo, who, in the preceding generation had stirred emotion in his audience with the tragedy of *Pia dei Tolomei*) was also the author of sentimental dramas. No longer performed are his *Celeste* or his *Raffaello e la Fornarina* [*Raphael and La Fornarina*], who was Margherita Luti, a model loved by the artist. The Roman Pietro Cossa (d. 1881) had far more dramatic ability. His *Nerone,* in which he endeavored to present the esthete and the sensual side of Nero rather than the tyrant and in which the tragic scenes alternate with the comical and humoristic, seemed a bold novelty.

Paolo Ferrari (d. 1889) of Modena was prolific and varied in production: *Goldoni e le sue sedici commedie* [*Goldoni and his Sixteen Comedies*] and *La Satira e Parini* were his first works and the ones that won him an audience; they were followed by *La Medicina di una Ragazza ammalata* [*A Sick Girl's Medicine*], *Cause ed Effetti,* and *Il Ridicolo.* All the above were composed with the equal vivacity. Later he became attracted to the "thesis drama," in which art too often is subordinated to moral principles, as in the complex *Suicidio.* Giuseppe Giacosa (d. 1906) of Ivrea emulated him in quantity of production and surpassed him in poetic sentiment. In his numerous plays he followed the various currents which rapidly succeeded each other in literary taste or fashion, and he assimilated them all with considerable ability. Among his most celebrated works was the romantic *Una Partita a Scacchi* [*A Game of Chess*]. His *Tristi Amori* [*Unfortunate Love*] and *I Diritti dell'Anima* [*Laws of the Soul*] are quite strong; *Come le Foglie* [*Like the Leaves*] is considered his masterpiece and is perhaps the finest contemporary Italian dramatic work. Felice Cavallotti, a Milanese and an ardent republican who died in a duel in 1908, portrayed his social and political ideals in several historical dramas, such as *I Pezzenti* [*The Beggars*], *Alcibiade, I Messeni* [*The Messenians*]; but he was more successful when he let himself be guided only by his poetic feeling and his facile gift, as in *Cantico dei Cantici* [*Song of Songs*] and *La Figlia di*

Jefte [*The Daughter of Jephthah*]. Giacinto Gallina, a Venetian, wrote comedies in his native dialect carrying on the Goldonian hilarity with a delicate and simple passion which is his alone: *Le Barufe in famegia* [*Family Quarrels*], *Zente refada, I Oci del cuor* [*The Eyes of the Heart*]. For a comedy in Piedmontese, *Les Desgrassie de Monsù Travett* [*Monsieur Travett's Misfortunes*] is a well-done portrayal of the harassed and submissive employé of a past time. The name of Vittorio Bersezio (d. 1900) of Peverano in Cuneo province is still popular. Ferdinando Martini of Monsummano is sceptically shrewd and witty in his dramatic proverbs: *Chi sa il giuco non l'ins egni* [*Don't Give the Game Away!*], *La Strada più corta* [*The Shortest Way*], *Il peggior passo è quello dell 'uscio* [*The First Step is the Hardest,* or *The Beginning is Half the Battle*].

Narrative Literature

Between 1850 and 1900, the output of novels, novellas, short stories, and sketches was prodigious, but it is necessary to come down to the last decades of the century in order to find deft and sure writers. One of the principal writers of those before 1870 are the Genoese Giovanni Ruffini (d. 1881), an ardent follower of Mazzini. He lived for a long time in England and later in France. *Il Dottor Antonio* and *Lorenzo Benoni,* published in the decade following 1850, are interwoven with imaginary events but are representations of the Italian struggles. The former ends with the story of the Neapolitan revolution of 1848; in the second, there is a portrait of Mazzini under the figure of Fantasio. These novels, which are reminiscent of the Manzonian manner in the richness of their analyses and in the calmness of the narrative, were originally written in English.

The *Storia dei cent'anni* [*The Hundred Years*] of

the Milanese Giuseppe Rovani (d. 1874) is a lively exposition of the history of Milan from the peace of Aachen in 1748 down to 1848. Ippolito Nievo, journalist, poet, and associate of Garibaldi on the expedition to Sicily, died in a shipwreck in 1861 when only thirty years old. He left a long story in autobiographical form: *Le Confessioni di un Ottuagenario.* In it, an old man tells the story of his life from the times of the *ancien régime* through the years of the Revolution, the Empire, the Restoration, the wars of 1848 and 1849, and down almost to the eve of 1859. In content, this novel has a good deal in common with that of Rovani. What is needed is more rapidity, less analysis, and more vigor.

The historical novel, in the years around 1870, flourished, if for no other reason than that it lent itself to an expression of the political ideas of the time. Thus, Luigi Capranica, of Rome, derived the material of several novels from the history of Italy; they are dramatically interesting novels with an anticlerical bias. At that time, the history of ancient Rome awakened special interest, a fact which is very understandable considering that the city had been won back, or was on the point of being won back to laic Italy. And so there were dramas and novels on the Roman theme, such as the *Titus Vetius* [*Tito Vezio*] of Luigi Castellazzo, and the *Giulio Cesare* of Rovani. Raffaello Giovagnoli, a Roman, published a series of tales with a Roman flavor, such as *Spartaco* and *Messalina.* However, around 1870 there was also a literature interwoven with the political and national events. Two writers in this field deserve mention here: one of them slips into satire, and the other rises to the epic. The former, Ferdinando Petruccelli della Gattina, of Moliterno in Basilicata, was a fervent patriot who died in Paris in 1890. He published various novels, of which the most singular is *Memorie di Giuda* [*Memoirs of Judas*], and a satirical presentation of the members of the Sub-Alpine Parliament with the title of *Moribondi di Palazzo Carignano* [*The Dying Men of Palazzo Carignano*]. The other writer was Giuseppe Cesare Abba (d. 1911) of Cairo Montenotte, who followed Garibaldi in the expedition to Sicily and, with admirable simplicity and artistic sense, narrated the events of that undertaking in *Da Quarto al Volturno: noterelle di uno dei Mille* [*From Quarto to the Volturno: Notes of One of the Thousand*]; one of the noblest books of modern Italian literature.

But the bourgeoisie which had arisen after the struggles of the Risorgimento, in an Italy far less great than their fathers had dreamed of, preferred a facile narrative literature that would picture common life without probing it too deeply and would arouse emotion without too much excitement. A goodly number of novelists and story writers responded to this requirement, led by Anton Giulio Barrili (d. 1894) of Savona. He left a large number of novels—something like sixty—*Santa Cecilia, L'Olmo e l'Edera* [*Elm and Ivy*], *Val d'Ulivi* were among the most read. Salvatore Farina (d. 1918) of Sassari was restrained and lively. He took special pleasure in picturing customs and places of his native Sardinia: *Amore Bendato* [*Blindfolded Love*] is one of his best novels; there is also *Il Signor Io.* Edmondo De Amicis of Oneglia (d. 1908) seemed at one time the most worthy continuer of Manzoni, at least to those who judged Manzoni's virtues to lie in the easiness and clarity of his expression. De Amicis wrote a great deal. *I Bozzetti Militari* [*Military Sketches*] and the *Novelle* are among his best things, along with *Cuore* [*Heart*] which most Italian children have read and reread. Many of De Amicis' books deal with travel: *Spagna, Marocco,* and *Olanda* succeed in wearying their readers with an overabundance of descriptions. In the novel, as in the *Romanzo di un Maestro* [*A Schoolteacher's Romance*], he showed a lack of constructive ability. He was a fragmentary writer, and *La Carozza di Tutti* [*Everybody's*

Car] is so many fragments, tied together only extrinsically; this is a collection of daily observations which the author makes while riding in a streetcar. De Amicis' care in writing proper Tuscan is obvious, and he eulogized the superiority of the Tuscan variety of the Italian language in a very debatable book, *L'Idioma gentile* [*Pure Italian*].

Gerolamo Rovetta of Brescia (d. 1910) wrote several plays, stories, and especially novels, with little feeling for art, but with an abounding vision of modern life. Of his dramas, *Romanticismo* enjoyed great favor because of the patriotic spirit which animates it. *La Signorina* is one of the best of his novellas, *Mater Dolorosa* is very moving, and *Baraonda* gives broad coverage of the life of business and speculation.

Less well known than the preceding, but perhaps more inward and concerned, is Mario Pratesi of Siena, who died at the age of eighty in 1921. *L'Eredità* [*Heredity*] and *Il Peccato del Dottore* [*The Doctor's Sin*] are two of his best things, and, for those who want to know Italy and her beauties, misfortunes, and traditions, *Figure e Paesi d'Italia* [*People and Places of Italy*] is highly recommendable. The novelist of those whom life has defeated was Emilio De Marchi, (d. 1901), a Milanese, who was filled with human goodness and sadness. *Demetrio Pianelli* and *Col Fuoco non si scherza* [*Don't Play with Fire*] are two of his powerful books.

In the many novels of Matilde Serao, such as *Cuore infermo* [*Sick Heart*], *Fantasia, La Conquista di Roma, Il Paese di Cuccagna* [*The Land of Plenty*], there is abundant spontaneity and naturalness, but if there is plenty of imagination, there is equally abounding declamation. The Milanese Neera (pseudonym of Anna Radius Zuccari) was also a novelist and perhaps the most sincerely feminine contemporary Italian writer. Calabria had a typically regional storyteller in Nicola Misasi, who wrote some very striking tales of brigandage.

Around 1880 the novel began to assume more depth of spirit and less conventional forms; this was when the Realistic or Naturalistic school, originating in France, attracted many followers in Italy. This was a school that brought about the death of any poetry in the writing of mediocre authors, but in born artists took the form of intensity of inquiry and originality of expression. The principal representatives of this movement in the field of the novel are two men from Catania, Luigi Capuana (1839–1915), and Giovanni Verga (1840–1922). In several of his studies in contemporary literature Capuana supported the Naturalistic theories which he put into practice in novels and novellas, such as in *Giacinta, Spiritismo,* and *Un Uomo* [*A Man*]. His fables are especially lively and admirable for their truth and poetry, such as the collection *C'era una volta* [*Once Upon a Time*].

Giovanni Verga (F. F.)

Giovanni Verga was born in Catania on August 31, 1840 and died on January 27, 1922. When he was twenty-one he published a historical novel, *I Carbonari della Montagna,* but his literary career really began with *La Peccatrice* [*The Sinner*], which was published in 1886 when he had left his native Sicily for Florence, where he remained for about a decade.

In 1871 there appeared the famous *Storia di una capinera* [*Story of a Blackcap*], and in 1873 both *Eva* and *Tigre reale,* all these being love stories, as was *Eros,* published in 1875. With these books Verga had not yet attained his originality as a writer although he gave signs of it in some passages. In these, for the most part, his characters resemble the many heroes of French romantic literature.

But in 1874, the Sicilian sketch *Nedda* [*Nell*] had announced a more original Verga. Now the writer, who was more at ease in short themes (like Maupassant) had begun to write tales drawn from material of his native Sicily.

In 1876 the volume *Primavera ed altri racconti* [*Spring and Other Tales*] was published, and it reappeared in 1880 with the title *Novelle.* As a mature writer, he had conceived the short narratives which appeared in 1880 with the title of *Vita dei Campi* [*Country Life*]: included were *Cavalleria Rusticana, La Lupa, Ieli il Pastore* [*The Shepherd Ieli*], *Rosso Malpelo,* and others – all masterpieces of Verga. They are hard and dark vicissitudes caused by elementary passions – vengeances taken against anyone who violated the sanctity of the house and the honor of the family.

While he was continuing to develop the subjects for his *Novelle,* in a tone which had now risen to a powerful originality, Verga wrote in 1881 a vast novel *I Malavoglia* [*The Malavoglia Family,* English translation: *The House by the Medlar Tree*] considered by many to be his greatest work, of which the plot might be called essentially a harmonious series of Sicilian novellas.

Then, in 1882, *Il Marito d'Elena* [*Helen's Husband*] appeared and seemed to go back, in part, to the topics of the youthful novels. But for several years Verga was to continue being faithful to Sicilian material in a rapid succession of novellas and plays.

In that same year, *Pane nero* [*Black Bread*] appeared; it was included in the collected tales of the *Novelle rusticane* which also contained, with other things, two new masterpieces: *La Roba* [*Stuff*] and *Malaria.* In 1883, *Per le Vie* [*Through the Streets*] appeared, and in 1884, *Cavalleria Rusticana,* scenes among the people and *Drammi intimi* [*Inward Dramas*]; then in 1887 came the novellas of *Vagabondaggio;* 1888 brought a new and vigorous novel, *Mastro Don Gesualdo,* which appeared in the *Nuova Antologia* and reappeared the following year in a revised edition.

In 1891 *I Ricordi del Capitano d'Arce* [*Recollections of Captain d'Arce*] came out; in 1894, *Don Candeloro e Compagni* [*Don Candeloro and his Companions*]; then in 1896 the dramas *La Lupa* [*The She-Wolf*], *In Portineria* [*In the Porter's Lodge*] and so on. Finally in 1902 the scenic sketches *La Caccia al Lupo* [*The Wolf Hunt*], *La Caccia alla Volpe* [*The Fox Hunt*] and, in 1905 in the *Nuova Antologia* the novel *Dal Mio al Tuo* [*From Mine to Thine*] which had been staged in Milan in 1903 in play form. All these appeared in print.

Verga's tone is that of heart-felt sentiment before the wearisome sadness of living as he sees it in simple souls bent beneath a religious sense of duty, honor, and labor. When these men and women sin, when they revolt against their destiny, there is yet in them an obscure recognition of the laws which they have broken and, sometimes resignation, acceptance of a punishment whose reason is mysterious and fated. A dismay which only habit has made serene is in the wisdom of their proverbs, which are the truths and the commands transmitted from their forebears. These people for whom Verga shows tenderness (and what is their life except the very sentiment which Verga feels of things?), these humble folk, in all their vehement passions as in their daily labors, are afraid of enjoying or at least restrain any excessive joy as though from an inborn modesty and from a distant terror.

This is how Verga appears in his principal works, especially in *I Malavoglia* and the great novellas of his later years. Consider the desolate and mournful situation of the Malavoglia family, the family of fisherfolk marked by a sorrowful destiny: 'Ntoni (Antonio) and his son Bastianazzo, his daughter-in-law, and the five grandchildren. Bastianazzo's boat is overturned by the sea with his load of beans which were not paid for and which the code of honor commands must be paid; one of the grandsons is led astray by the city in which he was doing his military service and he ends up in prison; another one was a casualty in the battle of Lissa; and the girl runs away and is ruined. Finally, the head of the family 'Ntoni, who has handed over the "house by the medlar tree" in payment of the debt, dies in the hospital. It is the common life of a whole Sicilian town in the first years of Italian unity, but it is sensed in the simple passions of those whose deep and intense lives ingenuously reflect the universe, or rather the painful toil of the universe, in good and bad.

If in *Mastro Don Gesualdo* Verga assembles, so to say, the world of his early novels in the figures of the wife and the daughter of the protagonist, the latter, who is a man of the fields who has become wealthy, represents the life of the humble Sicilian folk in its very depths, dominated by the same difficult laws, and tormented by the same destiny.

Verga's art adheres to this world of the peasant with a mournful serenity, with a restrained almost reluctant musicality, which for that very reason is more inward and has strength of relief and rhythm that neither deforms nor constrains the different characters.

Yet it sometimes happens that Verga restricts his expressiveness within the mental horizon of his humble characters. Then he constricts and freezes expression in a sort of jargon of the people, in proverbs, in clichés, in rough dialectal images, as though a townsman were trying to speak the way the peasants do, without being aware that inevitably he is distorting their accent. Then Verga expresses himself in a dialectal language, negating that lyrical and musical virtue wherein lies the best of his strong and sober style. The result is his monotony, which critics mention.

In his freer moments, Verga displays, even in his novels his incomparable expressive strength, with that melancholy and melodious dirge-like chant which passes into the accents and the pauses of his humble prose. Consider the beginning — I almost said, the prelude — to the novella *La Roba* [*Stuff*, or *Possessions*]:

> The wayfarer who made his way along the Biviere di Lentini, spread out there like a piece of a dead sea, and the parched stubble of the Plain of Catania, and the ever-green orange trees of Francoforte, and the grey cork-oak trees of Resecone, and the deserted pastures of Passaneto and of Passinatello, if to beguile the boredom of the long dusty road under the sky dark with heat, at the hour when the little bells on the stretcher on wheels litter sound sadly in the immense countryside, and the mules let their heads and tails droop and the driver sings his melancholy song to keep from being overcome by the drowsiness of malaria. If he asked: "To whom does this belong?" he would hear the answer: "To Mazzarò."
>
> And passing close to a farm as big as a whole town, with storehouses like churches, and flocks of hens huddled in the shade of the well, and the women with hands lifted to their eyes in order to see who was passing: "And here?" "To Mazzarò."
>
> And going on and on, while the malaria weighed heavily on his eyelids, and suddenly the barking of a dog struck his ears, passing by an endless vineyard which spread up the hill and out over the plain, motionless, as though the dust were weighting it down, and the guardian stretched out face down upon his gun by the heavy wall, and opened an eye to see who it was: "And here?" "To Mazzarò."
>
> Then came an olive grove as thick as a wood, where the grass never sprouted and the harvest lasted into March. They were the olive trees of Mazzarò.
>
> And toward evening, when the sun was going down red as fire, and the country was veiled in sadness, the long lines of the plows of Mazzarò would be met, returning slowly, slowly, from the fallow lands,

> and the oxen crossing the ford, slowly, muzzles in the dark waters; and far off in the pasturelands of the Sansiria, on the slope, were visible the huge, whitish masses of the herds of Mazzarò, and the whistle of the herdsman was heard echoing in the gorges, and the cattle bells sometimes tinkled, sometimes not, and the lonely song dying away in the valley. "All Mazzarò's possessions."
>
> It seemed as though even the setting sun belonged to Mazzarò, and the cicadas that were whirring and the birds flying to huddle behind the clumps of turf, and the hissing of the horned owl in the wood.

This is a notable example of the spirit and the form of Giovanni Verga. In this broad rhythm, with an entirely different character, is found that "poetry in prose" which was mentioned in connection with Carducci. When it reaches this tone level, a narration belongs by right to the history of poetry.

Historians and Critics

Positivism had much influence on historical research, but at the same time it hindered a full knowledge of events. Pasquale Villari, a Neapolitan, was one of the great representatives of the new direction. His most outstanding works were *Savonarola e i suoi Tempi* [*Savonarola and His Times*] and *Niccolò Machiavelli e i suoi Tempi*. On the other hand, Michele Amari of Palermo was a historian of the old manner; he wrote the *Guerra del Vespro* [*The War of the Vespers*], which is full of learning and inspired by the most fervent love of country, and the *Storia dei Mussulmani di Sicilia* [*History of the Sicilian Moslems*].

Some autobiographies are directly connected with the history of the times; for example, the *Ricordi autobiografici* by Giovanni Duprè of Siena, a classical sculptor, and the *Ricordanze della Mia Vita* [*Recollections of my Life*] by

Settembrini. Luigi Settembrini of Naples was one of the noble spirits of the Risorgimento. In his youth he was imprisoned because of membership in the Young Italy group. In 1849, following the failure of the Neapolitan revolution of 1848, in which he had actively taken part, he was condemned to death; the sentence was commuted to life imprisonment in Santo Stefano. He consoled himself for the horrors of the prison by translating Lucian's *Dialogues.* In 1859 he was about to be deported to America with other prisoners, but in a most romantic way, he succeeded in fleeing to England whence, after 1860, he was able to return to his now free and Italian Naples. He became a teacher of Italian literature in the university there and died in 1876. He told his life story in the above-mentioned *Ricordanze,* a book which expresses all the sufferings and the invincible goodness of the patriots and the horrible moral conditions of the kingdom under the last Bourbons. Literature was the great love of Settembrini, second only to his love of the fatherland. His *Lezioni di Letteratura Italiana* is a clear, lively book, more a work of art and poetry than criticism. There are some historical inaccuracies in it, and its judgments are not invariably objective, being often obscured by political and anticlerical passion.

Settembrini was lacking in the critical habits which were outstanding in another southerner, Francesco De Sanctis (d. 1883), of Morra Irpina, which today is called Morra De Sanctis. He emigrated to Turin for the Italian cause after 1850, and then he went to Zürich, (where he taught at the Politechnic). After 1860, he was distinguished by the Italian government with many offices and honors, which for him were just obligations to make him work still harder. He was the foremost historian of Italian literature. For him, a work of art is resolved in its historical environment, and even more, in the mind of its creator. For him, poetry is a spontaneous product, and its content and form are inseparable: precepts and rhetoric are all contrary to the poetic process and to the understanding of poets. His *Storia della Letteratura Italian* (which is to be taken as part of a whole including the numerous critical essays and the *Lezioni sulla Letteratura Italiana del Secolo XIX*) remain a fundamental book for anyone who wishes to know more about Italian literature than names, anecdotes and dates. It helps to give a full understanding of the individual merits and significance of Italian writers, and at the same time show the rise, development, decadence, and reconstitution of the national consciousness through the literature.

Italian Literature Between Carducci and the Twentieth Century (E. M.)

It is necessary to pay great attention to distinguishing the writers who in the middle and late nineteenth century still belong to Romanticism from those who are already working in the culture of Positivism or, indeed, are taking part in the Realistic movement.

Notwithstanding their attitude as poets *maudits* and the influence upon them – still vague – of Baudelaire, the poets called *scapigliati* must nevertheless be included in Romantic literature. They represented either the romantic Bohemianism of Italy, or they adapted the ironic-fabulous moods of Heinrich Heine to their own poetry. Heine was beloved and translated by Carducci himself and was a strong influence on Italian Romanticism, together with other German poets of *lieder* (from Goethe to Platen to Uhland). These *scapigliati* liked to consider themselves Satanists and rebels, destroyers of the petty bourgeois morality and the Philistinism of the orthodox *benpensanti* or right-thinking persons. As a consequence they brought into the Italian literary tradition prose-poetry and even erotic and blasphemous obscenity. But there is discernible in the real poets another kind of inspiration, something between fable and idyll tempered by irony. It invades their personal memoirs, even those of adolescence, or represents pathetic and light fantasies, something in the nature of melancholic *divertissements.* This bohemianism was known as *la scapigliatura,* and its knights-errant were Cletto Arrighi (that is, Carlo Righetti), among other things the author of a novel appropriately entitled *La scapigliatura e il 6 Febbraio* based on the Mazzinian uprising which broke out in Milan on February 6, 1853; and Giuseppe Rovani, author of the novel *Cento anni.* As a narrator, in moods running from whimsical to affectionate, Rovani conjures up his Milan of the "good old times." So, too, Emilio Praga writes poems against the ideal drowned in mud, opposing it with "a strange and sublime blasphemy." But already the fact that the blasphemy must be "sublime" betrays the old romantic Prometheism and the old masters of European Romanticism (Shelley, Byron). Of course Positivism had already inspired Carducci's poemical lines against the hypocritical and farcical romantic idealism, starting off with the line made famous in *Intermezzo*: "O idealismo umano, Affògati in un cesso." [O human idealism, Go drown yourself in a watercloset]. But the poems of Praga that are remembered are those which turn back to good old religious and popular legends (*I re magi*: the fine old men with their golden scepters), or back to family affections remembered with elegiac tenderness: *Tavolozzo, Penombre, Fiabe e leggende.* The anguish of living supplies the material for the poetry of Giovanni Camerana of Casale Monferrato (1845–1905), but this is all sentimental, not problematic. Anguished and not conceptually mediated, like Praga Camerana also likes to stretch out and rest amid the spectacles of nature. When the landscape darkens and even grows gruesome, he hints of the Romantic manner which once was that of Alfieri and Foscolo. Another Bohemian poet is Arrigo Boito who in his operatic librettos and his poems conjures up the historical ages with sentimental impetus and stern sadness.

The spiritualistic and ironic-fantastic tones of the bohemians, therefore, do not carry us to realistic and social poetry. Furthermore, the realism that prevailed in the theater and in narrative literature in the late nineteenth century did not have a widespread parallel in Italian lyrical poetry, which remained firmly bound to the Classical-Romantic literary tradition. The most vital book of poetry inspired by polemical realism is Carducci's *Giambi ed Epodi,* in which the battle against the Romanticist languors, the hypocritical piety, and the financial speculation of *la terza Italia* (post-1848 Italy, "the Italy of the Italians" following the Italy of the Romans and that of the Church) sometimes becomes prosaic in gait and crude in language. The numerous poets of the Carduccian school (Marradi, Ferrari, Guido, Mazzoni, Panzacchi, Giacinto Ricci Signorini, Giuseppe Chiarini) were, rather, evokers of historical landscapes or poets of personal fantasies. Nor do poets like Costanzo, an elegiac, or Stecchetti, who is too facile and lenient, forsake the old Romanticism: in both, the social, or rather, socialistic accents lose their edge and become diverted to other and different motifs. The same thing happens to writers of the time who dissolve their realistic-social notions in idyllic or elegiac effusions, or in a social novelette which, at most, reflects the patriotic and homely oleograph of the lesser Italian bourgeoisie. And yet, there is also a realistic poetical line, for example, Vittorio Betteloni (see p. 454), who, to be sure, gives way to idyllic loves and impressionistic pictures, but at the same time betrays a corrosive irony. This irony does not restrict itself, as happens with the bohemians, to tempering daydreams and reveries, but rejects the dream and the oleographic artifice in the name of truth, by virtue of a new consciousness of the art of living. Hence the significance of the prose-poetry, of that concession to popular, dissilusioned language; in Betteloni the illustrious and literary locutions are pure parody. They foreshadow the classicism in a key of irony of one of the writers standing on the threshold of the Italian school of the so-called "decadent" poets; namely, Guido Gozzano. For another reason socialistic realism appears evident in the poetry of the Milanese Pompeo Bettini (1862–1896), translator of the Communist Manifesto, anti-militarist, anti-Dannunzian, who, without making concessions to the fad for novelettes, to Romanticist piety, or to sentimentalism, enfolds in his verses the figures of poor children, petty laundresses, and socially disappointed schoolteachers.

The two most typical and popular means of expression, the epic and the comic: that is, the meeting in the common people of heroic chant and comic laughter that De Sanctis had noted, are present in the twenty-five sonnets of *Villa Gloria* (1866) and the fifty sonnets of the *Scoperta dell'America* by the Roman Cesare Pascarella (1858–1940). In modern Roman dialect a man of the people narrates the undertaking of the Cairoli brothers in defence of Rome in 1848 and the discovery of America by Christopher Columbus. In the comic-epical song of the Roman commoner, Pascarella does not always succeed in conveying all the historical reality; sometimes the poet's critical intelligence dominates the popular material (in this regard another collection of modern Roman dialect sonnets is more coherent: *Er Morto de Campagna,* 1882). However, this work by Pascarella has raised dialect to epic heights, and we should add, to the level of the popular epos in its comic dress.

An even greater poet was the Neapolitan Salvatore di Giacomo (1860–1934). In his poetry, the musical and pictorial tradition of Naples is continued through the popular song. It is as though a long secular heredity of songs, music, and colors had been uncovered integrally in the soul of the Neapolitan populace or rather of those people who lived and moved around him, day after day, clamoring to resolve their own evocative poetry in choral poetry. Therefore, the realistic and social poems which present the crowds, streets, courtyards, even the lower classes and the underworld of Naples and the tragedies of the people, are not far from exquisitely musical and contemplative *canzoni* and *ariettas.* Melancholy ecstasy, picturesque images, love of life as it is, without pharisaic hypocrisy and without sentimental mawkishness recur in both branches of poetry. Tragic love and gently passionate love are always real. With Di Giacomo, the idyllic-elegiac poetry of the *scapigliati* is clearly repudiated. In Betteloni, Carducci had already distinguished a poet who had given a new direction to reality, the first to break away from Romanticism; he could have repeated those same remarks, and even more rightly, in connection with the poetry of Di Giacomo. Di Giacomo, a dialectal poet, raised his dialect to such epic tragedy and to such melodic purity, that after him (and after the other two great examples, of Belli and of Porta) no one would dare repeat the old purist prejudice that poetic language can never be dialectal; on the contrary, the true aesthetic principle is that the real poetic and communicative language is always dialectic and appertains to all the historic dialects, so structurally dialectic is the national literary language. The collection of Di Giacomo's sonnets (1848) *'O Funneco Verde* represents in his youthul production a moment still literary but formative. His major poetry, that which reveals in the common people a sense of reality that is both sorrowful and imaginative, is collected in *Ariette e Sunette* (1893), in *Vierze nove* (1907), and also in short narrative poems, such as *A San Francisco,* made up of seven sonnets of tragic inspiration.

Realism was brought to Italy by the dramas of Verga and Di Giacomo. Here we note the latter's *Mese Mariano* and *Assunta Spina.* The first of these two has as its protagonist a mother who goes to the charity home to get her child, but the child is dead and the most that human pity can do is to try to hide the truth from the unhappy woman. The protagonist of the second drama is an adulteress, a woman of the people, the victim of a passionate love affair. The dramatic action represents reality without any show of cruelty and without sentimental attenuations: the author interprets the events by making the action move on and by letting the dialectic dialogue, rapid and terse, burst alternately from the lips of the actors; dialogue which, by allowing a hidden psychological reason to be glimpsed behind the factual circumstance, creates a wondrous feeling of a humanity far richer than our daily humanity, oppressed and saddened by conventions.

Realistic expressions and motifs, limited to personal, individual psychology, are found in the comedies of the Neapolitan Achille Torelli (1841–1922). Among them is one entitled *I Mariti* [*The Husbands*] written in 1867, which tries to prove that a good husband will have a good wife. It is a "thesis comedy," but the old psychological casuistry of the Romantic theater (Ferrari, Giacosa) is raised to a social situation subtly investigated and resolved in action with a certain inventive inspiration. However, the theater in dialect is that which assumes this realistic search for human truth, and which becomes national theater inasmuch as it flourishes in all the regions of Italy and thus welds them into an ethnic and culturally historic unity. This may be said of the plays of Giacinto Gallina and Vittorio Bersezio (see p. 490), alongside which may be placed the Milanese theater of Carlo Bertolazzi, *Nost Milan, La Gibigianna.* The first of these represents the psychological complexity and profusion of the poor people, starting from the fringes of Milan and moving on through the bleak circle of the mountebanks, the public sleeping-house, and refectory. A psychological, rather than social, realism, that is still ideologically rich, inspires the theater of Marco Praga, son of the poet Emilio. His finest comedy, *La Moglie Ideale* [*The Ideal Wife*], investigates with bitter pessimism and yet with temperate moderation a drama with a conjugal background.

The entrance of Realism into narrative literature was still more determinant. A similar realism, understood as research and discovery of psychological and social truth, is not observable in the prose memoirs of the *scapigliati* which include: the *Memorie del presbiterio* [*Memoirs of the Presbytery*] by Emilio Praga; the two volumes of tales by Camillo Boito, the brother of Arrigo; *Storielle vane* and *Senso,* in the fantastic and gruesome tales of Iginio Ugo Tarchetti (1841–1869) of Alessandria which are related to those of Poe and Hoffmann rather than to those of Baudelaire. Because it is autobiographical, his novel *Fosca* is more original and direct. Nor was such realism observable in the impressionistic and witty sketches of Giovanni Faldella (1846–1928) of Vercelli, who was especially famous for his *Figurine*; nor in the extravagant stories of Vittorio Imbriani of Naples (1840–1885), who seems to have have gone back to the baroque grotesque style of the Neapolitan seventeenth century (*Per questo Cristo mi son fatto Turco, Mastr' 'Impicca: For this Christ I became a Turk,* Master Hangman). The representation of Italy under King Humbert is external in the famous book *Avventure di Pinocchio* by Carlo Lorenzini under the pseudonym of Collodi, a Tuscan of Pescia (1826–1890). The value of the book lies in the whimsical and witty adventures of the hero, the puppet-urchin Pinocchio. The customs represented by Edmondo De Amicis (see p. 492) are those of the petty Piedmontese bourgeoisie. A similar remark is in order concerning the Tuscan memoirs of Ferdinando Martini (see p. 490) in *Confessioni e Ricordi* [*Confessions and Recollections*], but praise is due him for his fine book on Africa, *Nell'Affrica Italiana,* which was justly admired by Carducci. In the genre of historical commemoration (which still persisted in the historical drama and novel, and in books and letters about travel) is to be placed the conservative writer

Edoardo Calandra (1852–1911) of Turin, who was faithful to the old Piedmontese monarchical traditions: two of his books were *Reliquie* and *Vecchio Piemonte* [*Relics* and *Old Piedmont*].

On the other hand, realism is at work in the tales and novels of Luigi Capuana (see p. 494), whose *Marchese di Roccaverdina* (1901) is especially important; in the stories of Matilde Serao (see p. 493); in the so-called "humble" realism of Emilio De Marchi (see p. 493); in the narrative of Mario Pratesi (see p. 493); in that of the Neapolitan Federico De Roberto (1861–1927), the author of a psychological novel *L'Illusione* in 1891 and a historical novel, *I Vicerè (The Viceroys)* in 1894; in the varied and often bitter tales of the Pisan Renato Fucini (1842–1921), author of *Veglie di Neri* (1884), of *All'Aria Aperta* [*Outdoors*] (1887) and, after a visit to Naples in 1877, *Napoli a occhi nudi* [*Naples Seen with the Naked Eye*]; and, finally, in the novels of Alfredo Oriani (see p. 514). It is obvious that realism works differently in different writers and often in different works of the same writer. In the narrative of De Marchi, it lightly touches inward intimations and elegiac tones, even though in his best novel, *Demetrio Pianelli,* one may find pages of high and tense drama in a terse and rapid style. In one of Capuana's characters, the Marquis of Roccaverdina, who gives his name to the book in which he appears, feudal tyranny blends with a harassing sense of sin and something like religious terror, so that there results a lonely, shut-in psychological portrait, introverted and rich in complicated ambiguities – forerunner of the decadent psychology of the *fin de siècle. The Viceroys* of De Roberto belongs to the positive-historical genre, but the historical pessimism, lit by gloomy, bitter irony (the last of the Uzeda, of the feudal family which is the protagonist of the novel, is forced to pretend to be democratic in order to keep his personal privileges), announces a crisis that is deeper and more disturbing than is generally stated by the historical-social narrative and theater. The character of Don Blasco, who lives and dies almost overwhelmed by his violent lasciviousness and greed, expresses a wretched gloom which later the decadents were to find an essential and perpetual part of man. A bitter scepticism, without any possibility of expiation, is caught in the more bitter tales of Fucini, which are also his best; the other Fucini of the good-natured, idyllic stories (in *Acqua Passata* [*Bygones*], *Foglie al vento* [*Falling Leaves*], and also in *All'Aria Aperta*), does not redeem himself by the facile Tuscan novelette manner. These stories are Tuscan even in language, a manner much in vogue in the nineteenth century. Perhaps the most authentic realism is that of the tales of Capuana (*Le Appassionate,* of 1893, and *Le Paesane*) and that found in the stories of Serao who after Verga, was the greatest artist (see p. 493) and who gives epical dimensions to realistic material and reveals in the so-called humble people a laical religion of high, tragic power.

The age of Positivism tended to lead poetry and the other inventive arts back to the exact sciences and in particular to physiology. The founders of the Positivist philosophy were the Frenchmen Auguste Comte and Hippolyte Taine; the precursors of psychological realism had also been Frenchmen, the two great novelists Balzac and Flaubert. The theorist of positive or naturalistic aesthetics had been the Frenchman Emile Zola, a doctor of medicine and a novelist. The theories of art as physiology and of the experimental novel as a documentary novel cropped out in the principal Italian authors as well, in Verga and Carducci, and in literary criticism (remember the use of sociology recurring in the historical-literary outlines dear to Carducci and in general to the Positivist school). But the Italian theorist of realism was Capuana, whose two important volumes of criticism must be remembered: the *Studi sulla Letteratura Contemporanea* and *Gli "ismi" Contem-*

poranei [*contemporary "isms"*]. However, Italian Realism let itself be modified or amended according to whether it was being theoretically considered or was being actually used in an artistic work. Just as Capuana the theorist never renounced his rights of invention and was always influenced by the historistic criticism of De Sanctis, so Italian Realistic narrators and playwrights, in the realistic structure of their works, either marshalled the old and decrepit romantic forms of the historic or psychological genres, or clung to the novelette style, or foreshadowed decadentistic motifs. In the youthful narratives of D'Annunzio (see p. 535), realism is already corrupted by the aestheticism of the solitary craftsman. We have seen what equivocal meanings may be grasped in the characters of Capuana, De Roberto, and Pratesi; even the narrative of Oriani, perhaps because of the overly crude and excessive thickness of blood-color tones, announces the exhaustion of realism, compelled to feed upon itself.

It is also foretold in Arturo Graf, a Positivist critic but a perplexed poet baffled by the impenetrable mystery of human fate (see p. 487). Another bemused poet is Domenico Gnoli (Giulio Orsini) author of the *Odi Tiberine* 1898. In these two poets and in Betteloni in his elegiac and ironical manner, but most especially in Graf, recur the wondering, tired tones that would later be found in the poetry of Gozzano on the threshold of the twentieth century. In the narrative corrosive humor the road begins to open to the great humorists of the decadent school: not so much that of the Mantuan narrator Alberto Cantoni (*Il re umorista, L'illustrissimo*), as that of Carlo Dossi (1849–1910) of Pavia, who inserts into his deconsecrating humor a queer equivocal cult of childhood in ways which foreshadow Proust, both in *L'Altrieri* [*The Day Before Yesterday*], written when he was eighteen, and *La vita di Alberto Pisani* written when he was twenty-one. Dossi's language is at the same time colloquial and refined, dialectal and yet affected. So we arrive at the spiritualistic reaction against the age of Positivism with Pascoli, Fogazzaro, and D'Annunzio. The spiritualism in question is an equivocal spiritualism, irresolute or tentative, which represents the direct antechamber of "the Decadents."

Antonio Fogazzaro (F. F.)

Spirits very different from those of the so-called *verismo* [realism] animated the art of Antonio Fogazzaro. He was born in Vicenza on March 25, 1842.

His first teachers in literature were an uncle and later the poet Giacomo Zanella. The uncle eventually was represented in his nephew's novels by the figure of Don Giuseppe Flores. His first literary step was *Miranda* (1874), a short narrative poem which was very successful; this was followed in 1876 by the lyrics of *Valsolda;* then began his series of seven novels and the two collections of short stories: *Malombra* (1881), *Daniele Cortis* (1885), *Fedele ed altri Racconti* (1887), *Il Mistero del Poeta* (1888) *Piccolo Mondo Antico* (1896), *Piccolo Mondo Moderno* (1900), *Il Santo* (1906), and *Leila* (1911).

But he did not give up poetry entirely, and the verses he wrote from time to time were collected by him in the volume *Poesie Scelte* (1898) and, ten years later, in the complete collection. He also wrote short pieces for the theater, and he published the discourses which may be considered as his philosophy and criticism: *Discorsi* (1898), and *Ascensioni* (1899).

He was not merely a novelist who was satisfied with artistic production; he was also a restless spirit who needed to set forth his religious ideas. He was a devout Catholic, but inwardly he wanted to reconcile his faith with positive science — Saint Augustine and Darwin — the concept of the Christian soul and that of the soul in spiritism. In *Il Santo* there are modernistic motifs which the Church promptly condemned: Fogazzaro was wounded by this condemnation, but *humiliter se subiecit.* He died at Vicenza on March 7, 1911.

More than the others, three novels reveal the particular art of Fogazzaro: *Malombra,* the first; *Daniele Cortis,* the second; and *Piccolo Mondo Antico,* the fourth.

Malombra is the novel in which Fogazzaro reverses all the experiences accomplished in his youth, and at the same time it is the one in which he gains awareness of himself and finds his vocation. In this regard, there is no other work among Fogazzaro's writings richer in motifs. As a document of the author's personality, this is truly the fundamental book. He was not only seeking the road to art, he was also asking for an answer to his religious and moral questionings. He thought he could solve his problems by imagining the story of Marina, a restless and sick creature, who believes in reincarnation and is convinced that she is the reborn soul of a certain tragic Cecilia. Around this central nucleus revolves a long series of episodes, dialogues, descriptions, and climaxes. However, vivid as it is in its details, its sketches, its anecdotes, and its short "lyrics" of landscape or of love, the novel possesses no real unity.

Daniele Cortis is the second of Antonio Fogazzaro's novels and therefore profits by the experience which the author had acquired in *Malombra.* But here, that which concerns the protagonist, the themes of religion, love, and politics, are not tied together nor sufficiently subordinated among themselves; in addition, there is a filial drama which torments Daniele. There are four dramas, then, each somewhat independent of the others, and it is not enough to recount them one after the other, or alternately; the final drama which from these elements arise and dominate the whole is not felt. The development of major prominence remains the love of Elena and Daniele; an illicit love which imposes on Elena a final renunciation that is morally fine but artistically too unexpected. While the love is drawn with ability, the obstacle to this love and the duty to which Elena sacrifices herself by renewing her fidelity to a worthless husband do not have the necessary fullness of psychological content. However, the style of the novel is considerably more sober and purer than that of *Malombra* and often develops a tone of human tenderness which is deeply touching.

Piccolo Mondo Antico (*Little Ancient World,* Eng. tr. *The Patriot,* 1906) is the greatest of Fogazzaro's novels, and the one in which his virtues as narrator are best proportioned. The story is lively and varied, yet everything tends toward an emphasis on the effects which are produced on the personalities of the protagonists, Franco and Luisa, by the unexpected death of their little daughter Maria, who was affectionately nicknamed Ombretta and who is pictured with ineffable grace. Her mother rebels against that destiny: Franco's faith is stronger, and he bows to God's design.

The scene in which Luisa learns of the accident, and that in which she and the doctor attempt to restore the drowned girl's breathing, are among the most powerful that the narrative art of the nineteenth century has produced. The scene near the clump of chestnuts, when Franco hears the Austrian guards speak of the accident, and then his meeting with his wife, and the sight of the dead girl, are inspired pages that keep this work ever young. What is most enchanting is the affectionate and melancholic pity with which he had watched over and followed the little creature, and the delicate weft of affections which are woven around that little head. The tragedy and the sense of the divine are felt as shadow or as light by the adult protagonists of the story. Also appealing is the presence of the countryside, that lake, that sky, those hills, and the variety of persons who move and have their being around the aristocratic protagonists; there are even some moments of amiable comedy. Thus in this work the gifts of Fogazzaro at his best are harmoniously composed.

Alfredo Oriani (F. F.)

At this point Alfredo Oriani must also be discussed; he is the author of several novels, although his major work is a vast historic narration. He was born at Faenza on August 22, 1852. He made his début in the literary world as a narrator, with a book published in 1876 entitled *Memorie Inutili* [*Useless Memoirs*]. It was followed in 1877 by *Al di là* [*Beyond*], in 1879 by *Gramigna* [*Couch-grass,* or *Weed*], in 1881 by *No,* in 1883 by *Quartetto,* then *Sullo Scoglio e altri racconti* [*On the Reef and Other Tales*]. They are all dark, gloomy narratives, emotional, shaken by an anarchical drive of revolt against society. Describing troubled, mad characters, the author seems to cling with angry spite to their immorality and their destructive nihilism; on the other hand, his deepest spirit opposes and loathes their lives. Indeed, it comes about that while his narrations present figures upset by evil passions, as soon as he begins to set forth a social thesis he manifests the highest human ideals and the most orthodox principles. His book *Matrimonio* (1886) defends with copious exemplification the indissolubility of the marriage bond. The work consists of a curious letter of 444 pages addressed to Alexandre Dumas *fils.*

In these books Oriani's style shows the strong influence of French social literature, not only that derived from the nineteenth-century novelists, from Balzac to Hugo and Zola, whose realism seemed sometimes to take pleasure in indecent things, but also from French journalism, and from parliamentary speeches to popular, political, and trade association meetings. Oriani's style, no matter what he writes about, is that of a great tribune.

It would be well to note here that, while the myth of rebellion for Carducci took the name of *Satana,* for young Oriani it was called *Giuda* [*Judas*]. In the betrayer of Christ (although the idea was not new) Oriani saw the man who made use of hatred as a defence of the weak. His were somewhat abstract ideas of revolt in which anarchical and humanitarian principles were confused and which he manifested in the letter *A Giuda di Simone da Carioth* [*To Judas, Son of Simon of Kerioth*].

Alfredo Oriani also participated in the literary press that developed in Italy in the second decade of the united kingdom, and his writings, under the pseudonym of Ottone di Banzole, appeared, for example, in the *Fanfulla della Domenica* [*Sunday Fanfulla*].

Despite all this, he was constantly out of his element, a sort of man without a country, a man who had not found himself. He felt himself alone. His scorn for his contemporaries, who did not confer on him the eminent position to which he aspired, had flashes of greatness, but it was also an attitude in which he took pleasure.

In 1900 he asked the Duke of the Abruzzi to take him along as historian of the Polar expedition, but his request was refused. Only in his old age did Oriani gain the fame which thereafter was to grow immeasurably down to our own days; then criticism took heed of him, and the young began to look for his books.

Oriani continued his career as a storyteller with *Il Nemico* [*The Enemy*] in 1894, then with *Gelosia* [*Jealousy*] in the same year. Troubled and illicit passions were still dealt with, but the spirit of the artist seemed to be more mature. The material would be of like nature when, in *Vortice* [*Vortex*] Oriani would tell of the last day of a suicide: a vice-ridden gambler, who wages his fortune and contaminates his honor so that even his suicide is not a redemption. Nor would the material be more savory in

Olocausto (1902), which tells of the vile prostitution of a human creature.

So then the novels of Oriani are twisted and distorted, as though prey to a fury which takes the form of a need to say or, rather, to shout scandalous things, things in which his heart does not participate. For indeed there is a severe moralist in Oriani, as is shown by the works of his maturity and especially his historical works. Nonetheless, between *Gelosia* and *Vortice,* in 1906 Oriani's novel *La Disfatta* [*Defeat*] came out; it is a novel made of very different material, a novel which reaches a high level of human drama.

La Disfatta is unanimously considered to be his best novel. Here he no longer uses the dark motifs; instead he uses the life of a thinker, of Professor De Nittis, who was incapable of uniting the sense of action among men with profound speculations and the widely varied experiences of his thought. He finally found himself stranded in sorrowful solitude, as the life about him took from him his son and his friends before he could reach the glory to which he had aspired. And yet the man did not lose himself in that sorrow, but "taking up his pen, as an ancient pilgrim his staff within sight of the Holy Sepulcher, he pressed forward on the footprints of God."

There are also the stories of *La Bicicletta* (1902), which are among the most serene of Oriani's writings. He also wrote verses entitled *Monotonia,* which have no poetic vitality. He wrote various dramas, some of which, for example *L'Invincibile,* were played but without too much success.

The real strength of Oriani is in history rather than in novels and short stories. He had a philosophical temperament of fine inspiration; if indeed he did not have inventive strength in the field of ideas, at least he did not succumb to the most ambitious and perishable part of Positivism. Through the rather strange Vichianism (cf. G. B.

Vico) of Giuseppe Ferrari and the Hegelianism of Angelo Camillo De Meis (who taught at Bologna and with whom Oriani developed a friendship), he cultivated an idea of history which is tied to Hegel's idealism. This idealism, which he expressed in a French manner, here again following the example of Ferrari, animated his historical vision and gave it a nobility which the common historiography of his times had, for the most part, lost.

All the writings of Oriani which involve problems of morals and of politics are tied to his conceptions as a historian, including *Fino a Dògali* [*All the Way to Dogali*] which he published in 1889. This is a writing of the utmost eloquence, in which Oriani looks at Italy in her new destinies and in the mission which awaits her in Africa. Oriani the historian collected certain of his essays in 1901 with the title *Ombre di Occaso* [*Sunset Shadows*].

La Rivolta Ideale is dated 1908. It is a book in which themes dear to Oriani recur and are sometimes developed further, such as the significance of the aristocracy in the ancient and modern worlds; the character of modern industry; social classes and political parties; the meaning of Christianity; Italy's mission in Africa, and so on.

The work was intended to be only a premise for examining the origins of contemporary struggle, but it should be considered, rather, as a continuation and annotation of *La Lotta Politica in Italia* [*The Political Struggle in Italy*], which appeared in 1892 and is Oriani's real masterpiece. This famous work is a dramatic presentation of Italian history down to the Risorgimento. The author relates how Italy passed inevitably from the communal federalism of the Middle Ages and from all the other federal tendencies, including the last one in 1848, to national unity, the unity which Mazzini wanted to be republican and which ended in the monarchy.

A few excerpts will give the spirit and the style of this book:

> Italy, in fifteen centuries of the most complex of all histories, finally attained her own political individuality by becoming a Nation.
>
> The number of Italian revolutions is so enormous that even today science has difficulty in verifying it; the range of her political forms is so extensive that no progress in it can be impeded; the crowd of her great men is so dense that fortune, and not merit, must award them immortality.
>
> But Italy, withdrawing from the vanguard of civilization, covers her retreat by launching Columbus on the discovery of America and Galileo on that of the heavens. So, after having given the world Roman and Christian unity, she adds thereto the unity of geography and planetary universality, surpassing Christianity itself, with which she had saved the world from medieval barbarism.

More than any particular thesis, the great worth of the book lies in the lofty sense of the Italian spirit which is unfolded there at every turn, that loving eulogy of Italy at the very moment when evils disdainfully assail her, a persistent, implied comparison between Italy and every other nation, with a sentiment of the superiority of Italy. *Lotta Politica* is a continuous affirmation of the primacy of Italy. He nursed this idea with such passion that even when he shot his arrows against the Italy of his own time (following the custom which free spirits have always had, never satisfied with what was already accomplished and always reaching for something better), he recognized that "the fact of her reestablishment as a unity and the fall of the temporal power" gave Italy "a greater significance than that of the new German empire." This idea caused him, in 1909, to write widely admired words to celebrate "the new triumph of the third Italy, which Europe must indeed accept as a great nation amongst the greatest, all athrob with a sudden wealth, with fields everywhere furrowed, with new roads, ports open to the expansion of life, cities noisy and smoky with factories, another industrial nation, free, sovereign, which no longer fears foreigners," and so on.

Oriani was a writer of great eloquence, a sort of oratorical athlete or vehement tribune who had a taste for the showy expression, the broad and manifold comparison, the spirited antithesis clothed in songlike declamatory style.

Above all, he was uplifted and inspired by his Italian faith and passion, which brought from his pen pages like that on the men who fell at Dògali:

> In all the heroisms made immortal by chronicles or made sacred by poems, passion is the soul when despair is not the only strength: in the five hundred there at Dògali the immobility of the battle and of death give proof of a conscience lifted above life by one of those sudden revelations which history makes in the heart of a nation. They felt themselves great, and they were great. Their colonel, riddled with wounds, swept up in the great African whirlwind, gathered within him all his pride to salute them, a salute which neither Rama, nor Achilles, nor Siegfried, nor Orland would have understood. "Present — arms!" And the last wounded, perhaps poor country boys from Abruzzo or Sicily, understood his gesture, and presented arms to their dead comrades, offering themselves, unarmed targets, to the last shots of their slayers. Immortal poetry has protected the life of one of those obscure heroes to save from oblivion those words which not one of its greatest poets, from Valmiki to Firdausi, from Homer to Dante, from Shakespeare to Hugo, in the most fervent inspirations of genius, had been able to find, and which the heroic colonel pronounced in front of his own dead, forgetful of the world for whose civilization he was dying.

This page may also serve as an example of his emotional style in abounding and solemn eloquence. Alfredo Oriani died at Casola Valsenio on October 18, 1909.

Giovanni Pascoli (F. F.)

Giovanni Pascoli was born at San Mauro in Romagna on December 31, 1855. A tragic event saddened his childhood when he was about twelve years old: the murder of his father, who was administrator of the La Torre estate of the princely Torlonia family. Ruggiero Pascoli was returning home, driving his carriage himself; he was alone, and the "dapple-grey mare" [*La Cavalla Storna*] who was drawing the carriage went on until she reached home. In many of his verse or prose works Giovanni Pascoli recalled that crime which was never punished and which brought death and ruin to others of his dear ones: first his sister, aged eighteen, and a month later, his mother. In the Preface to *Myricae* (1894), dedicated to his father, the poet wrote: "Reader, there were men who opened that tomb. And in it a whole flourishing family came to an end." And in the Preface to the *Canti di Castelvecchio,* published in 1903, he added: "Other men, who remain unpunished and unknown, willed the death of a man not only innocent but virtuous, sublime in his loyalty and goodness, and the death of his family. And I refuse. I will not let them be dead."

After the death of his father, the studies on which he had embarked at the Collegio degli Scolopi (Scuole Pie) in Urbino continued in that same "excellent school." He went on later to a *liceo in* Rimini and to a *liceo* in Florence. Then, by winning first place in a competition judged by Giosuè Carducci, he obtained a scholarship granted by the Commune of Bologna to the first six admitted to the University. In a page included in the *Anthologies,* Pascoli told of this meeting with Carducci, whose most distinguished pupil he later became.

Young Pascoli's dreams were full of the great human ideals of solidarity and equality, and he took a position alongside the rebels who were inciting to social revolt, feeling that here was his only way to avenge himself on a society that had brought no light to bear on the killing of his father. In 1879 he was arrested in a demonstration and had to remain in jail for three months. Thus he lost his scholarship, but regained it later. In 1882 he took his degree and started off on a career as professor of Latin and Greek, first for two years in Matera, then at Massa, and after that for eight years in Leghorn. Then he wrote those Latin verses which, when sent to the competitions in Amsterdam, revealed him as being the finest poet who in modern times had graced Latin letters: *Veianus* is dated 1892, *Phidyle,* 1894. At the same time, he was writing those Vergilian *Myricae* that had first appeared in 1891 and were added to in later editions. The honor of having pointed out the new poet to the Italians belongs to Gabriele d'Annunzio.

In 1895 Giovanni Pascoli was a probationary teacher at the University of Bologna, and in 1897 he was appointed without examination as professor of Latin literature at Messina. There he remained until 1903, at which time he was transferred to Pisa. In 1907, upon the death of Giosuè Carducci, he was called to take over the chair of his former teacher at Bologna.

During his life as a professor, Pascoli fled whenever possible to a humble cottage at Castelvecchio di Barga, where he stayed with his sister Mariú. There he wrote most of his poems.

His simple life, up to the day of his death on April 6, 1912 at Bologna, has no events of greater importance than those represented by the publication of his books. Of few other poets is it as true as it is for him that their truest history is that of their poetry.

What, then, was the poetical world of Pascoli? The poet said, concerning his *Myricae*: "They are the whir of birds' wings, the rustling of cypresses, the far-off singing of the countryside." And so they are. On the background of their melodies, desires and images of domestic goodness stand out in relief. Sometimes, in their accomplished brevity, the verses have the elegance of Greek handiwork. But in *Myricae,* as later in the *Canti di Castelvecchio,* there is an intimation of death, as though the tragic mourning of the poet was always in the offing of each vision. The poet was to write a powerful justification of this presence of death: "But life without thought of death, that is to say, without religion, which is what distinguishes us from the animals, is a madness, either intermittent or continuous, either expressionless or tragic."

The *Canti di Castelvecchio* also have the rural inspiration in their background, which stress the vocal gift of the birds. These too are *myricae* [sweet-gale, bay-berries]. But, in Pascoli, the birds are not those common to poets – nightingales or swallows, sparrows or larks – they all have other names and sounds – robins, blackcaps, goldfinches, cuckoos, wrens, finches, turtledoves, titmice, stonechats.

The *Primi Poemetti,* published in 1897, and augmented in later editions up to the fourth in 1906, sing praises of the life of the fields and of their people in a manner of narrative or elementary epic. They sing of the great difficulties of living, the struggles of men and their illusions, and they invoke human kindness. In this second group there are the famous *I due Fanciulli* [*The Two Children*]; *Digitale Purpurea (The Common Foxglove); L'Eremita* [*The Hermit*]; *L'Aquilone* [*The Kite*]. Later, some *poemetti* were transferred to the work *Odi ed Inni* [*Odes and Hymns*] in a new arrangement which the poet made of his compositions. Related themes are to be found in the

Nuovi Poemetti (1909) where, with other things, may be read the fine tercets of the *Staccio* [*Sieve*].

The *Poemi Conviviali* (1904) are mostly the poetry which Pascoli felt resulted from his vast knowledge of Hellenism and his love for the ancient poetry. Such compositions as *Solon* or *L'Etera* or *Psyche* are among the loftiest expressions arising out of the poetry of old in the nineteenth century. Here the poet has produced a work of consumate artistry, coming close to an Alexandrine elegance.

The *Odi ed Inni* (1906) are the civil praises of Pascoli. They begin with the proud honor which the poet pays to himself in *La Piccozza (The Ice-axe):* "I climbed the mountain without the din of companions' cries. Silence. No dark dejection — no voice but voices of the dead"; and he feels that he is rising alone "to stay alone with the eagle" and to die up there, while beside him the mountaineer's ice-axe "reflects the stars of the Bear."

Here the *Aurora Boreale,* in whose impalpable beauty the poet sees the mystery of God, stands next to the *Inno secolare a Mazzini*: the hymn *Al Re Umberto* next to the tercets *Nel Carcere di Ginevra* addressed to the anarchist Lucheni. The poet sings the praises of Giuseppe Verdi and Antonio Fratti, the Duke of the Abruzzi and Umberto Cagni and, with ineffable strength, the flight of *Andrée,* whose end is expressed in two unforgettable lines: "Then there was silence. The star shone above the pole, like a lonely lamp on a tomb." (The Swedish aeronaut, Salomon August Andrée set out for the Pole in a balloon from Spitzbergen, July 11, 1897 and never returned.)

There are themes, often powerful, and powerfully expressed in more than one point. But in these odes and hymns there is also something oddly out of proportion, either in the rhythm or in the image, and sometimes the loftiest passages are followed by tired, poor and even paltry lines. But this unequalness, as criticism has remarked, is a frequent characteristic in the work of Giovanni Pascoli.

An epical breadth is aimed at in the various parts of the *Canzone di Re Enzo* (1909) (illegitimate son of Emperor Frederick II, 1225–1272), but here the poet was less successful than elsewhere in hitting his target; quite apt passages are found in it, the verse is from the hand of a master of the art, and the literary details are treated with elegance; but all this is not enough to give the work an enduring life.

In the *Poemi Italici* (1911), we meet the *Paolo Uccello* which Pascoli had written some years earlier. Here the varied virtues of the poet are elegantly balanced around the figure of the painter, who was a Franciscan tertiary who took an oath of poverty. As a result, he who painted little birds was forbidden to own any of those blackbirds or woodpeckers and had to be content with pictures. Once he "took a fancy to a bed-warmer and could not buy it, so then he painted one." Later he stopped saying the Angelus in front of the wall on which he had "painted every sort of bird for the pleasure of seeing them, since he could not own them, and was tempted against poverty." Then Saint Francis came walking down the beautiful perspective which Paolo had painted and gently reproved him; as he was leaving "he showed him that the birds he had painted were also alive and real and belonged to him alone" and the "little and dear creatures" flew about and sang. All the poetry of the Pascoli of *Myricae* is here recast in new beauty.

To Pascoli's books already mentioned here should be added the *Inno a Torino* [*Hymn to Turin*], 1911, the posthumous collection of *Poesie varie,* (1912), and the *Traduzioni e riduzioni,* 1913 [*Translations and Adaptations*].

Together with the poetry of the humble *myricae* there are vast themes in Giovanni Pascoli that reach the deepest life of the universe. The poet tries to convert into concrete images the mysterious forms of the world; indeed, the life of the worlds. This poetry of cosmic themes has majestic outlines, and a sharpness of meaning which makes its imaginings corporeal and, contrariwise, confers the lightness of imagination on the bodies. It is not to be sought only in compositions like *Ciocco* [*Blockhead;* lit. log] or in several of the *Poemi Conviviali* and *Ode ed Inni,* but also in the poems of slenderer theme. The cosmic images respond to Pascoli's basic vision, even when he is looking at little domestic and rural things. In this poet the infinitely large and the infinitely small are truly identical because they sprouted from a single mystery (and that is sometimes the cause of lack of proportion and balance).

The vastest themes are those which proclaim the heroic and saintly life: *Il Ritorno di Ulisse, Alexandros, Andrée, L'Isola dei Poeti, La Buona Novella* [*Good News*]; and in most cases there is a corresponding height of form. Consider *Alexandros:*

He hears wild beasts roaring in the distance,
he hears constant, unknown forces
pass before him on the immense plain
like the tread of herds of elephants.

Heed the grand finale of this poem:

Meanwhile in rough and rugged Epirus
his virgin sisters
for the gentle Absent One
are spinning the Milesian wool.
Late into the night, among the busy maidens,
they twist the spindle with their wax-white fingers; and
the wind blows by and the stars go out.
Olympias lost in a dream
listens to the long babbling of a fountain,
listens in the infinite empty darkness
to the great oaks whispering on the mountain.

Certainly the power of vast imagination, of creating images which give outline and rhythm to the indefinite, belonged to Pascoli as to few others. It would be he who would end the hymn to *Antonio Fratti* with such lines as these, reminiscent of old fables:

> That was in the times when on the mountains
> still screeched the Chimeras
> when in the dark sunsets
> Centaurs came down to drink;

and he could compose a comparison in which this somber line occurs flashing *"Come le sfingi, fosche ossute atropi"* (Like the sphinxes, dark bony Death's-head moths). He was a poet who could transfer to his poetry images of the space in which the spirits live after their earthly death:

> let itself be rocked
> by the great sea of ether, by the brief
> swinging of the world, up there so soft.

The life of the universe tempted all his virtues as a poet capable of giving form to the impalpable:

> And among the worlds, like a grey veil, floats the
> smoke from every hearth.
> The Milky Way is exhaled out into the sky
> by the tremulous serenity.

In this poet of the stars the worlds really arouse emotion:

> . . . and now heed the dim murmur
> which the worlds whisper to each other.

And again: "There where the worlds, with lagging steps, like an immense harmonious herd, seem to graze quietly on the flowers of the sky, blessed by serene eternity." He saw tremendous struggles in the universe and gave them figures: "and an incessant fray continues hotly mid the smoke of the ruins, as though Titans, aeriform, at the corners of the Cosmos, burning to strike one the other, cleft space with uprooted stars." As a last example I cite this vision or, rather, this myth of the earth:

> And the Earth was fleeing on a dizzying course along the soft road and rolled on all tightly retracted upon herself from the pricking of the eternal gadfly. And rolling on to escape the arrow of sharp fire turning over and over in her heart, panting she exhaled through cold space her azure breath. So, in the hard breathing of the race, she saw the glittering of the stars, and in the empty darkness of the Cosmos she saw gleams from green dragons' scales and loosing of red whips by charioteers, and flashes from the archers' arrows and sparkles from the crowns' jewels, and a glimmer from the strings of the golden lyres, and the watchful eyes of lions and the drowsy gaze of bears.

While the poetic imagination of Pascoli ranges to such heights, another fundamental characteristic of his art is a new phonic insistence (which is not always free of perils) with which he sharpens sight and sounds and odors. If he writes *E le ninfe divine, anime verdi d'alberi, cristalline anime d'acque* [And the divine nymphs, green souls of trees, crystalline souls of waters], here the poet's phonic adherence to the word, I should say his way of emphasizing every syllable, enlivens the sense pull of the things said. This is most noticeable in a more extended passage, such as this example from *Il Ritorno di Ulisse* [*Ulysses' Return*]:

Ulisse: Diceva, e un improvviso ululo acuto
da boschi e botri si levò, di ninfe;
e dei torrenti risonò lo scroscio.
E il grande olivo, con un frullo lieve,
versò nell'aria un pigolio d'uccelli.
E uscian dall'antro al nuovo sol ronzando
l'api, volando al murmure del fonte.
E i meli, al mattutino urto del vento,
piovvero i bianchi petali dei fiori.

[He spoke, and a sudden sharp howling rose
From woods and stagnant ditches, a howling of nymphs;
And the rushing waters of torrents resounded.
And the great olive tree, with a light whir of wings,
Poured out on the air a chirping of birds.
And from the grotto the bees flew out buzzing,
Flying to the murmur of the spring in the new sunshine.
And the apple trees, shaken by the morning wind,
Rained down the white petals of their flower.]

To achieve this new phonic virtue, various devices are adopted. He uses the unusual adjective: *"l'acri zanzare e l'esili tignuole,"* [the acrid mosquitoes and the frail moths (estile: slender, weak)]; *"l'arzillo vino"* [the brisk wine]; *il cielo canoro* [the canorous sky]; and he will write a phrase like *il lor canto era fanciullo* [their song for a boy]. The result of this device in cases in which the adjective seems to be opposed to the noun is still more intense: *"Quel labile tuono è del fiume"* [That ephemeral thunder is the river's], or *"l'esile strido"* [the frail scream], or even *"con qualche voce ruvida"* [with some rough, coarse words], and so on.

Then, the adjective is used to produce rare analogies, the same the new poets attempt today: the "glaucous pallor" of the olive tree, the "gracile stalk," the "labile shore," the "sunny cry" of the cicadas, the "gracile whispering," the "vocal spring" [of water], the "empty sleep," the "opaque evening," the "dubious [uncertain] night," the "opaque night," the "opaque silences," and the "opaque silence of the road."

The poet counts on the daring of certain juxtapositions which are irreconcilable to each other, such as *scampanare fioco* [faint tolling of bells]; *ronzio di campane* [buzzing of bells]; *singulto ermo del mare* [solitary sob of the sea]; *strepere nero d'un treno* [black roar of a train]; *Stanotte per le vie non c'era/che qualche scalpiccio del vento* [Tonight in the streets there was only some shuffling of the wind]; the *grufolare fragile di verri* [fragile rooting of boars]; the *stridulo ansare di grilli* [shrill panting of crickets]; the *grave gracilar delle galline* [solemn clucking of the hens]; and *il sottile stridio dei pipistrelli* [the thin squeaking of the bats]; *il sibilìo de' fragili canneti* [the whistling of the fragile reed thickets]; even *Dei fulmini fragili restano cirri di porpora e d'oro* [Fragile cirrus clouds of purple and gold are left behind by the thunderbolts]; and again, ... *e nel cielo turchino già ridono l'aspre civette* [... and already in the turquoise sky the asper owls are laughing]; and *mordean le bigie nuvole del cielo* [they were biting the gray clouds of the sky], and so on. And with a more acute sensibility, . . . *e vicine strider udiva l'ombre delle foglie* [. . . and heard nearby the shadows of the leaves shrieking].

Sometimes there are several analogies in a single period, as when he writes: *Su la campagna solittaria tremava il pianto delle squille* [Over the lonely countryside trembled the weeping of the bells] — here the sound of the bells is intimated in the image of trembling and again in that of weeping. Again, if he writes, *Così scoppiò nel tremulo meriggio il vario squillo d'un'aerea rissa* [So burst forth on the tremulous noonday the varied pealing of an aerial affray], there is a still greater number of images. The shrill sound of the birds is called *squillo* [peal], and their flight and song which suggests a contest is called *aerea rissa* [affray or brawl in the air]. The peal is expressed in the unusual verb *scoppiare* [to explode]; the first image then, that of *tremulo meriggio* [tremulous noon] says two things: the quivering of the light, and the sharp, brief sounds vibrating in the air.

Other images can be analyzed in the same way: . . . *e sentii come il frusciare in tanto di mille cetre, che piovea nell'ombra* [. . . and I sensed as the rustling of a thousand zithers that it was raining in the shade]; or even, *nel sibilo assiduo dei fusi* [in the persistent whistling of the spindles]; *stelle che accese in un attimo e spente rigano il cielo d'un pensier di luce* [stars instantly lit and extinguished furrow the sky with a thought of light]; *un aureo stelo con in cima un astro* [a golden stalk with a star atip]. Consider *Nebbia* [*Mist*], which is expressed in images of high fantasy: *tu fumo che ancora rampolli su l'alba, da' lampi notturni e da' crolli d'aeree frane* [thou smoke that dost still rise above the dawn from nocturnal lightnings and from crumblings of aerial landslides]. Finally, I quote a complex and vivid image:

scoppio donde era resta una nuvola
grigia che pigra fuma nel vitreo
serale silenzio, tra i salci colore d'assenzio!

[an explosion behind which still lingers a gray cloud
which drifts lazily like smoke in the glassy silence of the evening,
amid the absinth-colored willows!].

In Pascoli there is a great strength of imitative harmony which sometimes is obtained by an unusual use of nouns and verbs and constructions: *Bianca l'aria vola come in un molino* [The air flows whitely as in a mill], giving a vivid sense of light; *un tuon sgretola l'aria* [a thunderclap shatters the air] – here is a graphic image with a novel use of the verb *sgretola*. And here we have the same thing: . . . *con l'aeree grottee intronate dal cupo urlo del vento* [. . . with the airy grottoes resounding with the mornful howl of the wind]. And elsewhere: *S'è sfatto il cielo: a scosse v'entrano urlando i venti e vi sbisciano i lampi* [The sky has broken up: in gusts the winds come howling in and the lightnings flash snakily] which is perhaps too forced. Here is a longer period with a vaster series of imitative words:

Quando s'udì l'ingorda sega un giorno
rodere rauca torno torno il tronco;
e il secco colpo rimbombò del mazzo
calato da un ansante ululo d'uomo.

[When one day was heard the greedy saw
Gnawing raucously all around the trunk,
And echoed and reechoed the dry blow of the sledgehammer
Brought down with a panting grunt of a man.]

And the poet uses even alliteration and puns:

a la terra, nell 'aprir d'aprile,
rotta e domata ai piedi ansa e rifiata.

Rather more apt is

Il tuo trillo sembra la brina
che sgrigiola, il vetro che incrina
[Thy trill is like the hoar-frost
which creaks, the glass which cracks].

He even said, "*qual di querule querule ranelle*" [like peevish, peevish little froglets].

One step farther, and we reach the dangerous onomatopeia which Pascoli abused: *Tient'a su! tient'a su! tient's su!, stacci, stacci; trr trr terit tirit,* of creaking; *tac tac,* of blackcaps [birds]; *tin tin,* of robins; *zisteretetet,* of titmice; *ce ce ce,* of the canapina, a bird of the sparrow family; *tellterelltellteretelltell,* of sparrows; *rererere,* of goldfinches; *uid uid,* weed of the lark; *tri tri,* of the crickets; *ce n'è, ce n'è,* of the finches; *siccecè siccecè* of the stonechat; *Addio addio dio dio dio dio* of the nightingale; *vita da re!* of the early cockerels; *ku ku* of the turtledoves; *gre gre* of the little frogs.

Together with this capacity for unusual and continual sounds (I am not referring to those of onomatopeia), the poet also possesses the opposite virtue, that of making words so light that they seem almost a design of air, in the air.

For example, *Psyche,* "lighter than the light shadow that smoke casts on the earth as it vanishes in the sky. "She in her own house occupies no more space "than a shadow" and makes no more sound "than a breath," no more than "the fingers of air." And in *I Gemelli* [*The Twins*], the poet says that Narcissus' neck "was so tired that it bent beneath his mother's eye."

Here is Helen who *con mute orme di sogno* [with silent footprints of dream] goes to the dying Anticlo: *Ella passava tacita e serena come la luna, sopra il fuoco e il sangue* [She passed unspeaking and serene as the moon, over the fire and the blood]; and in other passages: *Passava il canto tra la morte e il sogno* [The song passed midway between death and dream]; . . . *e lucido com'astro e soave come ombra era il suo canto* [. . . and shining as a star and as soft as shadow was his song].

He wrote, as if freeing the word from its sound: *E tra le dense foglie aliano i falchi* [And amid the dense leaves the hawks flutter]; *S'ode qui l'erba che cresce* [Here the grass is heard growing]; *Sotto l'ali dormono i nidi, come gli occhi sotto le ciglia* [Under the wings the nests are asleep, like the eyes beneath their lashes].

And these are not the only melodic devices of Pascoli, sometimes even the omission of the article gives something new to a line, as when he writes: *Campana si sente sonare* [Bell is heard ringing].

Such in its more important elements is the poetical structure of Giovanni Pascoli. Vastness and depth of lyric themes, novelty of forms, and a sensitive sharpness of the image which in this regard places him ahead of any other European poet of his time—characteristics immediately evident in his poetry. And yet, he was lacking in that divine balance which would give full value to his most illustrious gifts. Along with his tremendous feeling and perception, there was in Pascoli something commonplace, a familiarity, something of the people, which slanted too far toward the childish and was mannered and affected and seemed downright mawkish.

Yet Pascoli was also a man of great learning, highly literate, and had few peers in the classical literature. He had a deep feeling for words. He had a full Humanistic culture and a vigorous and thoughtful mind, a fact which was not sufficiently stressed by his critics, who were misled by certain appearances of his broken and fleeting prose. His historic judgments and his artistic observations have a strength which is rare in poets. Although with less balance, Pascoli possessed mental virtues more powerful than those of Carducci or of D'Annunzio. It is precisely this lack of balance, accentuated by his poetry, which obscures his prose writings: *Minerva oscura,* 1898; *Sotto il Velame* [*Under the Veil*], 1900; *La Mirabile Visione* [*The Marvelous Vision*], 1902; *In Or San Michele,* 1903; *Pensieri e Discorsi* [*Thoughts and Lectures*], 1907; *La Grande Proletaria s'è mossa* [*The Great Proletariat has Started*], 1911.

It is necessary to know how to see in those prose

writings, besides his vast erudition, the sureness of his theoretical, critical, and historical principles, which reveal his lucid conception of the world; it would be more exact to say, his lucid philosophy.

The very material of his poetry is, here and there, an indication of the strong mind of a poet who could be original even in scholastic anthologies: *Fior da Fiore, Sul Limitare* [*On the Threshold*], *Lyra,* and *Epos.* No Italian poet since Leopardi had had such high poetic ambitions.

Is it possible now to forget the verbal life that Pascoli gave to robins and blackcaps and wrens? All the good, though somewhat sugary, language with which he expressed their sounds and told of their flights, in the country which, it was rightly asserted, has become, to a degree, Pascolian? Is it possible to forget the great cosmic visions and the astral poetry that Pascoli composed with ineffable transparency?

Time will sweep away the caducous parts of Pascolian poetry, but it will leave this lofty marvel of images, of the eternal and, finally, this rich savor of the language that all those coming after him, beginning with D'Annunzio, have directly or indirectly learned from him.

Gabriele D'Annunzio

The life of Gabriele D'Annunzio, a poet who dreamed of making life itself a poem, is even more varied and adventurous than that for which George Gordon (Lord Byron) was famous in the early nineteenth century. D'Annunzio was born on March 12, 1863 at Pescara, to Francesco Paolo and Luisa De Benedictis: it was on a Friday, and the young mother, affectionately accepting a common prejudice, exclaimed: "My son, you are born on a Friday and in March. Who knows what great things you will do in the world!"

His childhood was lively and full of great dreams.

When he was five years old, his teacher was Filippo de Titta; in 1874 he entered the Real Convitto Cicognini [Royal Cicognini Boarding School] at Prato, where he completed his secondary education. In 1879 his first printed work appeared, the *Ode a Re Umberto* [*Ode to King Humbert*].

In 1880, the poet's first volume was published: *Primo Vere,* which attracted the attention of Giuseppe Chiarini, who, in the May 2 number of the *Fanfulla della Domenica,* dedicated an enthusiastic article to it, thereby quickly publicizing the name of the young poet.

For his part, the youth fanned the fire of his nascent fame, going so far as to spread the news of his presumed death. Then, being henceforth known to the world of letters, D'Annunzio began to contribute to newspapers and reviews. In 1882 his *Canto Novo* came out and gave further evidence of the new poet's originality. In that same year his collection of short stories appeared: *Terra Vergine.* By then, the mundane life of D'Annunzio was well under way, and around him that legendary atmosphere was being formed which is an indication of the charm exercised by a name on human imagination, inciting people to talk about the public and private events concerning its bearer.

The publication of the *Intermezzo di rime* aroused a storm of polemics: Chiarini, who had been the first to call attention to the new poet, now accused him of having betrayed his expectations with an immoral work. The literary world was all astir, and the fame of the poet profited thereby.

In June, 1884, *Il libro delle vergini* appeared, which likewise aroused discussions about its contents and also on account of a dispute between the poet and his publisher, Sommaruga, over the book's cover. The year after, in his second duel, D'Annunzio received a head wound, to which, as Matilde Serao relates, the poet's early baldness was attributed. In 1886 the short stories of *San Pantaleone* and the affected stanzas of *Isaotta Guttadauro* came out, followed as usual by polemics concerning new books by D'Annunzio.

In 1888 he published *L'Armata d'Italia* [*The Italian Fleet*], maintaining that Italy "would be either a great naval power or nothing at all." This work marks the first signs of D'Annunzio's political activity.

In 1889 his first novel was published: *Il Piacere* [*Pleasure;* Eng. tr., 1898, *The Child Of Pleasure*] which he had written the year before at the "Covento," the house of painter Francesco Paolo Michetti. This was a product of the experiences of his worldly life in Rome and created the first hero characteristic of that particularly Dannunzian morality which confuses art with life and exercised such fascination on youth. The morality of D'Annunzio was more precisely stated later in a theory of the Superman, which seemed drawn from Nietzsche but was really his own spontaneous conception of life and differs profoundly from that of the German philosopher-poet.

Toward the end of 1889, D'Annunzio was called up for his year of military service. Meanwhile, his *L'Isotteo e la Chimera* came out. During his army experience, throughout which he had been unable to pay much attention to art, the poet wrote a novel of a quite different nature from the preceding one: *Giovanni Episcopo* (Eng. tr., 1806, *Episcopo & Co.*), and then *L'Innocente* (Eng. trs., 1898, *The Intruder,* and in 1914, *The Victim*), a book which seemed quieter and easier than the others.

Three new works came out in 1893: *Poema Paradisiaco, Odi Navali,* and the novel *Il Trionfo della morte* (Eng. tr., 1896, *The Triumph of Death*).

In July, 1895, with Edoardo Scarfoglio, Guido Boggiani, Pasquale Masciantonio, and his translator Giorgio Herelle, the poet embarked, aboard Scarfoglio's yacht "Fantasia," upon that voyage to Hellas which, poetically transfigured, he later exalted in the book of *Maia.* His novel *Le Vergini delle Rocce* dated 1896 [*The Virgins of the Rocks*] appeared in the summer, a book which apart from its real artistic center reveals in what an unusual way D'Annunzio conceived of political action. His hero dreams of the conquest of Rome.

Meanwhile, he also took part in militant politics. In 1897 he was elected to the national parliament and was one of the majority members; someone hailed him as "the representative of beauty." But in 1900 he noisily broke away from the majority and, with the cry of "I go towards life!" went over to the opposition. He was not reelected, but his parliamentary *intermezzo* had helped to draw renewed attention to him and to his books.

His way of announcing forthcoming publications, and the exceptional art he employed to create suspense prior to their appearance, served as propaganda for his name whatever they may have done for his books. Then, to impress that name upon a still larger public, the theater was a useful tool. D'Annunzio had met Eleonora Duse, the great actress who played such an important role in his life, and their theatrical collaboration began. After the *Sogno di un Mattino di Primavera* (Eng. tr., 1902, *The Dream of a Spring Morning*), they worked together in writing and presenting *La Città Morta* (Eng. tr., 1902, *The Dead City*), *La Gioconda,* and *La Gloria.* The vicissitudes of that collaboration between poet and actress were many and varied, and in 1899 their relations were broken off. However, D'Annunzio was to continue to write for the theater for a while longer, alternating with novels and poems.

In 1900 the novel *Il Fuoco* appeared (Eng. tr., 1900, *The Flame of Life*), which recounts the love of a poet and an actress and is a prelude to the heroic theater which D'Annunzio was to write. In 1901 the tragedy of *Francesca da Rimini* (Eng. tr. 1902) appeared, one of the poet's finest. In 1903 two volumes of *Le Laudi* came out: the first contains *Maia,* the second, *Elettra* [*Electra*] and *Alcyone* [*Halcyon*]. The poet had reached the highest point of his poetry.

D'Annunzio's enthusiasm for the theater continued. In 1904 *La Figlia di Iorio* [*The Daughter of Iorio*] was presented; it seems a continuation of *Le Laudi.* It was followed in 1905 by *La Fiaccola sotto il Moggio* [*The Torch under the Bushel*], which was enthusiastically received at the Costanzi Theater in Rome. In 1907 the poet read his new "adriac" tragedy, *La Nave* [*The Ship*], and later the circumstance assumed for him the character of a portent. On January 12, 1908, the play scored a triumphant success at the Argentina in Rome.

In 1909 D'Annunzio collected his short stories, previously published singly, and published them in a volume entitled *Novelle della Pescara.*

A man who had taught superhuman morality, life as a poem and as a danger, could not but be attracted by the new miracle of flying which had recently become possible. In September, 1909 the poet flew for the first time. The newspapers gave much publicity to the event, but the poet transfused his impressions as a flyer into his novel *Forse che sì, forse che no* [*Perhaps Yes, Perhaps No*], of which the protagonist is an aviator, and included the first elements for an Italian nomenclature of the *velivolo,* as he called the airplane. The novel was published in January, 1910.

Vicissitudes in his personal affairs, which were to lead to the sale of his villa *La Capponcina,* disgusted the poet. In 1910 he left Italy and went into "voluntary exile" in France. And in the country which gave him shelter he wrote some fine things in the French language.

In 1911 he had *Le Martyre de Saint-Sébastien* [*The Martyrdom of Saint Sebastian*] produced in the theater, with music composed by the great contemporary French musician, Claude Debussy. In 1913 he put on some other dramas written in French: *La Pisanelle ou La Mort Parfumée* and *Le Chevrefeuille* [*Honeysuckle*].

In 1911, when war broke out between Italy and Turkey, the poet began the vehement *Canzoni d'oltremare* [*Songs from Overseas*] in tercets, published from time to time in the *Corriere della Sera,* and which appeared the following year in *Merope,* the fourth volume of *Le Laudi.*

On December 16, 1913, *Parisina* was put on at La Scala in Milan, with music by Pietro Mascagni. But the poet himself was still in France; in France in 1912 he had written *La Contemplazione della Morte* [*The Contemplation of Death*].

Then came the European war, which was to transform the poet into a soldier. On the outbreak of the war, Gabriele D'Annunzio's voice calling for Italian intervention on the side of the Entente was one of those most listened to. From day to day his work assumed such importance that he became the very symbol of the interventionist will in Italy. All the parties endeavoring to lead their country to war against the central powers turned toward him. He was invited to make the commemorative speech for the inauguration of the monument to Garibaldi on the rock of Quarto. On May 3, 1915 the poet left for Italy, where on the following day he was received with wild enthusiasm. On May 5 he delivered the speech of the *Sagra dei Mille* [Festival of the Thousand], in which there is foreboding of imminent war. Reaching Rome on May 12, his presence and speeches inspired the interventionists to action — war was declared on May 24, 1915, and the poet left for the front.

What he did in the war, his flight over Vienna, the "error of Buccari" (near Fiume, occupied Februray 10–11, 1918), his actions before and after Caporetto, the shock which the loss of an eye caused him, his gold and silver medals, the work of passion which he carried out during the hideous conflict are now known to all Italians. And even during that time he wrote poems of combat, which appeared in the *Canti della Guerra Latina,* and prose writings, which were gathered in the book *Per l'Italia degli Italiani.*

However, in 1919 when, at the Peace Conference, Fiume appeared to be irrevocably lost to Italy, Gabriele D'Annunzio conceived and carried out the audacious plan of occupying the city. On September 12, at the head of his 287 legionaries who later were reinforced, he entered Fiume; thus he carried into action a great part of the political concept which he had once expressed in *Le Vergini delle Rocce* and in *La Gloria.*

The Fiume exploit is one of the most singular events of his life. The poet became a legislator, and not only did he deliver those speeches that would appear in 1920 with the title *Contro Uno e Contro Tutti* [*Against One and All*], but he prepared the *Costituzione della Reggenza Italiana del Carnaro* [*Constitution of the Italian Regency of Quarnero*], which is one of the most unexpected documents emanating from his multiform nature.

In 1920 the Italian government threw troops around Fiume, and fraternal blood was shed. On December 29, D'Annunzio turned over his powers to the communal authorities of Fiume; on January 28 of the following year, he left the city.

He established his residence in the Villa Cargnacco at Gardone, today called *Il Vittoriale.* In 1924 the king conferred the title of Prince of Montenevoso on him. In that calm abode he busied himself with his art until his death on March 1, 1938. In 1921 *Notturno* [*Nocturne*] appeared, one of the best of the latest D'Annunzio; in 1924 *Il Venturiero senza Ventura* [*The Unlucky Adventurer*]; in 1928 *Il Compagno dagli Occhi senza Cigli* [*The Companion with the Lashless Eyes*]; in 1931 *Il Sudore di Sangue* [*Bloody Sweat*] and *L'Urna inesausta* [*The Un-*

exhausted Urn]; in 1935 *Cento e cento e cento e cento Pagine del Libro Segreto* [*The Four Hundred Pages of the Secret Book of Gabriele D'Annunzio*].

Now it would be well to follow the varied road of the art of Gabriele D'Annunzio.

Although the poetry may go unheeded and the ingenuousness of the beginning is evident, *Primo Vere,* the poet's first book, shows the motifs and ways of feeling which later appear to be those closest to the personality of D'Annunzio.

Canto Novo vividly expresses the sense of universal life, in which the poet participates bodily. Here, in proclaiming his own originality, he liberates himself almost entirely from the great model of Carducci.

D'Annunzio expresses the same feeling for natural life in the tales of *Terra Vergine,* in which people of his land of Abruzzi appear. An ardent and sincere vigor flows in that prose, which at times is exuberant, but most of the time it shows a still simple and wholesome art.

The *Intermezzo di Rime* was considered as a moment of weakness in the wholesome poet of *Canto Novo;* but in truth, D'Annunzio was more sincere than before and had won both technical and stylistic craftiness and cunning. Here he had found real mastery of his legato rhythm, and freed himself entirely from the tyranny of Carducci.

The *Isotteo* and the *Chimera,* to which *Intermezzo* is a prelude, reveal more clearly the outpouring of D'Annunzio's musicalness. In the *Isotteo* there are the elegant ways of enjoying the swirl of the lines with a hint, a suggestion, of ancient modes, which will return, more limpid, in *Francesca.* They have a rare freshness:

Piegare d'erba è lieve
men che dolor d'amante.
Bevon l'acqua le piante;
cuor di donna oblio beve.

[The bending of the grass is slight,
Less than lover's sorrow.
The plants drink water;
A woman's heart, forgetfulness.]

In the *Chimera,* D'Annunzio finds ways that are humble but have the preciousness of madrigals. The preciosity is more that of rhythmic flavor than of the dictionary; often it is a way of suggesting things seen and sounds heard as they are in the triteness of everyday life which, when they are put into poetry, acquire a sense of melodious fable.

The book of *Novelle della Pescara* seems to be by an author surer of his art than he was in the preceding works; there is an observable refinement of style, which is useful to the poet as a writing exercise. The themes of blood and violence portend certain tendencies which in future books were to become paroxysmal.

After much experience of life and art, the poet dreamed of appeasing *en bloc* his hunger for beautiful visions, for love affairs, for luxury — for pleasure in life and in art. He wrote his first novel *Il Piacere,* at the center of which he put the esthete Andrea Sperelli. The book is poor in qualities of soul but rich in sensuousness and powerful in certain unforgettable descriptive pages, such as those about Rome after a snowfall.

The *Elegie Romane* present in verse the Rome of *Il Piacere,* and anyone who limits his appreciation of poetry to virtuoso bravura cannot wish for any more tempered forms than these hexameters.

The *Elegee* was followed by the very gentle *Poema Paradisiaco,* which is pure rhymed vocalism and, largely, a prelude to the more inward music of D'Annunzio.

A good deal simpler than *Il Piacere,* the novel *Giovanni Episcopo* came later; it is a novel which, besides a certain interrogative and exclamatory breathlessness and a certain monotony, has pages of stupendous narrative power.

Then came *L'Innocente,* which may have been the most read of D'Annunzio's books, perhaps for the sort of sick goodness expressed in its characters, perhaps because its style is less high-flown than in other stories by D'Annunzio and closer to the spoken language. Certainly the book has passages of undeniable beauty.

In *Il Trionfo della Morte,* the poet's art reached a higher level; as the most vital themes of D'Annunzio come flowing into the book, from that of Mother Earth to that of sensual death, the first terms of a masterpiece are reached.

Le Vergini delle Rocce followed. At times the unity of this book is found in that wave of tired melancholy diffused through all its pages, like a slow, soft, gentle pleasure akin to that of sunsets and of solitude; in it there is a sensuous musicalness which cannot be called inward, but yet is intense and persuasive.

The cantos of *Elettra* have a connection with the heroic motifs of the *Vergini delle Rocce*; they are the poetry of the heroic morality. Here it must be said that the civil compositions of D'Annunzio, except in rare cases (such as the *Preghiera per i Cittadini* [*Prayer for Citizens*] written during the war), are eloquent but do not reach the level of great poetry. In *Elettra* there appears, among other things, the song of Garibaldi, *La Notte di Caprera.*

Laus Vitae [*Praise of Life*], the first volume of the *Laudi,* contrasts the myths of Hellas with Christianity in an ideal journey toward Greece which the poet undertakes. This is an angry motif of that paganism which earlier elated Carducci, and, in fact, *Laus Vitae* ends with praise of Enotrio Romano (that is, Carducci). But the strength of *Laus Vitae* does not lie in the polemical contrast, it lies in its adherence to the world of nature in which the poet's senses expand joyously.

The novel *Il Fuoco* has passages of subtle sensitivity, and dynamic and resplendent pages; it is tied to the dramatic activity of the poet. We recognize those characteristics of sensation which are encountered in the other works in the theater of D'Annunzio; however, they are exacerbated to the extreme limit: from *La Città Morta,* which develops in a Greek landscape with the troubled love of Leonardo for Biancamaria; to *Fedra* [*Phaedra*], who is tragically enamored of Hippolytus; to *La Nave,* in which the love of Basiliola generates fratricide; to *Il Ferro* [*Iron*]; to *Parisina*; to *Francesca*; even to *La Figlia di Iorio.* In *Più che l'Amore,* the thesis of Corrado Brando, which asserts the necessity of crime for a superhuman morality, is all feline, untamed sensuousness.

In these dramas there are moments of vivid beauty, but in their overall effect there is something wearying and forced. Only *Francesca* and *La Figlia di Iorio* reach the level of pure poetry, as though they were great odes of the *Laudi.*

In *Forse che sì, forse che no,* the poet turned again to the novel. It is a book that has pages of endearing melancholy and an underlying tone of heartache. But the most beautiful prose in the last style of D'Annunzio is in the tale *La Leda senza Cigno* [*Leda Without a Swan*] and *Notturno.* Here the poet has reached an incomparable sobriety and flexibility, which put some moments of the *Notturno* on the plane of most exquisite lyrics of the *Laudi.*

The art of D'Annunzio, that which forms the originality of this poet, is above all in the lyrical music which he has imparted to many images and elementary sensations.

The best of D'Annunzio is to be sought in the musical moments of his entire work, and will be found in its greatest intensity in *Le Laudi, Maia,* and *Alcyone*; it is found in many lyrics written in prose, especially in *Notturno.* It is found even in his most youthful writing, in a page of the *Canto Novo* and of *Terra Vergine,* or in *Il Piacere* or in *Le Vergini delle Rocce,* or in *L'Isotteo* or the *Poema Paradisiaco.*

In reading those pages, we feel the joy of the world which D'Annunzio expresses tranquilly flowing back into us, since at every dawn his senses recreate the universe, so that he could say "I was born every morning." And in his joy of the world we can feel and seize two moods which correspond roughly to the two D'Annunzian motifs of action and of contemplation. The first tends toward the "Act," and to its subjects, even the power of the "Word," which is then a manner of performing, of working; the other tends toward the idyll in which action exists in a state of desire or, one might say, of dream.

In the first mood, the poet defies the rainclouds and the Fates, is willing to overthrow the common laws of life, proclaims himself the equal of Ulysses king of the tempests, king of men, strains toward conquest of the heavens, for the sun's vulture grasps him in its claws; he is intoxicated with flight, he invokes Icarus and noble death as he eulogizes Hermes machinator. In the other mood he takes shelter by the domestic hearth where his mother and three sisters watch over his childish innocence; the journey of the king of the tempests is replaced by that of the simple shepherds who come down along the cattletrack to the sea; to Hermes machinator correspond the cities on lonely hills "encompassed in their silence like one who adores." Then he can delight in the sweetly languid joy of the countryside, sing the praises of the olive tree and the ear of wheat and the work and the days of the good old gaffer, the husbandman of the venerable earth, and contemplate the grace of the sky born from the cloud, or the rain falling in the pine wood upon his fresh thoughts, or in the new moon, the face of the celestial creature which wanly bows and dies.

One mood will lead him to ask: Where must I yet

climb?" The other will awaken the melancholy question: "Who will console me for the days gone by, for the lost days?" Savage myth of the centaur and the stag will be compared with the arboreal myth of Versilia, with the sea in which the power of the great families will be severed is the sea of Undulna of the wingèd feet and her crescent-shaped writing.

Thus the poet who has dared the song of *Felicità* enthralls us in his earthly myth of joy:

Di cose fugaci e segrete
sei fatta, di silenzi
e di murmuri, lieve
come i frutti piumosi
della viorna, come
le lane del cardo argentino,
O Felicità del cor prode.

[Of fleeting and secret things
art thou made, of silences
And murmurs, light
as the feathery fruits
of the viburnum, as
the fuzz of the silvery thistle,
O Felicity of the heroic heart.]

Seeking his own self and the land on which the common men cannot land, the poet finds Felicity, that is to say, his very own law. And so it is that happiness appears to him personified in a woman made of rustic essences and aromas, of the most subtle and vaporous elements of holy nature, like the nymphs.

I do not believe a poet exists who has ever eulogized Felicity with such gratitude, since it is indeed an everlasting theme of poets to show how vain that play of syllables is that says Felicity. In the past, whoever wanted to recognize her and to sing her praises, placed her in the celestial spheres, in another life, called her unattainable on earth, and called her the *summum bonum* of God. Rather than a personified idea, the Felicity of D'Annunzio is a women or a nymph, a pleasure on earth, a joy attained; and the existence of Felicity, for him, is as legitimate as the existence of Sorrow is for other poets.

But even for D'Annunzio, no sooner is it touched by poetry than it changes into the melancholy of which Carducci spoke, in his verses to "little Mary": "Exit poetry, when melancholy knocks on the door of the heart." And then the music of Gabriele D'Annunzio is melancholy of the senses.

This music is evident in the *Oleandro,* which is perhaps the most finished lyric of D'Annunzio, and it is evident in *Il Fanciullo* [*The Boy*], and in the hymn to Felicity which is in *Maia.* It is this music that makes the strength of *La Morte del Cervo* [*The Death of the Stag*] and of *L'Otre* [*The Wineskin*]; it is this that gives ineffable youth to the *Sera Fiesolana* [*Evening in Fiesole*], to *L'Ulivo, Versilia,* to *Undulna,* and to *Il Novilunio* [*The New Moon*].

What is the particular music of D'Annunzio? It is really the ethereal ringing of the word, its resounding so as to create, before the syllable and after it is spoken, a continuous space, a shivering shuddering of sound that expresses the melancholic tired halo and takes a trembling pleasure in the melancholy.

"And have you ever considered that the essence of music is not in the sounds?" asked the mystic doctor. "It is in the silence which precedes the sounds and in the silence which follows them. Rhythm appears and lives in these intervals of silence. Every sound and every chord reveal in the silence which precedes them a voice which can be heard only by our spirit. Rhythm is the heart of music, but its beats are heard only during the pauses of the sound." It is something absorbed, especially in the novels and in the tragedies, like the figure and the glance which accompany and illuminate a speech by a woman with a beautiful voice.

Observe the resumptions of his periods in the novels or verses: they have a pronounced phonic tie, they count on repetition for an increased affective and melancholic power.

His music is the sweetness of singing, which extinguishes what is harmful, as Francesca says, "From our earliest childhood, music bent our soul as the water of the stream bends the grass." And her mother said, "Sweet singing wipes out what is hurtful." D'Annunzio himself stresses the term *musica:* he feels that his sensibility lies more in musical modes than in verbal modes.

"Who was it who once called you 'L'Imaginifico'? [the creator of images]" asks someone in *Il Fuoco.* "Ah, images!" exclaimed the poet, flushed with fruitful warmth. "In Venice, since they can hear only in musical ways, so they can only think in images!"

He energetically emphasized the value of the sound of the syllables: ". . . the syllables, beyond the meaning which they convey, have an evocative and emotive power in their composite sounds."

Here, sketched briefly, are the poets of D'Annunzio, which extol the musical quality of the Italian language and assert that in it writers "have musical elements so varied and so effective as to compete with the great Wagnerian orchestra in evoking that which only Music can evoke in the modern soul."

9.

The Twentieth Century

The "Decadents" and the Twentieth Century

The Romanticism which we shall call "classical," that which in Italy is identified with the thought and the poetry of Foscolo, Leopardi, Manzoni, and Carducci, had not substantially broken the spiritual synthesis of the Renaissance because consciousness of the infinity of the universe was balanced by faith in the capacity of man to communicate with all men and with nature or, at least, to suffer nobly the adversities of nature when it appeared an enemy. The Italian and European Romanticists of the early and middle nineteenth century believed in the rationality that inspires and activates the history of man, or they believed in the providence of God which works with justice and goodness within the vicissitudes of human beings in their earthly life: Therefore, by virtue of their awareness of history and religion, alongside affections sublime and heroic or, at any rate, magnanimous and deeply felt, they placed truth as the content of all literary or artistic manifestations and works.

In short, the Romanticists believed in the full and perfect harmony between content and form: that is, style. The greatest Romantic historian of Italian literature, Francesco De Sanctis, gave as one of the bases of his criticism the famous definition *like content like form,* and this principle was continued and philosophically enriched by Benedetto Croce, the founder of historicism in Italy.

It is true that already in the full flood of Romanticism assertions were made which tended to corrode the splendid synthesis inherited from the Renaissance; when, for example, the equilibrium between the individual and the universe was compromised, bringing about the superiority of the former over the latter, or when, in comparing oneself with the universe, amazement no longer aroused a feeling of deeply moving wonder but only a sentiment of bewilderment or anguish. Nevertheless many writers, to whom there is a tendency to attribute decadent premises, exacerbate certain Romantic sentiments and interpretations of reality, do not turn them upside down and do not destroy them. The Parnassian artists, the Pre-Raphaelites, the cultivators of aestheticism, the ironic poets who disenchant the fables and, in short, all the exponents of extreme European Romanticism: Leconte de Lisle, Swinburne, Oscar Wilde, Ruskin, Dostoyevsky, Wagner, Heine, had reached an objective; that is, an historical, solution of their own individual ways of creating poetical reality and of resolving it into a style. They drew from their restless and refined spirituality a lyric or dramatic myth which was put down as a reality and was erected into a cultural institution. These Romantic European motifs were transformed into myths precisely by force of the penetration which they had into contemporary culture; that is, they did not become simple subjective projections and personal aspirations, provisional ways of eulogizing a state of mind, feigning a conquest or an illusory certitude.

Outwardly, the school of the decadent poets continues some Romantic tendencies: rebellion against the classical ways of understanding reality and poetry, the aesthetic conception of life that offers the artist only a beauty indifferent to moral values, the titanic cult of individual energy and intelligence (Prometheism, Satanism, Faustism), the theory dear to the Pre-Raphaelites of "art for art's sake." But what is new in the decadents is the realization that a split has intervened between the individual man and universal reality; an awareness, that is, that man is not identified with existence, that he does not correspond with God nor with human history nor with nature – down to the extreme negation that man can not even correspond with man. The prime reason for the decadent school lies in the declaration of the solitude of human beings and their inability to communicate with one another.

But the declaration by itself is a pure statement of negativeness. It is pure rationality which retires within itself, not rationality applied to investigation of history and the discovery of its reasons. Therefore, the masters of the decadent school worked hard at rebuilding upon a foundation of negation, at attributing symbolic values to things so as to make them fit, somehow, into the sequence of reality. They rejected historical and social institutions, yet cultivated their spiritualistic leanings; they aspired to the construction of an ideological system or, at least, a series of ideologies; they worked out a cultural apparatus formulated on rigorous literary selections; they sketched a philosophy of existence, and when they really decided to renounce systematic reason, they grasped at safety anchors, at the faculty of intuition, at salvage of memory, at the will to exist, to be, in some way or other. The European masters of the decadent school were Heidegger and Bergson,

Proust and Nietzsche, so listed in sequence in order to call to mind an equal number of "decadent" theories: existentialism, intuitionism, theory of memory, and that of the pure volition to be.

On the philosophical plane, decadentism did not express an authentic system of thinking in Italy. In philosophy, Italy was, above all, a follower of Croce. The only alternative to his historicism was the Italian Marxism of Labriola, the only system that Croce felt to be in dialectical opposition to his thought. Twenty years before and ten years after the *Estetica* of Croce, (approximately within the period 1880–1910), the decadentistic movement withdrew from positivism, historicism, or Marxism; that is, from the three fundamental systems for judging reality rationally. More than anything else it was an effuse literary sensibility, incapable therefore of resolving itself into a system. It concerned itself, also, with the cultivation of feeling, but of feeling that erected symbols by which to express itself. The most determined cultural engagement of the Italian decadents was in fact a problem of style: the problem of establishing a verbal analogy between the first, direct image, and the super-sense that applied to it. Therefore, decadentism came close to two equivocations: the first, which identified style with poetry and destroyed the relationship between content and form; the second, which separated style and language, contrasting the common language as an institution common to all speakers, with a language all style, artistocratic, and comprehensible only to the initiated.

Alessandro Manzoni had maintained that the language of writers should identify itself with the national language; that what had happened in France should happen in Italy also. He had established a positive relationship between the dialects and the national language, and the relation between the spoken and the written language. Before decadentism opened a breach between style and language, Italian writers were all Manzonians because they sought to establish the language of national culture by antonomasia, and defined good writing as the ability of the writer to communicate his ideas and images with clearness and propriety of vocabulary and syntax to the whole nation in order to raise it to the plane of culture. Think of the untiring and educational work of Ferdinando Martini, journalist, popularizer, and curator of scholastic texts. Think of the vulgarizing and popular books of Stoppani, De Marchi, De Amicis, or Farina. In this sense Carducci was a Manzonian who felt the necessity of making the language of classical education fit the present day, who understood the importance of the indispensable popular foundation of the language of culture.

Forced to project behind things the illusion of a faraway truth, to create within the fact an illusory meaning, to imprint upon the significant word a super-sense, the decadent school set up an arcane, elusive language, a wholly poetical language in contrast to the common language adapted only to communicate sentiments and practical notions. The twentieth-century search for poetical style rests upon this breach between language and style, a search which has been called the salvation and almost the restorer of reality to music and language.

European and Italian Schools of Decadents

In 1885 in France a little book called *Les Déliquescences, poèmes décadents d'Adoré Floupette* was published. Perhaps because of this title the word *Décadent* bobbed up as the title of the heading of a magazine founded in 1886 by Anatole Baju. In that same year, several reviews inspired by symbolism appeared; the Belgian *Wallonie* and the French *La Pléiade, La Vogue, Le Symboliste, La Décadence.* In *La Vogue,* Arthur Rimbaud's *Les Illuminations* appeared. The *Manifeste* of Jean Moréas announced symbolism publicly and made an official movement of it. French critics and writers, more or less in agreement, stressed that there were two key elements in symbolism: the analogy that resolves the object in its super-sense, and music, or the highest and most comprehensive quality of style. It was as though the poet drew his Good, his reality, from stylistic invention. Meanwhile (all this was somewhere around 1886), the *Revue Wagnérienne* was coming closer to symbolism, attributing to Wagner the invention of a purely musical dimension of reality.

In France, therefore, the school of the decadents took as its own the poetics of symbolism and thus was opposed to naturalism because, as the objective of art, their aim was not the fact but the super-sense of the fact: the fact in allegorical key. According to the symbolists, the mind, which is both imagination and reason, discovers a hidden truth behind the sensory perception, a truth that can be communicated only to a few initiates through the medium of arcane expressions, mysterious and magical, which elude the traditional knowledge of things and put obscure relationships between things instead of direct ones. Therefore, the symbolists foreshadow almost all the decadentistic movements: neoprimitivism, Dadaism, Expressionism, Surrealism, Cubism, pictorial and plastic deformation, dodecaphonic music, and the application of psychoanalysis and of the philosophy of existence to the arts. In all these contemporary *isms* the new relationship which is established between rationalism and irrationalism is fundamental: reason is evaded by pure intuition, but then the enlightenment of magic, of the symbol, of intuition, aspire to reconstruct rationally a sense of reality, perhaps even an interpretation of life.

The great master of the symbolists was Charles Baudelaire (1821–1867) who continued and transferred to Europe the poetics and the work of the American poet,

Edgar Allen Poe (1808–1849). For Poe and Baudelaire, reason, passion, moral truth, and the representation of nature are elements that have nothing to do with art. Thus the autonomy of art is asserted—art entirely independent of logical and moral philosophy. The world of poetry is something quite different from nature and rational truth, from the sentiments which men commonly affirm and upon which they build their knowable history. Artists seek new and unknown values. Hence there arises, alongside the declaration of human solitude and incommunicability, the always uneasy and sometimes anguished an anxious necessity which only the artist—poet, painter, musician—can illumine by means of a prodigy, an enchantment, in the most secret folds of dreams (oneiric science, related to psychoanalysis) and of pure private psyche. Therefore, at a certain point reality is the allusive and symbolical language of the super-senses.

Was Baudelaire conscious of how much his *Fleurs du mal* represented what was new and revolutionary in contemporary literature? The answer is certainly in the affirmative, if the poet who had also written "in this terrible book I have put all my heart, all my affection, all my (disguised) religion, all my hatred" could assert the principle that "there is in the verb, the word, something sacred" and could make Beauty say: "I am beautiful, O mortals, like a dream in stone." Passion, therefore, and liberation comes through the liturgical pathway of passion: "horror of life, ecstasy of life." He also said that he was "passionately smitten with passion and coldly determined to seek the means to express it." The lines of Baudelaire:

La nature est un temple oú de vivants piliers
Laissent parfois sortir de confuses paroles;
L'homme y passe à travers des forêts de symboles
Qui l'observent avec des regards familiers,

[Nature is a temple where living pillars
Sometimes utter indistinct words;
There man passes through groves of symbols
Which observe him with familiar glances,]

give the kernel of the poetics of symbolism. Rémy de Gourmont and Joris-Karl Huysmans asserted that all symbolist poetry is Baudelairean. Alongside the "absolute poet" there is in Baudelaire the "accursed poet", the "poète maudit": in him Romantic satanism still persists. Corbière, Rimbaud, Mallarmé, Marceline Desbordes-Valmore, Verlaine, and their companions were to become ever more "absolute" and less *poètes maudits;* they were to stress shifts from contentual search for a new reality to the search for form and style. Expression is the magic moment which reveals the new surrealist analogies in the act which defines them in the word, the outline, the plastic, the architectonic mass, and in music. Thus we have reached Rimbaud's "alchemy of the verb, the word," the music of the nuance which strips the flesh from Verlaine's word. Rimbaud was fond of discussing the loves of vowels and colors, and René Ghil, discussed the loves of sounds and their corresponding words. Along this line the Italian futurists were to move later with their poetics of sound. According to Mallarmé, it was necessary to "yield the initiative to words": driven out of poetical content, reason reappeared in the word, "the intellectual word at its apogee." We are just a step from the poetical technique of Paul Valéry, a fervent admirer of Mallarmé. Surrealism too, founded as a movement by André Breton, Louis Aragon and Paul Eluard, makes the immediate and almost automatic expression correspond to the intuitive search for one's own ego. And this inward literature, resolved in diaries and confessions, includes the vast work of Marcel Proust, *A la recherche du temps perdu* which, through memory, defines in the individual's childhood the ancestral reasons that explain his whole existence. This literature also includes the "intimism" of Gide.

In Spain the romantic sorrow of Miguel de Unamuno and Antonio Machado is replaced by the *novecentismo* of the poet Juan Ramon Jimenez, who was open to symbolism which still persists in the poetry of Rafael Alberti. With the school of the decadent may be classified two theorists of the importance of Eugenio D'Ors and Ortega y Gasset.

In England, the revolt against the Victorian age is represented by two deconsecrators: the playwright George Bernard Shaw and the essayist Gilbert Keith Chesterton. Chesterton is a Catholic, but Catholics in general, through existentialism and the liturgical concept of reality preached by the symbolists, found themselves at ease in decadentism and participated in even its extreme consequences. This is also true of another English storyteller, Hilaire Belloc and of the Frenchmen, François Mauriac, Georges Bernanos, and Paul Claudel. The revolutionary impetus was carried into English literature by David Herbert Lawrence, more or less properly considered as the narrator of psychoanalysis, and by James Joyce, who has destroyed the parisaic framework of contemporary civilization in order to draw from the life of the unconscious the most pitiless psychological introspection; the objective truths are no longer bitter nor joyous. In all these writers, as in Virginia Woolf or the Catholic Graham Greene, the deconsecrating irony and the search for ancestral reasons for our living amount to stylistic research; hence the analogical writing of Joyce which facets sensations in an inexhaustible catherine-wheel of instinctive emotions and impulses; hence the magical and musical transfiguration of reality in Woolf. With the poet and dramatist Thomas Stearns Eliot, the desolation of the ravaged earth, now in ironic, now in anguished moods, attains epical force. And not far removed from Eliot stands the poetry of Wystan Hugh Auden.

In Germany, the anti-naturalistic and symbolical poetry is represented by Stefan George and Rainer Maria Rilker, while an idyllic current is noticeable in Hermann Hesse and Ernst Wiechert. In Hugo von Hofmannsthal the current is idyllic, to be sure, but more involved. In his earlier work, Thomas Mann showed a leaning toward the decadents, then the great events of the wars and the upheavals that stemmed from them led him to interpret and judge with lucid penetration the psychological and moral causes of human vicissitudes. In Germany, also, expressionism was born in 1910; it produced its finest results in the theater of George Kaiser. The inspiration for expressionism is anarchical: individualism substitutes for natural and historical reality a purely subjective reality. But later, expressionism also, like the youthful surrealism of Aragon and Eluard, turned toward historical values and, with Bertolt Brecht, went on to undertake politico-social messages.

Franz Kafka is an artist who pictures the solitude of man in a close-packed play of expectations and equivocations until he succeeds in giving the feeling of an effusion of muffled dramatization. In Russia the poets Blok and Sologub were symbolists; Boris Leonidovich Pasternak may be considered approximately an intimist. And before the bolshevik revolution, Vladimir Vladimirovich Mayakovsky and Sergei Aleksandrovich Yesenin were futurists. But already the movement of Acmeism had inspired poets faithful to a melancholic psychological realism, such as Gumilev and Anna Ahkmatova.

Definitely, the Russian literary movements, bound to social realism, and the narrative and poetical literature of the United States worked on Italian literature only after the Second World War: of the two, the American narrative was the more effective. The literature of the decadents was influenced not only by the French symbolists from Huysmans to Mallarmé and to Valéry, but especially by the most refined stylists; that is, by the writers of intimism and of confession, the French and Flemish crepuscular poets; in short, by all those who, after having disavowed reason, sought after a magical, allusive reality.

Historicism and Benedetto Croce

The really literary twentieth century, then, falls between the exhaustion and breakdown of nineteenth-century Romanticism (which we have defined as classical and historic) and the new poetics, such as primitivism, which operated in Italy during and after the Second World War, coming especially from North American literature, social realism, and so on. This does not mean that in Italy, between Pascoli and the writers of surrealism and *Ermetismo* (a modern Italian school of obscure poetry; cf. Hermes Trismegistus) there were no other movements than that of the decadents. In the same field of poetry, of the narrative and of the theater, the work of D'Annunzio represents a private or personal decadentism, which in our opinion it would be an error to classify with that of Pascoli or of Luigi Pirandello. Nor was there any lack of "traditionalistic" poets and narrators. More than anything else, Italian culture rests on two fundamental philosophic movements: on the one hand, the historicism of Benedetto Croce, on the other, a system which is likewise historical but which stands between renewed liberalism, such as that of Piero Gobetti, and Italian Marxism, like that of Antonio Gramsci.

These two lines of Italian historicism were greatly strengthened by the sharp, open opposition of both of them to Fascism; that is to say, to the political movement which for two decades represented anticulture in Italy. The best Italian minds were opposed to Fascism or outside it, and by itself it could express only a false culture made up of facile and rash myths (nationalism, imperialism, demagogy, even a national pseudo-virility and swaggering arrogance) deteriorated by rhetoric. Even Giovanni Gentile, chosen as the theoretician of Fascism, gave it only remasticated Hegelian cud, while his pedagogy had been shaped in a liberal spirit and his gnosiology and aesthetics, notwithstanding the proclamation of their historical and rational contents, finally courted mystico-decadent attitudes. Other writers, whom the dictatorship filed away as its cultural exponents, even in a periodical of "encounters" such as the *Primato* published by the minister Giuseppe Bottai, maintained a state of coexistence between their superficial attachment to Fascism and their more congenial decadent sentiments; among these were for example, Pirandello, Bontempelli, Panzini. Finally other hierarchical and official representatives of the Fascist pseudo-culture, such as Bottai himself, Giovanni Federzoni, Arturo Marpicati, Gioacchino Volpe, Francesco Ercole, shrank to the status of theoreticians and academic historians of the most obsolete nationalistic and lictorial mythography; yet these were talented and well-educated men.

Italian culture, on the contrary, belonged to anti-Fascism, whether that which was cautiously at work in Italy, in the prisons and in clandestine meetings, or the anit-Fascism working in Europe and in America by virtue of exiles, whom the Fascists scornfully called *fuorusciti* [political refugees]. As for Catholic culture, it was active, on the one hand seeking an agreement with Fascism, on the other opposing it. However, official Catholic thought shut itself up in academic and university circles, while the more spiritually restless Catholics attached themselves to decadent poetics.

Benedetto Croce was born at Pescassèroli in the Abruzzi region in 1866. After the death of his parents and sister, he went to Rome to live with his uncle Silvio Spaventa and attended classes at the law school of the university. In 1886 he moved to Naples, where he began his long, persistent activity as philosopher and critic, which absorbed him entirely. He made several journeys to various European nations for reasons of study; he also took part in political activity and was Minister of Education from 1920 to 1921. In 1924, when Fascism had assumed absolutist and dictatorial forms, he retired from public life, and yet, in the field of thought and culture he represented the national anti-Fascist resistance. He returned to politics from 1943 to 1945, in the first two years, that is, following the fall of Mussolini and his régime. Then he returned definitively to his studies, rarely leaving Naples, where he died in 1952. He was a member of the Lincei Academy and a senator.

Croce's work is enormous (over forty volumes). It comprises speculatives works: *Estetica come scienza dell' espressione e linguistica generale,* 1902; *Logica come scienza del concetto puro,* 1909; *Filosofia della pratica; Economia ed Etica,* 1909; *Teoria e storia della storiografia,* 1917; *La poesia,* 1935; *La storia come pensiero e come azione,* 1937; monographs on the philosophies of Vico and of Hegel and on historical materialism; the historical studies, among them the *Storia dell'Italia dal 1871 al 1915,* 1928; the *Storia d'Europa nel secolo XIX,* 1932; the literary studies such as the *Saggi sulla letteratura italiana del Seicento,* 1911; *La letteratura della nuova Italia* (in six volumes, beginning with 1914); *Conversazioni critiche* (in five series, from 1918 to 1939); *Ariosto, Shakespeare e Corneille,* 1920; *La Poesia di Dante,* 1921; *Poesia e non poesia,* 1923 (essays on the poets of the Italian and European nineteenth century); *Storia dell'età barocca in Italia,* 1929; *Poesia popolare e poesia d'arte,* 1933; *Poesia antica e moderna,* 1941; *La letteratura italiana del Settecento,* 1949, and so on. A fundamental and valuable volume is

Contributo alla critica di me stesso [*Contribution to Criticism of Me Personally*], 1915. His historical interpretations, vast erudition, and anecdotage are fused in such volumes as *I teatri di Napoli, Storie e leggende napoletane, Uomini e cose della vecchia Italia, Varietà di storia letteraria e civile,* and *Pagine sparse.* In these books the intellectual and moral reaction of Croce is so lively that the numerous learned notes dissolve in a witty conversation of diversified humanity. The reactions of the free man to tyranny and his participation in the tragedy of war and the heroic, bloody struggle for the liberation of Italy from the foreigner give us famous vibrant pages, such as those against the use of violence, which not only evades the dialectics of liberty but completely destroys it. These may be read in *La Storia come pensiero e come azione* [*History as Thought and as Action*]. Those on the liberation are found in the volume *Quando l'Italia era divisa in due* [*When Italy was Split in Two*]. Finally, in 1903, Croce founded his review *La Critica,* which survived until 1944 and turned out to be a cultural institution of historical significance. From 1944 to 1952 it was continued as *Quaderni della critica.*

The fundamental theories of Croce, besides his theory of aesthetics, are: the theory of the *distinti,* which arranges itself with that of "the opposites" in defining the human cognitive process; the theory of vitality; and especially the theory which identifies the real with history, and philosophy with historiography. Now that the philosophic system of Croce has been absorbed and is present as vital pith or essence in contemporary culture, all the gnoseological residues that are still met with in the organic system of the philosophy of the spirit no longer interest us. Today the old philosophical system has given way to specialized monographic problems posed one after the other by the internal development of our culture itself in relation to precise political, sociological, literary situations; in short, to the situations of civilization. But the identification of philosophy with historiography and the relationship studied by Croce between theoretical and practical activities of the spirit form the bases of modern historicism and worked prolifically even in that part of the culture which, because of its counter-reformistic and innovating spirit, considered and proclaimed that it had rid itself easily of Croce's philosophy. The moral vigor which Croce reveals in another of his famous identifications, that of thought with liberty, is so full and eruptive, yet contained within the lucid strictness of theoretical research, that today it is difficult to think about the tragic and fundamental moral problem of liberty without receiving enlightment and comfort from the thought and educative activity of Croce.

Let us now look briefly at Croce's aesthetics. Art is intuition; therefore, it belongs to the life of the spirit and is a cognitive activity, but it is quite distinct from logic, from the practical sciences. Hence it is extraneous to any intellective, technical, or moral discrimination. Art is intuition of sentiment, and in this sense it is always lyrical. In the work of art, content and form are always a single thing, they constitute a concrete unity that resolves into the work of art, into its historical objectivity. Language as a linguistic institution is a practical codification of speech, which, on the other hand, is always a creation of the individual lyrical intuition and belongs therefore to aesthetics. Grammars, dictionaries, literary genres, and the rules of rhetoric are breviaries which, reducing selected literary examples to a common denominator, propose or suggest some practical standards which, therefore, are neither cognitive nor absolute.

Literary criticism is the history of poetical contents, because there exists no history of poetry: poetry is reality in each work of art; it lives and is complete, and is not repeatable. In considering a work of art, criticism confines itself to pointing out and distinguishing what is poetry from what is not poetry; that is, distinguishing poetry from literature. The latter is writing for a practical purpose (such as eloquence, historiography or philosophical prose, scientific prose). Croce's literary criticism reveals here and there some limitations; for example, his unacceptable opinion which holds that Dante's poem is a theological novel and, as such, unpoetical, while the lyrical episodes which cover the theological structure are poetical. On the poetry of *Le Grazie* of Foscolo and on the poetry of Leopardi we observe other limitations in Croce's opinions, which disclose some severe conclusions, while, on the contrary, they praise as poetical some things in Carducci which we judge merely eloquent. With what he sensed as the healthy classicism of Carducci as poet, Croce compared the wind of morbid insincerity that he regretted in the poetry of Pascoli and progressively in the poetry of his contemporaries. Therefore, where the critical opinion of Croce does not convince us, it is often necessary to consider the historical and moral values which the critic – always an historian of human reality – attributed to the same poetry in an aesthetic section. Moreover, Croce's studies on the Renaissance and Ariosto, on the Baroque, on the eighteenth century, on European Romanticism, are fundamental. In *Poesia e non poesia* [*Poetry and Non-poetry*] one may read essays of extreme historical characterization; also, the essays on the writers of "the new Italy," in addition to the opinions considered in themselves, are fundamental because they describe clearly the literary and civil atmosphere of the Italy of the late nineteenth century.

Croce's prose is limpid, clear, and constructed on the very rhythm of his thought. It is capable of tonal transitions, ranging from the severity of the philosopher, and from the wit of the narrator and the anecdotist who conjures up men and events, to irony. The prose is rich in varied and inexhaustible anecdotes and in covering different times and nations shows Croce's enormous acquaintance with European literatures from their origins down to his own times; a knowledge, moreover, nimble and full of movement, of striking comparisons and rapid, unexpected antitheses and contrasts.

The romantic European tradition (with a vein of Hegelian philosophy) are fused in Croce's thought and in his historical criticism, with the Italian philosophic and historiographic tradition, treated from Vico, Foscolo and De Sanctis, and by a certain inclination toward reaping the dialectical components of culture, to Gioberti and Carducci — so total and universal is the system of Benedetto Croce.

Giovanni Gentile and Antonio Gramsci

Giovanni Gentile was born at Castelvetrano in Sicily in 1875. He was a pupil of Alessandro d'Ancona and thus was brought up in that positivist and historico-erudite school to which Carducci also belonged. Soon, through the philosophy of Hegel, Gentile matured the philosophical system of neo-idealism. After several years of discordant collaboration he detached himself from the "historicist" Croce in 1926. His philosophical and critical activity was spread over three decades, a period roughly corresponding to his teaching of philosophy at the university of Rome. Thereafter he allowed himself to be absorbed by ministerial and editorial activity, and by political activity, for which he was labelled the philosopher of Fascism. He was minister of education (October, 1922 — July, 1924) and engineered a famous educational reform which was ingenious on the strictly pedagogical plane, but was unrelated to any social necessity. He was chairman of the Istituzione Treccani, which published the monumental *Enciclopedia Italiana*. He was also a senator. After the fall of Fascism, when the Italian Social Republic was founded under the protection of German arms, Gentile was an adherent. He was killed in Florence on April 15, 1944 by anti-Fascist partisans.

His principal works are: *Sommario di pedagogia come scienza filosofica,* 1913–1914; *Teoria dello spirito come atto puro,* 1916; *Sistema di logica come teoria del conoscere* 1917–1921; and *Filosofia dell 'arte* 1931. In this discussion, where literary culture is the issue, we shall mention the volumes *Dante e Manzoni,* 1923; *Manzoni e Leopardi,* 1928; *Gino Capponi e la cultura toscana nel secolo XIX,* 1922 (2nd ed. 1926) ; and, finally, *Giordano Bruno e il pensiero del Rinascimento,* 1st ed., 1920, 2nd ed., 1925. The divergence of Gentile's neo-idealism or actualism from the historicism of Croce is chiefly this: Croce took only the dialectical method of thought from the philosophy of Hegel and transferred it to the Italian tradition from Vico to De Sanctis. Gentile fundamentally kept to the philosophy of Hegel, from which he drew the inauspicious doctrine of the hegemonic state and, therefore the theoretical principle on which Fascism stood. Consequently, Gentile was inclined to deny the autonomy of art, which Croce stubbornly defended. Gentile tended to consider poetry a minor philosophy which, as Hegel holds, represents an inferior phase of the human spirit. In the poets — Dante, Leopardi, Manzoni — Gentile saw the man of thought rather than the poet. He had a predilection for the doctrinal poets who, in his opinion, were exponents of a philosophical poetics of life. Finally, started with the concept that the human spirit performs in the *act* and there expresses its whole self circularly and globally. Gentile contradicted the "distinti" of Croce and ended up favoring vague theological tendencies, which in some of his pupils became frankly mystical and decadentistic. This was in opposition to the rigorous laicality and rationality of Croce's historicism.

Antonio Gramsci, on the contrary, represents the evolution of Croce's historicism towards the Marxist interpretation of reality. Gramsci was born in Sardinia at Ales (Cagliari) in 1891. In Turin he represented the revolutionary socialist movement of Palmiro Togliatti and Umberto Terracini, publishing his ideas in the movement's periodical *Ordine nuovo*. The separation of Gramsci and his companions from the official socialist party was caused by the realization that neither the democratic movement during the Risorgimento, nor the socialism of the Treves and Turatis had ever represented an authentic "Jacobin" movement, that is, a party which would unite the working classes and the peasants in an enduring bond. Thus the Communist Party came into existence and was organized initially among the workmen of Turin. In this mission, Gramsci spent his most ardent spiritual and moral energies. After his arrest and condemnation by the Fascists, he spent the rest of his life in prison, where he died in 1938. His works, written in the years of his imprisonment, were published posthumously by Einaudi in Turin. Among his philosophical works, *letteratura e vita nazionale* [*Literature and National Life*] is very important, and the pages on Machiavelli and the literature of the Risorgimento are noteworthy. These present a new interpretation of Italian culture which is so well grounded that today even historiography of liberal-radical or Catholic persuasion has adopted it as its own. But the masterpiece of Gramsci's literary work is *Lettere dal carcere* [*Letters from Prison*], 1947. This poetical document expresses faith in the historic evolution of man, strength of mind, spiritual fervor, a sound but subtle sensibility, and, in short, the portrait of a martyr who, like authentic heroes, has divested himself of the ostentation of martyrdom. To the theory of historiography, Gramsci's new contribution is the fundamental relationship existing between political reality and culture on the one hand and the social structure and vital contribution of the people on the other. In this sense, Gramsci not only has not destroyed Croce's philosophy but has enriched and completed it in that part of it which had been left unresolved: dialectical relationship between political facts and economic-social facts. Certainly in Gramsci's thought the historical materialism founded by Karl Marx is present in all its fullness, but it is drawn out of the rigid sociological schemata of Hegelian orthodoxy and, as Croce might have said, born into the tradition of Italian thought from Machiavelli (on whom Gramsci wrote some illuminating pages) to Vico and also related to the Italian illuminists, to Cattaneo, De Sanctis, and to Croce himself, the hostile yet influential teacher of this rebellious scholar.

Notes on Literary Criticism of the Twentieth Century

The school of Croce chiefly produced histories of political and economic sciences, law, letters, and the arts. This should not surprise us because, as we have seen, the fundamental principle of Croce's system identifies philosophy with historiography. In this section, however, we must not deal with political, but rather with literary criticism. Therefore we shall limit ourselves to remembering that the historians who were educated along Croce's lines, with the exception of some few "orthodox" writers (Fausto Nicolini, a Vico and Manzoni scholar and recent biographer of Croce; Guido de Ruggiero, and others), welcomed ideological enticements emanating from radical liberalism. Among these are Adolfo Omodio, Luigi Salvatorelli, the author of *Il pensiero politico italiano dal 1700 al 1870*, 1935 (which also concerns Italian literature); Delio Cantimori; Federico Chabod; Arturo Carlo Jemolo; Antonio Monti, and so on. Representing Marxism are: Cesare Spellanzon, Ludovico Geymonat, Eugenio Garin, who represent with respect to Croce, a definite progress beyond the old liberal schemes which Croce's philosophy, with its political conception of liberty, had not surpassed. The historian Gaetano Salvemini was an independent.

Among the thinkers who most energetically renewed the concept of liberty, Piero Gobetti deserves particular attention. He influenced literary studies as well. And as initiator and promoter of "Rivoluzione liberale," he changed the course of the old liberalism toward a new democratic vitality, a fact borne out by his writings (*Opera critica*), 1927, which were published posthumously, for he was attacked and killed by Fascists in 1926.

From the Gentile school of actualism, on the other hand, came mostly theretic philosophers who followed other paths and went on to enrich diverse philosophical currents: that of Christian spiritualism (Armando Carlini, Augusto Gusto), another, of existentialism (Vito Fazio-Allmayer) still another of neo-illuminismo and critical philosophy (Giuseppe Lombardo Radice and Ernesto Codignola, pedagogists (Giuseppe Saitta, Guido Calogero, Ugo Spirito), and, finally, that of Marxism (Galvano della Volpe).

We shall briefly examine the principal historians and critics of letters. Alfredo Gargiulo was a follower of Croce. Already in his study of *D'Annunzio* (1912) he revealed an interest in the forms and components of style and continued this interest in his *Letteratura italiana del Novecento* (1940), where he presents himself as a critic of "pure poetry," attributing to the Crocian concept of *liricità* [lyricism] a restrictive interpretation which Croce never accepted. The name of Gargiulo draws our attention to other cultivators of stylistics. These certainly never claimed to reduce the work of art to pure style or to pure form, but did consider that they could interpret the psychological content of poetry through analysis of stylistic forms. In addition to the aesthetics of Croce, the influence which the masters of stylistics in Germany exercised on Italian stylists is plain; especially Carlo Vossler and Leo Spitzer. However,

Italian scholars rejected the sociological schemes dear to German stylists and transferred analysis of the forms to the historical development of the literature as it had been theoretically defined by Croce himself. The following are some exemplary works of historical stylistics. The essays on Cellini's life and on the prose writings of Giordano Bruno in *Poesia e letteratura* (1916) and *Saggi di letteratura francese* by Tommaso Parodi, and especially in the *Saggi sulla forma poetica italiana dell'Ottocento* (1929) by Cesare de Lollis; the stylistic-psychological essays on the poetry of the baroque writers, on Parini, on Carducci, and on of the writers of the decadent school in the two volumes of *Dal Barocco al Decadentismo* (1957) by Domenico Petrini; the study on the expressive technique of the *Decameron* of Boccaccio (considered a form required by the poetic vision of the author), which is included in *Tradizione e poesia nella prosa d'arte italiana dalla latinità medioevale al Boccaccio* (1934) by Alfredo Schiaffini; the more recent studies on the style of Vico in *Stile e umanità di G. B. Vico* (1946), in *Stile, linguaggio, poesia* (1948) and in *Critica e poesia* (1956) by Mario Fubini. Giacomo Devoto defended stylistics as an autonomous science in his *Studi di stilistica* (1950); and his *Nuovi studi di stilistica* (1962) which proposes that an author chooses the forms of his poetical and literary output from within the language of the collectivity – the community.

These new researches into style are apparent also among the academic scholars of linguistic institutions. They are observable in Giulio Bertoni, a Gentile disciple and author of *Lingua e pensiero* (1932); in Benvenuto Terracini, author of the *Guida allo studio della linguistica storica* (1949); in Bruno Migliorina, author of *Lingua e cultura* (1948) and *Storia della lingua italiana* (1960); and in still others. They are likewise present in the modern school of philology; in the Romanists, Angelo Monteverdi and Antonio Viscardi; in lovers of classical philology such as Concetto Marchesi, author of the famous *Storia della letteratura latina* and of monographs no less famous on Seneca and Tacitus; in Ettore Bignoni, Manara Valgimigli, and Giogio Pasquali, whom we shall meet further on; in the philologists of modern literature such as Michele Barbi, the celebrated Dante and Manzoni scholar.

A weighty reunion of philology, linguistics, and stylistics is revealed in the work of Gianfranco Contini who, for example, had detected a "system" in the poetical variants of Petrarch, *Saggi di un commento alle correzioni del Petrarca volgare* [*Essays On A Commentary Of The Corrections In Petrach's Vernacular Works*] 1943. He has investigated the stylistic work of classical and contemporary poets (for example, in *Esercizi di lettura,* 1939, and *Un Anno di letteratura,* 1942) . A student of De Robertis and Pasquali, Lanfranco Caretti, was known as a Tasso and Parini scholar and an advocate of a stylistic philology (*Filologia e critica,* 1955). A tendency to detect literary and even metrical disciplines or systems for the purpose of historicizing certain components of the stylistic invention of poets is discernible in the studies of Giovanni Getto (*Storia delle storie letterarie,* 1942; *Aspetti della poesia di Dante,* 1947; *Interpretazione del Tasso,* 1951; *Poeti critici e cose varie nel Novecento,* 1953). In sketching historical developments of determined stylistic compents from poet to poet, a greater severity is found in the studies of Emilio Bigi, of whose works we shall mention only *Dal Petrarca al Leopardi.*

The semantic trend which stresses expression more than intuition is represented by Guido Calogero in *Estetica Semantica Istorica* (1947). Also worthy of mention here are the *Saggi* and the *Nuovi Saggi di critica semantica* of Antonio Pagliaro (1953–1956). Guido Morpurgo Tagliabue contradicted Calogero in *Il concetto di stile* (1951) , firmly defending the technical concept of style. Many studies on the expressive forms of the arts take their inspiration from stylistic independence. Here it suffices to mention the *Discorso tecnico delle arti* (1952) of Gillo Dorfles.

Another "work group" emanating from the school of Croce has, on the contrary, plumbed the intuitive and lyrical concept of poetry. Style is considered in the totality of the work of art and hence denies an independent science of style and an equally independent science of language.

Francesco Flora was a theoretician of an aesthetics of the word (*I miti della parola,* 1931; *The Myths Of The Word;* and *Orfismo dell a parola,* 1953). He first studied contemporary literature in the light of the historicistic method (*Dal Romanticismo al Futurismo,* 1921 and 1926) and continued and completed these studies in the last years of his life: in his *D'Annunzio* of 1926, in his monographs on Pascoli (1959) and Carducci (1959), and in his collections of essays *Saggi di poetica moderna* (1949) and *Scrittori italiani contemporanei* (1952). His last book, published posthumously in 1962, is devoted to *Poesia e impoesia nell 'Ulisse di Joyce* [*Poetry and Non-poetry In Joyce's Ulysses*]. His aesthetic researches and vast readings in the major and minor classes of all epochs, Italian and foreign, developed his organic concept of the history of literature; hence his great *Storia della Letteratura Italiana* (1940, in three volumes, 1953 ff. in five volumes). Two fundamental concepts inspire this work: first, that the language of poets is the primitive, primigenial, and essential language of human civilization (which has caused some discussion of a humanistic aesthetics in Flora in relation to his aesthetics of language) ; second, that a history of poetry is permissible — it is permissible to study and ponder an activating literary tradition within the individual and independent separate works of poets and artists. The most vigorous quality of the *Storia* is the reading of the poetic and literary texts which are included in the historical exposition. It is rather like an ample anthology of supporting examples interpreted by virtue of a highly educated, stylistic, and musical sensibility.

Luigi Russo, whose principal studies are on Machiavelli (1949), Verga (1920), and Carducci, also wrote a commentary on the *Promessi Sposi,* the tragedies, and the lyric poems of Manzone and a study *I personaggi dei Promessi sposi* (1945). He chose to become a historian of Italian literature, and his essays range over a great part of Italian literature, including *Ritratti e disegni storici* in four series (1946–1953). He delved deeply into the relations obtaining between poetry and culture, between the lyric and the construction within the work of art. He revealed the personality of individual writers insofar as they are involved on the cultural plane and wrote of what he was pleased to define as "transcendental politics." Among his books devoted to study of the historiographical method we must at least mention *La Letteratura italiana e la storiografia contemporaneo* (1947).

Mario Fubini, whom we have met as a student of stylistics, is also an historian of literary culture (*Dal Muratori al Baretti,* 1946; and *Arcadia e illuminismo,* 1949). He is as well the author of important monographs on Foscolo (1928); and Alfieri (1951); besides that on Vico mentioned above. Walter Binni was a student of Russo and began his scholarly activities with *La poetica del decadentismo italiano* (1936), in which, contrary to Flora's view, he maintains that decadentism does not represent the decadence of Romanticism, but is instead a new poetics corresponding to a new sensibility, to a different and autonomous conception of life. Binni's studies on *Preromanticismo italiano* (1948) and on *Metodo e poesia di L. Ariosto,* (1947), are also concerned with the cultural significance of poetry, which puts itself into history only by that route. The *Cultura letteraria contemporanea* (1951), of Claudio Varese is on much the same ground.

Eugenio Donadoni, Attilio Momigliano, Manara Valgimigli and Pietro Pancrazi were influenced by Croce, but kept faith with a psychological sensibility of their own in interpreting the personality and the poetry of poets. Donadoni, the author of the present "History," is given special mention at the end of this work, a courteous but above all deserved homage to one of Italy's principal critics and scholars of her literature. In Momigliano's work psychological introspection tends toward evocation of tonal atmospheres which he notes and describes within the poetical texts; in so doing he is still a student of style, but for the purpose of tracing back the source of a psychological reason of a writer or of a cultural reason, and also to give vent to the sentimental sonorities of the text. His commentaries, especially that on the *Divine Comedy* (1945–1947), are the basis of this opinion. But the essay *Saggio sull'Orlando furioso* (1928), together with tonal analyses, brings a fundamental contribution to the study of the structure of that poem, through its merging of dream and reality and its wealth of human motifs. In a similar way, the picture of the personality and art of Manzoni is developed completely in his exemplary study *A. Manzoni – La Vita – Le Opere,* 1915–1919. An historical scaffolding supports the pages of keen analysis of his *Storia della letteratura italiana,* (fifth ed., 1946). Manara Valgimigli is a historian of Greek literature, but here we mention him for his psychological and literary evocations, which cross over from a learned note to the portrayal of men and affairs of the late nineteenth century and early twentieth century. This is especially so of Carducci, whose pupil he was, and in his *Uomini e scrittori del mio tempo* [*Men and Writers of my Time*], 1943, about the group in Emilia and Romagna which stands between Carducci, Serra and Panzini. Of Pancrazi, a polished writer and a keen but reserved critic, let us here discuss the collections of critical essays on the late nineteenth century and early twentieth century. *I Ragguagli di Parnaso* [*Re-*

ports on Parnassus], 1920; *Toscani dell'Ottocento,* 1924; *Scrittori di oggi* [*Writers of Today*] in six volumes, from 1942 to 1953, the last published posthumously; and *Italiani e stranieri* [*Italians and Foreigners*], 1957. The essays of Pancrazi embody many moderate and courtly characteristics of his taste and are inspired by a cultivated sense of civility which is both literary and customary with him. The name of Pancrazi brings up those of many critic-writers who are capable portraitists and polished conversationalists and the names of writers of literary articles on the "third page" of daily papers. We shall have to discuss some of these later on. However, it is fitting to record here those critics, polemicists, and essay writers whom we shall not have a chance to mention again.

Enrico Thovez, author of *Il pastore, il gregge e la zampogna* [*The Shepherd, the Flock and the Reed Pipe*], 1909, expresses in lucid, polemical language severe judgments on the poetry of Carducci and D'Annunzio, comparing learned and rhetorical poetry with the pure poetry of feeling of the Greeks and Leopardi. Carlo Linati was a diversified essayist, narrator, and describer of customs and landscapes. Two of his books seem particularly stimulating: *Sulle orme di Renzo* [*On the Footsteps of Renzo*], 1919 and 1927, in which the historical and natural places of *I Promessi Sposi* are described; and *Decadenza del vizio e altri pretesti* [*Decadence of Vice and Other Pretexts*], 1941. There is something akin to Linati in Cesare Angelini, who seems to make occasions and pretexts his starting points and presents states of mind and environmental atmospheres. His work is often seized with a keenness of sensibility and of language found in the style of the writer. He wrote much about Manzoni: *Il dono del Manzoni* dates from 1924, *Invito al Manzoni* from 1936. Ugo Ojetti has remained in the history of literature not as a storyteller, but as an essayist. His "third-page" articles, which appeared in the *Corriere della Sera* of Milan from 1921 to 1938, were published by the author in the seven volumes entitled *Cose viste* [*Things Seen*]. He is also well known as the founder of magazines of facile but pungent literature (*Dedalo, Pan, Pegaso*). Giuseppe Ravegnani is the author of *I Contemporanei,* of which the first series came out in 1930 and the second in 1936, it was revised and expanded in the 1960 edition. We might cite other works of his, but these *Contemporanei* clearly demonstrate the qualities of Ravegnani as a writer and a keen, measured reader of literary texts. A master of learned biography, beside Fausto Nicolini (*La giovinezza di G. B. Vico,* 1932, and *Benedetto Croce,* 1962), is Piero Nardi, author of *A. Fogazzaro su documenti inediti A. Fogazzaro* [*Revealed by Unpublished Documents*], 1930. Tommaso Gallarati Scotti is a portraitist who proceeds by psychological motivation; he is also the author of a life of Fogazzaro, *La Vita di A. Fogazzaro,* (1934). Let us mention Piero Bargellini's calling forth of painters and paintings: *Città di Pittori* (1939); *Via Larga* (1940); *Volti di Pietra* [*Stone Faces*] (1942). Other essayists of polished style and ardent intelligence are free of poetics and of schools, and therefore are quite different one from another: Giovanni Titta Rosa, who came from Abruzzo and became an honorary citizen of Milan, has reconstructed the Milan of Manzoni with both fidelity and poetic imagination; Arnaldo Bocelli was an educated and nimble writer of leading literary articles; Mario Bonfantini, a student of French literature and portraitist-critic of contemporary writers; Giuseppe Villaroel, poet and occasional writer; Giorgio Pasquali, whom we include here not as a philologist, but as the author who unleashed an enormous erudition in brilliant and intelligent conversations that are collected in his four volumes called *Stravaganze* [*Eccentricities*], 1933–1951, of which the fourth reveals a presentiment of death in its title, *Stravaganze quarte e supreme* [*Fourth and Last Volume of the Eccentricities*]; a friend both of Pasquali and Pancrazi and of a whole democratic group of scholars and writers of genius, Piero Calamandrei was an historian of jurisprudence, an essayist of varied human interests with the style of a narrator, an organizer of a culture of renewal, an anti-Fascist, and counter-reformist and the founder of the review *Il Ponte* [*The Bridge*]; Lorenzo Giusso was the author of *Il viandante e le statute* [*The Wayfarer and the Statues*] in two series, 1929 and 1942.

Other critics, while sensitive to historiographical necessities, devote the manner, terms, and lines of their study to spiritual values and problems, which are considered to be everlasting. Thus Carlo Bo, solaced by the new experiments of an active and especially French Christianity, has sketched a contemporary spiritual "problematics," in his works from the *Otto studi* on contemporary Italian poets, preceded by the essay *Letteratura come vita* (1939), through the *Saggi di letteratura francese* (1940), *Nuovi Studi* (1946), *Nuova poesia francese* (1952), *Riflessioni critiche* (1953), and the *Scandalo della speranza* (1957). Francesco Casnati, the author of the *Favole degli uomini d'oggi* [*Fables of Today's Men*], 1952, is bound to a traditional Christianity untroubled by doubts; he is a student of Claudel, Proust, and Baudelaire. Sergio Solmi derives inspiration from the cathartic function of poetry which faces the research and solitude of men projected into history. He feels the need for an essence and purity which diminish and rarefy the themes of lyric poetry — "a supreme illusion of song which miraculously maintains itself after the destruction of all illusions". Hence, the essays soul by supreme wisdom or by song as in *La salute di Montaigne e altri scritturdi letteratura francese* (1942 and 1952), in the studies of contemporary Italian poets, and in the study of the poetry of Leopardi published as an introduction to the works of Leopardi (1956). Solmi's book *Scrittori negli anni* [*Writers over the Years*] was published just before this edition of the *Storia* went to press. Luciano

Anceschi is a keen investigator of poetics, especially the contemporary poetics inspired by existentialist research and so also by a symbolic language. Representative are his *Autonomia ed eteronomia dell'arte* [*Autonomy and Heteronomy of Art*], 1936, and *Saggi di poetica e di poesia* [*Essays on Poetics and on Poetry*], 1942. The names that follow are those of readers and interpreters of symbolist poetry who are attentive to the direction of style or to existentialist overtones: Piero Bigongiari, *Studi* (1946) and *Il senso della lirica italiana* (1952); Aldo Borlenghi; Beniamino Dal Fabbro; Giacomo Debenedetti, *Saggi critici* (in two series, 1929 and 1945); Enrico Falqui, *Ricerche di stile* (1939) and *Narratori e prosatori del Novecento* (1950); Giansiro Ferrata; Mario Luzi, *L'inferno e il limbo* (1949); Oreste Macri; Adriano Seroni; G. A. Peritore, *Alcuni studi* (1961).

A most vigorous historical base supports the researches and the interpretations of the critics who, while stemming from the historiography of Croce or from technico-stylistic researches, have not been immune to other influences, especially of the Marxist aesthetics of Giorgio Lukâcs, or to that implicit in the historiography of Antonio Gramsci. Here we shall also restrict our attention to literary criticism and to the generation of older writers, with the exception of Pasolini. Natalino Sapegno must be named for several works and for an exemplary commentary of the *Divina Commedia.* He is the author of the *Trecento* in the series of literary centuries published by Vallardi of Milano (1934) and of a *Compendio di storia della letteratura italiana* in three volumes (1950). Both are masterly works which reveal great balance in sketching the ideological history of literary civilization. The ideologies are always related to the poetry and are presented as though dissolved in the culture which dialectically renews and enriches itself. The same balance is evident in the pages devoted to Verga, either in the *Compendio* or in the earlier *Appunti per un saggio sul Verga* (1945): his interest in the social art of the great Sicilian narrator never gives way to interpretations of content.

In his *Saggi critici* of 1950, Gaetano Trombatore reveals the temperament of a strong, clear critic who places the ideological content and the style of a work of art in its relation to an historical period of civilization with such keen adherence that the historical, universal fact and the individual fact of the work under consideration seem to become identical. In *Miti e coscienza del decadentismo italiano* [*Myths and Conscience of the Italian Decadent Poets*], 1960, Carlo Salinari has studied four poets and authors, D'Annunzio, Pascoli, Fogazzaro, and Pirandello, as illustrative of four expressions of the decadent civilization of the twentieth century. While the results do not always seem acceptable, nevertheless the great historical lines of the twentieth century are partially but surely marked out. Carlo Muscetta is a student of Romanticism, which he has covered in various ways from Monti to De Sanctis. Similar criteria have inspired the works of Giuseppe Petronio, who is led by his historico-ideological interests to study times and poets of volutive or involutive crises. He has been especially interested in Parini, Manzoni, and contemporary poetry. The work of Silvio Guarneri stems from analogous interests, his special subject being the post-Manzonian narrative. So too Antonio Piromalli, a student of Ariosto, Pacoli, and Fogazzaro. Pier Paolo Pasolini has collected his various studies and ventures in popular poetry under the title *Passione e ideologia* (1960). This treats Italian dialectal poetry of the twentieth century and contains his studies on poets and other writers from Carducci to the present. For each theme he concentrated on rapid, graphic information which is vibrantly intense, and on a constant dialectic symbiosis between style and content, between characteristic and repetitive stylistic construction and mental axiom. At times he seems to overturn old and academic historical sentence arrangement.

Supported by the aesthetics of Galvano della Volpe and Cesare Luporini, the ideological historians are congenially placed at the dialectic meeting point of Italian humanistic, historiographical, and Marxist tradition. They are opposed by critics and historians faithful to a positive historiography, according to which literary facts are arranged either in long national traditions or in sociological institutes. Giuseppe Toffanin, an historian of the Renaissance *(Il Cinquecento,* 1928; *La Storia dell'Umanesimo,* in three volumes completed in 1950; *Arcadia,* 1929, published 1946); Carlo Calcaterra, founder of the literary review *Convivium,* is a Catholic but much less prone to sociological schemes than Toffanin and is instead more congenial to stylistic-psychological design. He is the author of two fundamental works: *Parnasso in rivolta* [*Parnassus in Rebellion*] 1940, concerned with the Baroque and anti-Baroque in Italian seventeenth-century poetry, and *Il Barocco in Arcadia,* 1950 which consists of studies later continued in *Poesia e canto,* 1951, a volume containing the essay *La melica italiana dalla seconda metà del Cinquecento al Rolli e al Metastasio* [*Italian Melic Poetry From The Second Half Of The Sixteenth Century*]. He is also author of essays on the nineteenth century, on Romanticism, and on the early literary portents of the Risorgimento with special attention to Piedmont. Finally, he did a biographical study on Gozzano and Gozzano's Turin; he was even the publisher of that poet's works. All the following may be included. The historians of the Italian theater, Mario Apollonio, Silvio d'Amico, Renato Simoni, formulated their studies and researches in different ways. Apollonio with spiritualistic and Catholic purposes, the other two on the level of a tasteful chronicle of costumes. Alfredo Galletti passed from the old positivist and sociological criticism over to the esthetics of *De Sanctis* and to the comparative method between European literatures. He always held out against the esthetics of Croce. He authored *Le teorie drammatiche e la tragedia in Italia nel secolo XVIII (Dramatic Theories and Tragedy in Italy in the Eighteenth Century),* 1901; and then, with livelier and more articulate historical sensibility, *Poeti poesia e storia,* 1926; *Studi di letteratura inglese,* 1928. *Giosuè Carducci,* 1929; *Teorie di critici ed opere di poeti,* 1930; and *La poesia e l'arte di G. Pascoli,* 1918. Adriano Tilgher and Giovanni Alfredo Cesareo, defended a creative esthetics which ended by abandoning art to the irrational mystical rush of pure invention. The former was mostly concerned with the theater, *Studi sul teatro contemporaneo,* (1922) ; the latter with the Italian lyric poetry of the thirteenth century, *Le origini della poesia lirica e la poesia siciliana sotto i Svevi* (1924) .

The Crepuscolari

Brief examination of culture in Italy during the first sixty years of this century has shown us how the dominant lines of historicism and ideologism developed alongside existential, mystical, and sceptical movements which flowed together in different ways into decadentism. Passing now to the literature of invention — poetry, narrative, dramatic — and to the poetics more closely connected to the inventive literature, we shall determine how decadentism therein prevails.

Chronologically, the poetry of the twentieth century had its beginning with the movement known as *crepuscolarismo,* a name which Giuseppe Antonio Borgese applied to a vague lyrical disposition toward melancholy and morbid sentiments, toward a sad and tender vision of life, toward a pathetic life soon burnt out, and represented in the twilight when the objects and the lights of day soften in the first manifestation of approaching night. Sergio Corazzini (1887–1907) , author of sentimental laments, unrhymed in low-toned rhythm, almost muted psalmody, was called "crepuscular" for his *L'amaro calice* [*The Bitter Cup*], *Piccolo libro inutile* [*Useless Little Book*], *Libro per la sera della domenica* [*A Book for Sunday Evening*], and other collections of poetry later published by his friends in the posthumous volume of *Liriche* (1909). Others called crepuscular were Marino Moretti, whom we shall meet as a novelist; Angiolo Orvieto; Fausto Maria Martini, who pictured the group of Corazzini and other Roman "twilight" poets in *Si abarca a New York* [*New York Landing*], 1930; Guelfo Civinini, a novelist, as well as a poet; Bino Binazzi; and Carlo Chiaves. But far more vigorous poetical inventiveness was possessed by Govoni, Palazzeschi and Gozzano, who surpassed the intimite but fragile effusion of the *crepuscolari*.

Born in 1884, Corrado Govoni of Ferrara joined the crepuscular movement before passing on to futurism. He contributed to Marinetti's *Poesia*, then to *La Voce*, *Lacerba*, and other avant-garde reviews. He wrote novels, novellas, and plays. Above all he was a prolific poet, generous but intermittent. He engaged in many trades and lived in Rome for many years. In a way his books of crepuscular poetry are reminiscent of the "humble" D'Annunzio of the *Poema paradisiaco;* in another, they reveal his inclination for dense, whimsical images, which were to become a constant feature of Govoni as a lyrical poet. Indeed, his poetical inventiveness was to resolve itself into an outpouring of images which either follow each other in sequence or explode, so to say, around a theme. And Govoni's themes are characteristically of those landscapes, which seem congenial to him: countryside and gardens, plants, flowers, birds, peasant festivals, fairs. In short, his repertory, which is half rustic, half farcical, rich in colors, lights, and shadows, reminds us of pictorial impressionism. Only after his son Aladino was killed by the Germans at the Fosse Ardeatine do the choked accents of tragedy appear in his poetry with an effusive line of colloquy, of sorrowful meditation, of lengthened rhythm and recitative. His poetical collected works were published in this order: *Le Fiale* [*The Phials*] 1903 and in the same year *Armonie in grigio et in silenzio* [*Harmonies In Gray And In Silence*], which is crepuscular in tone but the title reminds us of the preciosity of the D'Annunzio of the *Isotteo; Poesie elettriche* and *Rarefazioni,* published by the Futurist Editions of *Poesia* in 1911 and 1915; then the more mature collections, from *Inaugurazione della primavera,* 1915, to *Brindcisi alla notte* [*A Toast To Night*], 1924, and in the same year *Il quaderno dei sogni e delle stelle* [*The Notebook of Dreams and Stars*]; *Il flauto magico,* 1932; and so on down to *Govonigiotto* in 1943. Then came the songs of sorrow, the colloquy-songs, which do not still the inventive inspiration of images: from *Aladino – Lamento su mio figlio morto* [*Lament For My Dead Son*], 1946, to *Preghiera al trifoglio* [*Prayer to the Clover*], 1953; and *Stradario della primavera* [*Roadmap Of Spring*], 1958; and *I canti del puro folle* [*Songs of Pure Madness*], 1959, but published later in the volume *Poesie,* 1961.

Aldo Palazzeschi was born in Florence in 1885. He joined the futurist movement, then broke away. He contributed to the futuristic *Poesia,* then to *La Voce, Lacerba,* and *La Riviera ligure.* In his youth he wrote more poetry than anything else. *I cavalli bianchi* [*White Horses*], 1905; *Lanterna,* 1907; *Riflessi,* 1908; *Poemi,* 1909; also *Incendiario,* collections published in *Poesia,* 1925 and 1930. The tone of an ironical fable which aims at pure amusement is peculiarly his own. Whether crepuscular or futurist, he was always faithful to this odd *impasto,* to this admirable inventive and stylistic agility and vivacity. Melody or recitative correspond to the two different tempos of the amazing fable and of the irony which does not spoil the fable but resolves it into a game, a happy inspiration.

In Guido Gozzano, irony is intended to keep the poet from yielding to sentiment. Instead, he becomes filled with it; yet, it is always related to his sorrowful consciousness of sentimental aridity. He was born in Agliè (Turin) in 1884. His life was divided between the city and the Canavese countryside from which his parents came. In Turin, a city which was provincial and subalpine in appearance, but with a restless European soul of its own, a whole historical and spiritual tradition was in crisis. The Turin which lay between Arturo Graf and Gozzano was transplanting its institutional traditions, those of the House of Savoy and the era of Mazzini, and those connected with the academic, positivist, and technical culture; for example, that which was represented by the *Giornale storico della letteratura italiana,* as well as by its old household virtues. Graf the critic remained faithful to the old positivist culture, but as a poet he eulogized the perplexed sadness that seizes upon us when faced by the enigma of the universe and of life. Gozzano takes a part the old sentimental world with his irony, but he is unable to renounce it completely, for in this world are included not only the famous "good things in the worst taste," (by which is understood furnishings and knickknackery) but Turin itself, remembered later when he was in India, with all its air of *fin-de-siècle,* of Humbertian nineteenth century. His poetry lies precisely in this affectionate and ironical recollection of the old and dear things, and definitely not where he makes a show of cynical intelligence and sentimental cruelty or indifference, which, incidentally, were things alien to his nature. His poems are collected in the *Via del rifugio* [*Road of the Shelter*], 1907, and *Colloqui* [*Conversations*], 1911. This latter volume contains the more famous short narrative poems, such as *Totò Merùmeni* and *La signorina Felicità ovvero la felicità* [*Miss Felicity or Happiness*]. The poetical language of Gozzano echoes Graf, the *scapigliati* poets and the

D'Annunzio of the *Poema paradisiaco,* but his composite ironic-elegiac tone is purely his own. His style blends a discoursive rhythm, which is sometimes very much like prose, with a secret melodic nostalgia made up of symmetries of images, of rich and serried phonetic evocations (rhymes, assonances, consonances, alliterations), and of limpid verbal surprises. Having fallen victim to tuberculosis, he went to India in 1912 for three months with the hope of effecting a cure. From this journey came the beautiful prose writings, more allusive than descriptive, contained in the volume *Verso la cuna del mondo* [*Towards the Cradle of the World*], published posthumously in 1917. But he returned to his beloved Turin sick and filled with homesickness for his city. He died in 1916.

The Futurists

The movement of futurism was born officially in Paris in February, 1909, with a manifesto signed by Filippo Tommaso Marinetti and others and published in the Parisian journal *Le Figaro*. The futurists proposed to repudiate the tradition of the past and to impose on all arts, including that of the word, an unprejudiced, impartial spiritual activism; therefore, they clamorously repudiated philosophical pessimism, pessimism of sentiment, diplomatic prudence in international and social relationships, neutralism, traditionalism, veneration for books, libraries, and museums. Futuristic works were to draw their inspiration from open-minded daring, from the conquest, ownership, and worship of machines, of speed, and of the swift analogies which bring with them perceptions and the most distant ideas. All values were to be resolved into one single anticonformistic, rebellious impetus; that of "modernizing, innovating, speeding."

Futuristic manifestos followed one after another, attacking all human activities from politics (the policy of the strong nation, the aggressive nation, of expansionism, of war), to economics, as well as all the arts – painting, sculpture, architecture, poetry, cinematography, music and the theater. The thing went as far as the *aerokitchen,* "born of the exhibitions of aeropainting."

Futurism caught on for a number of years as a way of life and in Italy merged with the style of D'Annunzio. These were the years preceding the war. A conservative and middle-class Italy was fond of camouflaging itself in *gallism [gallo: the cock],* in vitalism, energism, and in a period of amateurish aestheticism. Meanwhile, political relations between the great European powers were becoming troubled, international economic competition was growing sharper and exacerbated, and social struggles were growing furious. As a programatic movement, futurism belongs to decadentism through the cult of irrationality: the vitalistic *élan,* energetic and physiological, took the place of reason, which alone gives value and historic meaning to ideas and to programs.

Nevertheless two futuristic principles in the field of aesthetics profoundly affected the literature of the twentieth century and not only in Italy (consider the Russian poet Mayakovsky, Joyce, Lawrence, Rafael Alberti, the French surrealists and German expressionists, a certain narrative technique of the American Faulkner and even the poetry of Ezra Pound). The two considerations are the analogical relationship between images, and the figurative penetration of the word freed from the traditional syntactical structure. The futurist revolution was less successful in the theater, although furious arguments and even fistic brawls made many futuristic theatrical soirées memorable. Futurism did not stand up against the break with literary traditions; that is, with the cognitive structure of poetic language which is placed upon faithfulness to syntax and punctuation.

As we have seen, the official founder of futurism was

Filippo Tommaso Marinetti (1876–1944), who was born in Alexandria, Egypt. He had studied in Paris and there he published his first poems, such as *La conquête des Etoiles,* 1902, *Destruction,* 1904, and some plays. In 1905 he founded in Milan the review *Poesia,* which grew to become a publishing house as well. It welcomed many French poets, and many famous Italian books of futuristic poetry were published there: in 1910, *L'incendiario of Palazzeschi,* in 1911, *Il Codice di Perelà,* also by Palazzeschi and the *Poesie elettriche* of Govoni; in 1914 the poem of Marinetti *Zang-tumb-tumb,* which describes the siege of Adrianople (Edirne), and finally, in 1915 Govoni's *Rarefazioni.* Then Marinetti returned to Paris where, as we have seen, he launched his first *Manifesto.* In January, 1913, in Florence, the first number of *Lacerba* appeared, and the review lasted until May, 1915 when, on the declaration of war against Austria, the editors, who had fought for intervention, left for the front. Futurism flowed into *Lacerba,* but other tendencies, avant-gardism and a breaking with the past, merged with it. Among the contributors – Agnoletti, Boccioni, Carrà, Govoni, Folgore, Palazzeschi, Papini, Soffici, Sbarbaro, and still others – we find Marinetti. From then on he became the poet of wars, or rather of battles and thundering weapons; we shall mention only *L'Aeropoema del golfo della Spezia,* 1935, and *Il poema africano della Divisione 28 ottobre,* 1937, which celebrates the war of Fascism in Ethiopia.

Some poets of genius made use of a certain futuristic technique in order to endow a greater phonetic articulation and inventive speed to a much broader lyrical inspiration. We have already recorded the futuristic books of Govoni and Palazzeschi, which take their places in their own independent poetical development, although persistent opposition to this experience remained thereafter in their authors. The same may be said both of Ardengo Soffici, the futuristic author of *Bif zf+18, Simultaneità,*

Chimismi lirici, 1915, and of *Primi principii di una estetica futurista,* 1920; and also of Giovanni Papini, who was, however, a solid theorizer of futurism rather than a poet (*Il mio futurismo* dates from 1914, and other articles in *Lacerba* followed). Poets who were more faithful to the content, as well as to the technique of futurism, were Paolo Buzzi, Licano Folgore, Enrico Cavacchioli, Auro d'Alba, Gesualdo Manzella Frontini, Mario Bètuda, and others. Of Folgore (pseudonym of Omero Vecchi), we shall mention *Canto dei motori* (1912), *Ponti sull 'oceano* [*Bridges on the Ocean*] (1914), *Città veloce* [*Swift City*] (1919); of Buzzi, *Areoplani* (1909), *Versi liberi* (1913), *Poema delle Radio-onde* [*Poem of the Radio Waves*] (1940), and *Atomiche* (1952).

La Voce *[The Voice]* *Prezzolini and Papini*

The movement of *La Voce* is contemporaneous with futurism. This review saw the light of day in Florence, December 20, 1908, through the efforts of Giuseppe Prezzolini, who was its founder. It was published until October, 1914, remaining a review of varied culture. In November, it became political, changed hands, and survived until December, 1915. Meanwhile, in December, 1914, the literary *Voce* had been born and was called *La Voce bianca* [*White Voice*] because of the color of its cover, and it was directed by Giuseppe De Robertis. The history of *La Voce* expresses partially but clearly the history of Italian culture in the second decade of the twentieth century. It presented a philosophical orientation of existential and spiritualistic inspiration, with pragmatic veinings, which corresponded to the composite culture of Prezzolini and his collaborators, but had a chiefly literary interest, which, through De Robertis, foreshadows *La Ronda,* (born after the war and of which we shall speak later), and

Ermetismo (a modern Italian school of obscure poetry).

With Prezzolini *La Voce* became a national review, or, indeed, a European one. It contrasts the system of Croce, based on the reality of knowledge and on the logical solution not so much of problems as of historical interpretations, with the sense of the particular inspired by the more general problem of existence. It does not resolve the problem of existence through a principle of truth, but confines itself to proposing a means of living or an affective attitude; that is why we have spoken of laical spiritualism and of pragmatism. Prezzolini's collaborators and contributors were: Giovanni Papini, still drenched with pragmatism, who published his *Pagine di poesia* [*Pages of Poetry*] in *La Voce;* Giuseppe Antonio Borgese, who brought to it Romantic myths already corroded by irrational and individualistic vitalism, almost to the point of being anarchistic (through him the Dannunzian echo of a false Nietzsche reached the pages of the review); Carlo Michelstaedter, Scipio Slataper, Renato Serra, Piero Jahier; Giovanni Boine; Federico Tozzi. And there were others who brought intimistic prose to it and an ever unsolved aspiration to spiritual certainties. Emilio Cecchi, Pietro Pancrazi, and Antonio Baldini, a refined essayist who seemed to start from capricious cultural causes to delineate unusual happenings and persons. Finally, there were historians and philosophers engaged in the search for a rational reality: from Croce himself to Giovanni Gentile, Gaetano Salvemini and Giovanni Amendola. It is therefore impossible, in describing the review, to reduce such diverse contributions to a unitary physiognomy. Nevertheless, it is possible to single out with a certain rightness a group of *Voce* writers and almost a *Voce* atmosphere and to arrange therein those inward prose writings, those psychological confessions, those stylistically honed and spiritually unresolved essays that oppose metaphysically allusive and elusive aspirations for the problems of reality. Outside of this group stand Prezzolini and Papini.

Giuseppe Prezzolini, born in Perugia in 1882, was more than anything else a tireless organizer of literary reviews and schools. He was on the editorial staff of the *Leonardo* from 1903 to 1908, then until 1914 he was the animating spirit of *La Voce,* then went on to *Lacerba.* His change of domicile to the United States marked the end of neoidealism. In 1906 he had written *La Coltura italiana* with Papini, then, in 1907, *Il sarto spirituale* [*The Spiritual Tailor*], in 1909 a monograph on Croce and, in 1915, one on Papini, and in 1922, the volume *Amici* [*Friends*]. Instead he accepted the positive method of American historiography and so wrote *La vita di N. Machiavelli fiorentino* [*Life of N. Machiavelli of Florence*] in 1927, and other essays on militant culture, as well as the famous *Repertorio bibliografico della storia e della critica della letteratura italiana dal 1902 al 1932,* published in New York between 1937 and 1939. The two volumes published by the *Voce* of Rome, *Dopo Caporetto* and *Vittorio Veneto,* were inspired by the first world war.

Giovanni Papini was born in Florence in 1881, and died in 1956. During his youth he represented the most varied literary experiences, from the crepuscular to the pragmatist, *vocian,* and futuristic. And yet throughout, there was in him a constant and unitary strain: a lively and articulate but superficial culture, which could take in and allow the most diverse interests and unlike inclinations to coexist. A polemical writer, he proceeded by axioms, epigraphical pronouncements, and even by paradoxes. His writing never invites the reader to meditate, precisely because it does not possess true certainties nor true perplexities, but it is always effective on the plane of immediate reading and is usually sonorous. Today his criticism reveals itself as more journalistic than historical; still, his books are rich in keen psychological illuminations and in unexpected reflections, which dart like lightning although they are ephemeral. His linguistic Florentinism, lucid in argument, sparkling in imagery, filters through an expert literary form. However, figurative immediacy and prehensile quality of the vernacular are not renounced. His first books were more devoted to destroying old traditional philosophies and old Romantic myths than they were to rebuilding. But it is precisely here that Papini stands out as an exemplary writer; he gives voice to a time of crisis that destroyed the past without being able to create a present for itself – a crisis, we might say, fed by the white fire of pure intelligence which placed itself between the maceration of the nineteenth-century Romanticism and the founding of the twentieth-century decadentism. Among others, the books which mirror this Papini are *Il crepuscolo dei filosofi* [*The Twilight of the Philosophers*] of 1906; *Ventiquattro cervelli* [*Twenty-four Minds*], of which the first series dates from 1912; *Stroncature* [*Harsh Criticisms*], 1916. But it is especially in *Un uomo finito,* 1912, that, amidst so many harsh and crude judgments and words, there runs a true sadness and the consciousness of so many battles not only lost but rendered vain because they have destroyed without having rebuilt. Even the creative or inventive works (*Cento pagine di poesia,* 1915, and *Opera prima,* 1917) seem to attempt a poetical route to the certainties of the soul and of the intellect – but they only attempt. His conversion to Catholicism, falling within this time of disheartened crisis, might appear as an epical spiritual conquest. Instead, Papini brought his too facile, inert uneasiness even to this new discovery. The best work of this writer has defined itself in a sort of nimble psychological portraitism which is psychologically evident: the portrait of Christ in *Storia di Cristo,* 1921; of Saint Augustine in the book *Sant'Agostino,* 1929; of Dante in *Dante vivo* of 1933; of Carducci in *Grandezza di Carducci,* 1935; and of Michelangiolo in *Vita di Michel-*

angiolo, 1949. Other works are a whimsical series of essays born of moods and occasions which, when they are not checked and deepened by some pathetic inflection which reminds us of the inward and confessional tone of the best pages of *Un uomo finito* are spoiled by a too indulgent exuberance: the *Operai della vigna* [*Workers in the Vineyard*]; *Gog; Figure umane* [*Human Faces*], 1940; *Santi e poeti,* 1947. On the other hand there is the misty Catholic reformism of books such as *Lettere agli uomini di Papa Celestino VI, L'imitazione del Padre,* and *Il Diavolo* (which dates from 1953 and is the last of Papini's works in book form). The last portrait, and the most effective because it is moderate and sincere, is the one Papini painted of himself in *Mostra personale* [*Personal Show*] in 1941.

Finally, we must record Papini's work as founder and director of reviews. He founded and directed from 1903 to 1905, the years of his pragmatic vitalism, *Leonardo,* the Florentine review which had the declared purpose of "intensifying existence." He was one of the leading spirits of *La Voce* and of *Lacerba,* and the founder of *L'Anima,* 1911, and of three other Florentine reviews: *Il frontespizio,* 1929; *La rinascita,* 1938; and *L'ultima,* 1946.

Writers of La Voce

Ardengo Soffici, born at Rignano on the Arno in 1879, is generally considered a *vociano,* a collaborator on *La Voce.* A painter and man of letters, he was cofounder, with Papini, of *Lacerba* and was the author of critical essays on sculptor Medardo Rosso in 1909, on the poet Arthur Rimbaud in 1911, and on others. He is the composer of impressionistic poems in which crepuscular and futurist moods are approached, such as the previously cited collection *Bif zf + 18, Simultaneità, Chimismi lirici* of 1915, and *Marsia e Apollo* of 1938. He wrote allegories, whimsical journeys, meetings, and portraits, and especially books of capricious memoirs. These latter gained in stress through their diary form and from the rapid succession of images, isolated and projected by the keen ardor of an often sarcastic intelligence; for example, *Giornale di bordo* [*Logbook*], 1915, and the wartime book *Kobilek,* 1918.

But the *vocian* writers who were most exemplary are those who represent themselves and their characters as held tightly in an uneasy and anxious state of mind, as oppressed and exalted by their innner problems, and above all, as wearied by the decadentistic necessity of reopening the difficult spiritual colloquy between men. For after the exhaustion of classical Romanticism and of the Foscolian "correspondence of the amorous senses," extreme individualism seemed to dry up or to shatter the very relationship of man to man.

Carlo Michelstaedter, of Gorizia (1887–1910), the philosopher poet of "the indifferent waning of everything; is already far from the crepuscular, the "twilight" authors. The latter gave themselves up without resistance, and even with soft voluptuousness, to the sensations of sorrow, whereas Michelstaedter reacted to sadness, the uneasy problem of existence, with a desperate cognitive and moral will. Through his lyrical speech which is secretly pathetic, his definition of "the arid and lonely" life, his need to denounce and to suffer, and his peremptory verbal axioms, he comes between Leopardi and Montale. He represents the restoration of a classicism within decadentism before it fulfills and defines itself in the poets of the mid-twentieth century. He wrote the *Dialogo della salute,* 1912; *La persuasione e la retorica,* 1913; and *Le Poesie,* 1922. The dates indicate that all these works and others appeared posthumously (there now exists a definitive edition of his complete works).

Scipio Slataper was born in Trieste in 1888 and died

in December, 1915, fighting on the Podgóra (the Piedimonte del Calvario, in the province of Gorizia, a place famous for hard fighting during the Italo-Austrian war, 1915–1918. It is now Yugoslav territory). This is the same place where Renato Serra, a literary critic from Cesena, also met his death. Of Slataper's writings there remain the *Scritti letterari e critici,* the *Scritti politici,* and the *Lettere* (published after his death by Giani Stuparich, one of his friends). His principal critical study bears the title *Ibsen;* but the book most representative of this patriot is the poetical diary *Il mio Carso,* published by *La Voce* in Florence in 1918. The intimate tone of this confession and the lyrical pace of the prose link this diary to the *Voce* movement and to the poetics of art prose and to the lyrical fragment. But the most congenial poetical themes of Slataper are the love of life which exalts the spirit, the necessity of opening an essential colloquy with mankind and a contact with nature. Nature is especially loved in its harsh and reluctant forms (which are precisely those of the Carso), and is felt to be the secret source of moral energies and fresh vitality. His lyric speech moves ahead by means of closed and isolated verbal nuclei within a dry and lucid tonality, which is alien to the musical shadings and pleasures of impressionism.

Piero Jahier was born in Genoa in 1884, the son of a Waldensian shepherd. There has been a tendency to attribute the strong moral inspiration of his work to the sternness of his Protestant upbringing. It would perhaps be more correct to assert that in him, as in those going his way, the difficult winning of a spiritual reality depends on an affective and pathetic impetus that goes beyond the logical search for that reality; hence the high tension of the soul, the intellectual tragedy, and the moral stifling of the spirit. His syntax is lyrically scanned; on the logical plane it reveals that fragmentary character which was attributed, either in praise or in blame, to those inward prose writers tensed in an inner effort of search. He is the author of *Le resultanze in merito alla vita e al carattere di Gino Bianchi* [*The Outcome Concerning the Life and Character of Gino Bianchi*], 1913. He also wrote a war book in which, behind the rough simplicity of the soldiers, vibrates the tension of an opening conversation, the discovery of the most profound reasons for heroic simplicity, and the atavistic and instinctive wisdom of the *alpini: Con me e con gli alpini* [*With Me and the Alpini*], 1919. Finally, there are *Ragazzo* 1919, and *Ragazzo e prime poesie,* 1939.

Giovanni Boine was born at Finalmaria in 1887 and died at Porto Maurizio in 1917. A religious spirit thirsting for faith, he went so far in his rejection of any rational procedure as to appear to be a mystic, but one who loves life on this earth and constantly refers to it by means of ancestral images. *Il peccato e altre cose* [*Sin and Other Matters*] appeared in 1914; *Frantumi* [*Broken Pieces*], and *Plausi e botte* [*Applause and Brickbats*] belong to 1918; *Le ferita non chiuse* [*The Unhealed Wound*] appeared in 1921.

Renato Serra was born at Cesena in 1884 and died July 10, 1916 in the fighting on the Podgòra (cf. Slataper above). A pupil of Carducci at Bologna, he was much closer to Pascoli because of his melancholy temperament and his imaginative and subtle sensibility. His *Epistolario* (1934), and the *Scritti* [*Writings*] (1938) were published posthumously. In these we find profiles of writers and friends dear to him and here also the inclination to write his own confessions may be discerned, to report on the writers on whom he is discoursing in the light of his own feelings — not so much to inquire decadentistically into the secret recesses of the soul, as to pour himself forth in a hazy atmosphere and in a diffuse and gently emotional tonality. Serra's criticism is an intimate conversation, poor in historical interpretations, rich in subtle and pungent intuitions. In him, the religion of literature, which in the personality of a Carducci became a component of the *amor vitae,* colors the whole of life with itself. It is as if he might say that, confronted with the elusive irresolutions and ambiguities of reality, only poetry and the human profiles of poets offer consolation and the illusion of a certainty to the agitated soul. Among his most intense and best remembered pages are those dedicated to Carducci and Pascoli, the famous *Ringraziamento a una ballata di Paul Fort,* and the *Esame di coscienza di un letterato* [*A Writer's Self-Examination*], 1915. This work describes the conscience of a writer obliged to leave the twilight quiet of the Malatestiana library of Cesena (where he had been the director since 1909) for the war front. For some reason the absurdity of the war seemed to justify the existential scepticism of the writer and to make the joy of a personal poetical reading more affectionate and inward — the only joy that could be offered to his *sensi smussati* (blunted, dulled senses). Another reason was that the obscurity of death made it essential that amid the general collapse of faiths and ideologies, at least one idea should be defined, an idea that could be built into a system. Serra's style has the vagueness characteristic of inward prose writings, of the confessions, of the contributors to *La Voce* (in fact, Serra did contribute to the review). His work also has a sharpness in profiles and portraits which his critics attributed to the influence exercised on Serra by the great French critic and writer, Sainte-Beuve. Sensibility, irony, and melancholy hint at a slow, subdued melody in his refined prose, and that wandering amid landscapes and recollections suggests a hidden vocation for narrative in lyrical moods.

Giuseppe De Robertis of Matera (1888–1963) was a keen reader of poetry and was especially expert on style. He felt this to be not so much a question of language but rather a principle of the very personal refinement of a writer. Among his works let us mention *Italia nuova e antica* [*Italy, New and Old*], 1930; *Saggio su Leopardi,* 1939; *Scrittori del Novecento,* 1940; and *Primi studi manzoniani e altri scritti,* 1949. What he gave to the last phase of *La Voce* can not be separated from his personality, for during this phase he became the review's most exemplary personage.

At this point we might insert a brief exposition of the war literature; that is, a discourse on the poetry, the diaries, and on the diverse essays which took their inspiration from the First World War. Almost all these books are best considered in the outlines and portraits of their authors. Thus we have already talked about the war books of Jahier, Soffici, and Prezzolini, and we are going to consider further those of Alvaro, Baldini, Stuparich, Gadda, Gatti and Comisso, and, finally, Ungaretti. Then there are the poems, diaries, and discorses of D'Annunzio, a rhetorician and sometimes poet of his own personal war adventure (the prose writings are collected in the *Libro ascetico della giovane Italia,* the poems in the *Canti della guerra latina.* But let us mention some books by authors whom we shall not have a chance to meet again: *La Sagra di Santa Gorizia* [*The Festival of Holy Gorizia,*] 1916, is a short narrative poem in blank verse in which Vittorio Locchi (1889–1917) conjures up the conquest of Gorizia, alternating between the manner of the popular saga and an aestheticising manner very reminiscent of D'Annunzio; the *Lettere dal fronte* [*Letters from the Front*], 1915; and *Colloqui scritti al fronte* [*Conversations Written at the Front*] by Giosuè Borsi (1888–1915) of a religious inspiration with some tendency to a sort of mysticism; *Appunti di vita di guerra* [*Notes on War Life*] by Fausto Maria Martini (whom we have already met above) : a poet and diarist of the crepuscular group in Rome; *Scarpe al* sole [*Shoes in the Sun*], 1921, by Paolo Monelli, which relates, on the level of a facile reality, "gay and sad adventures of alpini, of mules and of wine." *La buffa* is a little book of realistic and whimsical verses, fable-like and bitter, which remind us of certain poetical moods of Palazzeschi. In this book the war is seen in its bare reality as anti-rhetorical and antilithographic; that is, antipicturesque. Indeed this character is implicit in the title, since the infantry was scornfully called *buffa* by the soldiers serving in special corps. Its author is Giulio Barni, born in Trieste in 1891, who died of wounds received in Albania during the Second World War, in 1941. *Trincee* [*The Trenches*] by Carlo Salsa, is somewhat similar at least in its motivating spirit.

Contributors to La Ronda: The Rondisti

La Ronda was published in Rome in the years between 1919 and 1923; its founder and director was Vincenzo Cardarelli. Among its contributors were Bacchelli, Baldini, Cecchi, Lorenzo Montano, the musicologist Bruno Barilli, and the painter Armando Spadini. *La Ronda* was opposed to futurism, lyrical fragmentarism, intimism, art prose, irrationalism, and *ermetismo*. It predicated the restoration of poetry and prose, as supported by logic and the intellect and trained by the classical tradition, by a taste for fine writing, for a clear style, for well-constructed syntax, for literary language. It raised the poetry and the aesthetic thought of Leopardi almost to the plane of a myth and a cult. But right in this literary Leopardism (which ended with more regard for the prose writings than for the *Canti* of Leopardi), stands revealed the tendency of the twentieth century toward the fine prose of art, the art prose more zealous of style than of human values. This road could be dangerous and could lead straight to academism, and to that academism of belles lettres which coexisted – precisely because it was alien to the most profound and tragic senses of civilization – with the culturally somnolent atmosphere of Fascism.

Fortunately the writers of *La Ronda* went beyond the equivocations of neoclassicism in their works. Perhaps only Vincenzo Cardarelli (born at Corneto Tarquinia in 1887, died in Rome in 1959) represents *La Ronda,* either through the myth of classicalism that inspired him to produce a literary poetry of high workmanship, or by his inclination toward art prose, to the stylistically perfect essay, to a temperate pleasure in formalism. Cardarelli is the poet of the seasons, of landscapes created by the light of the day and the night, of the vital rhythm of men. The nature which he senses does not express difficult relationships between men and things, or between things and things, nor does it inspire ineffable states of mind, but it is interpreted in relation to the common vicissitudes: birth, death, passing from age to age as the year progresses from spring to autumn. His best prose writings represent a stable, immutable situation, on which the course of history, the progress of civilization, the very transmutation of the landscape and of nature converge and seem miraculously to stop. His *Poesie* are now published in the definitive edition of 1949, while his most convincing prose works may be read in *Sole a picco* [*Sun Overhead*], 1929, *Cielo sulle città* [*Sky over the Cities*], 1938, and *Villa Tarantola,* 1948.

Riccardo Bacchelli was born in Bologna in 1891. First he was editor of *La Voce* of Florence, then of *La Ronda;* but he was the only one of the *rondisti* who, while cultivating a varied output of essays, braved narrative writing, a narrative of traditional structure, and so carried on the historical novel. However, a literary expression that was subtle in another way, called him to *La Ronda* and to the stylistic experiments of the twentieth century. From the events of history, Bacchelli drew characters that were reserved and often introverted. These were partly sons of their own century, partly sons of our own, psychologically complex and sometimes ambiguous and unresolved. Bacchelli's masterpieces are *Il diavolo al Pontelungo* [*The Devil at Long Bridge*], 1927, which is about the anarchists Bakunin and Cafiero and the unsuccessful revolutionary coup attempted at Bologna by Bakunin and Andrea Costa; and *Il mulino del Po* [*The Mill on the Po*], a vast cyclical novel in three parts that tells the story of a family of millers, the Scacerni, over a century of history from the Russian retreat in 1812 down to the battle of the Piave. This work is centered around a mill on the Po in the region of Ferrara. It was published from 1938 to 1940. Bacchelli is the author of numerous novels in which the historic theme sometimes constructs the book. At other times it constitutes the background. He is also the composer of poems and the author of plays. A volume published in 1962 contains his *Saggi critici,* in some of which keen judgments on poetry are alternated with pages of memoirs, striking in their vigor of images and temperate mildness and melancholy.

Emilio Cecchi was born in Florence in 1884. He engaged in journalistic activities early in life, showing most interest in literature and art. He was a contributor to the *Leonardo* and later to *La Ronda.* He lived for a while in the United States, teaching at the University of California at Berkeley, and he traveled in various countries from Mexico to Greece. His major works, omitting the more strictly critical books, and restricting our remarks to the more "extravagant" essays, fantasies, and travel journals, are *Pesci rossi* [*Goldfish*], 1920; *L'osteria del cattivo tempo* [*Bad Weather Inn*], 1927; *Et in Arcadia ego* [a book on his travels in Greece], 1936; *America amara* [*Bitter America*], 1941; and *Corse al trotto vecchie e nuove* [*Trotting Races, Old and New*], 1941. In recent years three volumes containing his "third page" articles have appeared: *Di giorno in giorno* [*From Day to Day*], 1957; *Ritratti e profili* [*Portraits and Profiles*], and *Libri nuovi e usati* [*New and Second-hand Books*], 1958. Cecchi is a subtle interpreter of art and poetry because he reveals their refined components on a psychological and stylistic plane. He is also a reporter of meetings with men, and an observor of customs and landscapes; in these he oscillates between the clear and exact lines of reality and a style with some magic change in coloration, between his taste as a Florentine and man of the Renaissance and the temptations of surrealism. No contemporary writer is his equal in evoking the atmosphere of suspense which envelopes a music lover listening to a concert. He evokes the fabulous transparence of an aquarium, the unexpected joyful or sad senses contained within a simple human vicissitude. These are glimpsed anywhere, at an elegant race course or in a poor courtyard, in the rooms of an art exhibition or in the printing room of a newspaper. His more properly critical essays deal especially with contemporary literary works, both Italian and foreign, but he also has written imaginative essays which commemorate diverse times and styles from Guicciardini to Cattaneo and D'Annunzio.

Bruno Barilli (born at Fano in 1880, died in 1951) wrote essays on musical criticism that resolve ideas and judgments in descriptions imbued with happy creativeness, as in his books *Il paese del melodramma* [*The Land of Melodrama*], 1929; *Il sole in trappola* [*The Sun in a Trap*], 1941; and *Il viaggiatore volante* [*The Flying Traveler*], 1946.

Antonio Baldini (1889–1962), a Roman, is the author of variously inspired prose works. Whether he tells a story about some personage (*Michelaccio,* 1924), or conjures up the war in which he served (*Nostro Purgatorio,* 1918), or outlines portraits of friends and men of letters (*Amici allo spiedo* [*Friends on the Spit*], 1932; *Italia di Bonincontro,* 1940; *Buoni Incontri in Italia* [*Lucky Meetings in Italy*], 1942), or whether he conjures up his Rome through perennial customs, (*Rugantino,* 1942), or finally whether he talks of poetry and art while pleasantly wandering amid criticism and recollection, between the impressions of his reading and the story (*Ludovico della tranquillità,* who is Ludovico Ariosto, *Cattedra d'occasione, Fine Ottocento*), Baldini is always the cordial, witty, smooth writer. He was brought up on the most moving, most inspired prose of Carducci, but for polemics he substituted good-natured sparkling satire. He resolves his impressions and his opinions in unhackneyed images with a wealth of creative élan.

Writers in the Tradition

The contributors to *La Ronda* belong to decadentism, notwithstanding their return to classical forms. In fact, classicism and Leopardism always represent a subtle choice, an aestheticising sentiment of reality, an aspiration to escape from historical responsibility, to unravel reality into psychological outlines and elusive transfigurations and into enchantments. The limit of the lesser *rondism* is therefore an aloof and aristocratic religion of literature: not the academism of the rhetoricians, but that of the esthetes – an exquisitely literary religion – without the uneasiness which morally deepens the pages of Renato Serra and reveals in him the sorrowful sense of existence, the elusive ambiguity of life.

A vein of genuine traditional literature does run through the twentieth century, a vein which has not yet produced writers of outstanding prominence. Among the poets, Giovanni Bertacchi (1869–1942) celebrated work and progress. By a sentimental combination of Mazzini and Marx, as he himself confessed, and a combination of Whitman and Heine, one of the styles of the late nineteenth century, he achieved lyrics of facile and melodic mood sometimes strengthened by incisive inventiveness and images (the *Canzoniere delle Alpi* dates from 1895, *Il perenne domani,* 1929). A stronger socialistic feeling is revealed in the poetry of Ada Negri (1870–1945), especially in her first books of lyrics, *Fatalità* (1892), and *Tempeste* (1895). Later, more personal and inward sentiments prevailed in her work without introducing any marked innovation in her poetry (from *Maternità* 1904, to *Il libro di Mara,* 1919, to *Vespertina,* 1931, to *Fons Amoris,* 1946), for she continued to be elegiac and slightly crepuscular. Angiolo Silvio Novaro (1866–1938) was a facile poet who assumed some vague reminiscence of Pascoli and turned it into melodic sentimentality. His best poems, in which some creative images occasionally spring up, are those written for children: *Il Cestello* [*The Basket*], 1910. Among the poets for children let us also mention Renzo Pezzani (1898–1951), who wrote pure poetry in the dialect of Parma. Mario Novaro (1868–1944), the brother of Angiolo Silvo wrote poetry only in his youth. His poems when compared to those of his more famous brother are a good deal more vibrant and original (*Murmuri ed echi,* 1912). He was also the director of an original review, *La Riviera Ligure* [*The Italian Riviera*], which lasted from 1899 to 1919. Diego Valeri of Padova, born in 1887, was a rather melodious poet of a refreshing "domestic grace," as it was said of him, having his own personal Venetian aura, golden, and of the sea." His *Poesie vecchie e nuove* were published in 1930 and his *Terzo Tempo* in 1950. He also wrote criticism of French literature and was translator of Mistral, Flaubert, Stendhal, and La Fontaine.

Painter and etcher, Luigi Bartolini (1892–1963) was also a poet of whimsical human vicissitudes. A native of The Marches, he had a taste for the satirical and the fabulous, not unlike Palazzeschi, and displayed this in works from *Poesie,* 1939; *Poesie e satire,* 1946; to *Poesie per Anita e Luciana,* 1953. Lionello Fiumi, born in 1894, was touched by futurism, but his poetry has remained fundamentally elegiac as regards language and meter (*Sopravvivenze* [*Survivals*], 1931, and *Stagione colma* [*Brimful Season*], 1943). Giuseppe Villaroel (b. Catania 1889) is an authentic voice amidst the minor poets: his rapture before nature (the hot and bright nature of his native Sicily) is in the purest moments of his lyrical utterance, resolved in images thickened with enflamed colors and tones and yet transparent. Such moments are met especially in *L'uomo e Dio* [*Man and God*], 1951. A neoclassical ideal, a position somewhere between Foscolo and Leopardi, is evident in the volume of lyric poems *La fontana nella foresta* [*The Spring in the Forest*], 1926, by Vincenzo Gerace (1876–1930), a Calabrian. The poetry of Giuseppe Ravegnani is sweet-sounding and elegiac, *I canti del cùculo* [*Cuckoo Songs*], 1914; *Quattro canti,* 1934, and so on. That of Giuseppe Lipparini is humanistic and in the Hellenistic manner, as shown in the *Canti di Mèlitta,* 1910.

Here we might list a long series of names of "traditionalist" poets; that is, poets who still like the extended lyrical utterance, images clearly mediated by feeling, and traditional meters. It is obvious that many of them have felt or are feeling the effects of new lyrical groupings, in particular crepuscular or pascolian, but not to such a point that sentimental perplexity and analogy prevail and become structural motifs in their poetry. Most of the dialect poets, originating in great number in the regions and individual cities of Italy, are also traditionalists. Besides, there was already a rich tradition of nineteenth-century poetry in dialect. Next to the masters (from Carlo Porta to Gioacchino Belli to Salvatore di Giacomo) and to competent poets (the Roman Pascarella, the Neapolitan Ferdinando Russo, the Veronese Berto Barbarani, the Venetians Pietro Buratti and Attilio Sarfatti, and Cesare de Titta from Abruzzi), stand the minor poets. These poets nevertheless constitute a literary and social institution and through a true Italian regional utterance represent the unity of the nation much better than the false myth of an academic cultural unity or a Tuscan linguistic unity, both of which turn out to be artificial. It is therefore obvious that in the twentieth century the dialectal poetry continued the nineteenth-century institution. However, we shall speak later about four dialectal poets (Tessa, Giotti, Dell'Arco, Pasolini) because in diverse ways they belong to nontraditional poetics. Other poets clung, or are clinging, to the melic, musical tradition: consider Murolo, Galdieri, Bovio, Capurro, Viviani, Mario, authors of the famous Neopolitan repertory of *canzonetta*. And remember Biagio Marin of Grado, and Aldo Spallicci of Romagna. A special place must be reserved for the Roman Carlo Alberto Salustri (1871–1950), known by his pseudonym, Trilussa. He is the poet of fables that symbolize men in animals, that attribute human characteristics to animals. These are fables of everyday happenings interpreted in a moralistic key and related to everlasting human nature and therefore may also be defined as satirical little stories with an ending which is often epigramatic. For the most part, they are effective and made deeper by the joining of satirical wit with a stern melancholy. The meter and the rhyme are well adapted to the composition of Trilussa who, in addition, has derived an excellent literary proficiency from Belli, and a language which transforms and continually develops the modern Roman popular speech in detail. Among others, the fables that may be called political are celebrated. These extol and regret the liberty extinguished by the Fascist dictatorship. The numerous poetical collections (*Le stelle de Roma* of 1887; *Quaranta sonetti romaneschi* [*Forty Sonnets in Modern Roman*], 1895; *Favole romanesche,* 1920; *Acqua e vino* 1944–1945) are published in the volume of the *Poesie* edited by Pancrazi in 1952.

It is not always easy to distinguish the traditional poets from the avant-garde (and in this case, from the poets of decadence). It is still less easy to single out from among the many storytellers and essay writers those who belong to the naturalistic tradition or to the literary tradition of the nineteenth century. A touch of corrosion, disenchantment, ambiguity, or perplexity has found its way even into the prose of writers whom we may consider conservative or traditionalists and, at the very least, a crepuscular manner is decernable.

Marino Moretti (born at Cesenatico in 1885) became known first as a crepuscular poet (*Poesie scritte col lapis* [*Pencilled Poems*], 1910; then he changed to narrative, and his next books were collections of short stories: *Il paese degli equivoci,* 1907; *I pesci fuor d'acqua* [*Fish Out of Water*], 1916; *Conoscere il Mondo* [*To Know the World*], 1919, and so on. The novels are: *Il sole del sabato* [*Saturday Sun*], 1916; *I puri di cuore* [*The Pure in Heart*], 1923; *Il segno della crose* [*The Sign of the Cross*], 1929; *La vedova Fioravanti* [*Widow Fioravanti*], 1941. He has been called the writer of the humble, though who suffer from the violence of the powerful and the bullies. His style has been judged calm and clear. Far removed from obscure and difficult psychology, the characters of Moretti reveal a sentimental perspective which they express and communicate in elegiac moods. However in his novels (and better in the novels than in the tale) there develops slowly, but surely, a tonal atmosphere which enfolds the protagonists in an effusion of feeling.

Francesco Chiesa, born in the Swiss Canton of Ticino in 1871, is, like Moretti, a writer of even and simple psychologies, which, however, indicate the very rhythm of the life of everybody. In the novel *Tempo di marzo* [*March Weather*], 1925, he relates the experiences of an adolescent who at a certain point shows himself to be wiser than the adults in grasping and feeling life — all that the "grown-ups" do not grasp or feel. Let us also mention *Villadorna,* a novel of 1928; *Racconti del mio orto* [*Tales of my Garden*], 1929; and *Racconti del passato prossimo* [passato prossimo, "recent past" is also the name of the present perfect tense], 1941.

Angelo Gatti (1875–1948) wrote books of military

history and a war diary (*Nel tempo della tormenta*). As a narrator, besides tales and sketches, he wrote the novel *Ilia ed Alberto,* 1930, which tells the story of the spiritual road traversed by Alberto after the death of his wife—from grief to peace, from the earthly chains of death to God. It is a slow-paced book with many inert pages and long psychological prolixities, but this story of a soul is truthful and affectionate, inspired by a quiet ardor, and slow patient research.

Umberto Fracchia (1889–1930) of Lucca was a crepuscular storyteller, but with a naturalistic vein of his own. In his novels *Angela,* 1923, and *La stella del Nord,* 1930, and in various tales, he presents the little vicissitudes of poor folk with shy pity. He achieves an elegiac, gray tone which, by means of its descriptive projections of reality, is more akin to the Lombard author of the late nineteenth century, Emilio De Marchi, than to the melancholy but blurred and antinaturalistic tone of Marino Moretti. Fracchia founded a weekly which was an immense success and which intended to set up a refined, educated society of writers: *La fiera letteraria* [*The Literary Fair*], 1925. In 1930 the weekly changed its name to *Italia letteraria;* from 1936 to September, 1943 it was published under the title of *Meridiano di Roma.* It resumed publication in the spring of 1946 under its original title and under the directorship of Vincenzo Cardarelli. At present Fiera is published by Rizzoli.

Alberto Savinio (pseudonym of Andrea De Chirico), the brother of the famous painter, was born in Athens in 1891 and died in Rome in 1951. He was more a writer of ideas than of events, of intelligence rather than of inventiveness. The caprices of his dry and swift imageries, his rapid flicker in setting the most distant and whimsical relationships between word and word, idea and idea, make him one of the most pointed writers of the traditional school. Sophism and intellectualism are joyous virtues in him because they become purified in the whimsical ardor of his intelligence. Of his works let us remember *Narrate uomini la vostra storia* [*Tell Your Story, Men*], 1942, and *Tutta la vita,* 1945.

Giovan Battista Angioletti (born Milan, 1896, died 1961), was a director of reviews (one of them *Italia letteraria*). In tales and lyrical prose works he recalled times, men, and things of the past, with a trend toward elegiac writing which opens, as though amazed, to the rushing, impetuous open-mindedness of the new times. Some of his books put forward, with ardent spiritual energy, the idea of a true cultural unity of Europe. We shall also mention his *Amici di strada* [*Friend on the Road*], 1935; *Le carte parlanti* [*Talking Maps*], 1941; *L'Italia felice,* 1947; and the recent *Inchiesta europea* [*European Investigation*] of 1953.

Ignazio Silone (pseudonym of Secondo Tranquilli), born near L'Aquila in 1900, wrote his best novels in exile, while fascism held the power in Italy. His novels picture the arid barren land of southern Italy on which the helpless and submissive poor dwell. But the portrayal takes on moral and tragic light from the livid, grotesque, hypocritical mask of the power of the lictor thrown by fascism over the face of that impoverished folk on the arid and barren land. So it was that *Fontamara* was born in 1930. *Pane e vino* in 1937; *Il seme sotto la neve* [*Seed under the Snow*] in 1940; followed by, in 1952, in another time and under the stimulus of a new and less revolutionary ideology, *Una manciata di more* [*A Handful of Berries*].

Bonaventura Tecchi, born near Viterbo in 1896, is a traditional writer in the sense that in his narrative works flow naturalistic themes and a certain dramatic dialectic of Good and Evil, perhaps inspired in him by his interests as an illustrious German scholar. From *Il nome sulla sabbia* [*The Name in the Sand*], 1924; to *Tre storie d'amore,* 1931; to *Villatauri,* 1935; to *L'isola appassionata,* 1945;

and on to *Valentina Velier,* 1950 and *Gli egoisti,* 1959, his intense, persistent narrative activity was not the consequence of an inventive inertia or a concession to mere craft, but was the expression of a fecund creativeness.

"Lettered" writers include Adolfo Albertazzi of Bologna (1866–1924), whose novels and stories run from 1896 to 1922 and are now gathered in a volume published in 1950; Antonio Beltramelli (1874–1930) of Forlì, author of a once popular novel, *Il cavalier Mostardo,* 1921; Fabio Tombari, born at Fano in 1889, the once famous author of *Tutta Frusaglia* (1929). The following are men of letters, but in a purely Tuscan sense, because of their attachment to the literary and traditional idiom of Tuscany. Ferdinando Paolieri, and Lorenzo Viani (1882–1936), a painter and writer of vivid impressions. Bruno Cicognani and Enrico Pea are especially naturalistic and jargonistic even in their colors and designs. Cicognani was known as the sketcher of the Tuscany of the Grand Dukes, portrayed by him with nostalgia and the liveliness of a man of the people, even though his whimsical and literary language does not always properly fit, with spontaneous fluency, the background of jargon. He was born in Florence in 1879 and was a persistent and prolific author; from the *Sei storielle di nuovo conio* [*Six Little Brand-New Stories*], 1917, to *Il figurinaio e le figurine* [*The Peddler of Statuettes*], 1920, to *La Velia* [*The Shrike*], 1923, to Villa Beatrice, 1931, to *L'omino che ha spento i fochi* [*The Little Man Who Put Out Fires*], 1937, and to *L'eta favolosa* [*The Fabulous Age*], 1940. Enrico Pea is less "lettered" than Cicognani, more inclined toward psychological representation in depth, even though his characters often have an impressionistic resemblance to figurines, and even though in his landscapes he reveals a strong inclination toward naturalism. His best novels are *Moscardino,* 1922; *Il volto santo* [*The Holy Countenance*], 1924; and *La Maremmana,* 1938. His best stories are contained in *Il trenino dei sassi* [*The Little Train of the Rocks*], 1936 and *Solaio* [*The Attic*], 1951. He was born at Serravezza in 1881 and died in 1958. Another Tuscan writer of a quiet and inward inspiration is Fernando Agnoletti (1875–1933), the author of a fine war book, *Dal giardino all'Isonzo,* 1918.

Unfortunately it is impossible for us to do more here than list other traditionalistic writers who enjoyed good repute and whose works may still be read in part without the help of historical devotion or of learned stimulus: Francesco Pastonchi, *Sul limite dell' ombra* appeared in 1905; Giovanni Titta Rosa, still praiseworthy in *Pietà dell' uomo,* 1952; Antonino Anile; Adolfo de Bosis; Sebastiano Satta, a wealth of impressions, tending toward reality, in *Canti del Salto e della Tanca,* which is Sardinian in inspiration and which came out posthumously in 1924; Ceccardo Roccatagliata Ceccardi, the poet of the sorrow still unknown and yet present in children, as in *Sillabe ed ombre,* published posthumously in 1925; Pietro Masti, like Orvieto close to Pascoli and the promoter, with Orvieto, of the celebrated Florentine newspaper *Marzocco;* Giovanni Cena; Giulio Caprin; Ugo Betti, whose *Canzonette* are dated 1932; Francesco Flora, whose *Canti spirituali* appeared in 1944; Emidio Piermarini, and so on. Also storytellers, such as Clarice Tartúfari; Paola Drigo, author of a strong novel, *Maria Zef;* Ugo Ojetti, *Mio figlio ferroviere,* 1922; Francesco Perri, *Emigranti,* 1928, a novel of recollection rather than social denunciation; Francesco Flora, *La città terrena* and *Mida il nuovo satiro;* Arturo Loria, storyteller who frolics between reality and the fantastic, for example in *La scuola di ballo* [*Dancing School*] of 1932; Corrado Tumiati, author of *I tetti rossi* of 1930, where outside of surrealism the innocence without logic of the inmates of an insane asylum is represented; Raul Maria de Angelis, from *Inverno in palude* of 1936, to *La brutta bestia* of 1944, to *Sangue negro* of 1949, to *Amore e impostura* of 1950, to *Il giocatore fortunato,*

1953; Arnaldo Frateili brings conventionally avant-garde experiences within the traditional narrative structure in *Clara fra i lupi*, 1939; Attilio Dabini, Mario Gromo, Bino Sanminiatelli, Francesco Serantini, Eugenio Vaquer, Nino Salvaneschi, Mario Sobrero, Renzo Martinelli, Dino Terra, Riccardo Marchi. Finally there are the capable professional storytellers and those of varied mundane digressions: Orio Vergani; Salvator Gotta; Luciano Zuccoli; Lucio d'Ambra; Virgilio Brocchi; Guido da Verona; Raffaele Calzini; Vittorio G. Rossi; Luigi Santucci; Alba de Cèspedes, whose 1938 novel *Nessuno torna indietro* [*Nobody Turns Back*] deserves special mention for dealing with the difficult and irreversible psychological development of certain girls; Piero Gadda Conti; Michele Saponaro, famous for some novelized biographies of Foscolo, Leopardi, Mazzini, Carducci, and Michelangelo; Delfino Cinelli; Mario Puccini; Luigi Barzini; Indro Montanelli, and a whole new generation of journalists.

Two poets and three writers of narrative deserve special comment because they have personalities that are independent of the schools of poetics or are otherwise distinct, even though they were exposed to naturalistic or avant-garde influences. Francesco Gaeta was born in Naples in 1871, and died by his own hand in 1927. Among his books of poetry let us mention *Sonetti voluttuosi ed altre poesie* (1906), and *Poesie d'amore* (1920). They are harsh poems, rich in verbal flights and roughness and weighed down by lines ending in truncated words, (e.g., *città, pietà*). His language often turns the slangy expressions of the lower Neapolitan middle class into something pompous. And yet the dialectical vicissitude between the life of the streets with its choral masses, and the personal impetus of the sad poet towards "joyfulness" is powerful and stands like a monument on the arhythmical course of the lyrical speech. And what is to be said of Riccardo Balsamo Crivelli (1874–1938) of Milan, the author of the poem *Boccaccino* in *ottava rima* and of other queer, satirical, comic rhymes? Only that his literary output, inspired by sixteenth-century models, is made personal and modern by his whimsical ardor, and by satirical flashes which seem to project the mysterious gloom of death upon the joys of living.

Gian Pietro Lucini (1867–1914), another Milanese, is usually accounted a follower of the Lombard *scapigliati* of the nineteenth century and of Dossi in particular. He did in fact draw from that movement his linguistic mixture, part literary, part jargon, with the felicitous contamination which is found in that strange nineteenth-century Neapolitan writer Vittorio Imbriani, and which would later be a characteristic of Carlo Emilio Gadda. But the urgent description of the state of mind from which he suffered is peculiarly his own and does not have the psychological evasion and the mysterious presence of the past that are found in the art of Dossi. He wrote verses, critical essays (his *L'ora topica di Carlo Dossi* is famous, and so is *Antidannunziana,* both published in 1911), and the novel *Gian Pietro da Core,* 1895 and 1910, which is, as the title suggests, a veiled autobiography.

Grazia Deledda was born at Nuoro in Sardinia in 1871 and died in Rome in 1936. Her narrative activity was tremendous. We shall mention here only a few principal novels: *Elias Portòlu,* 1903; *Cenere* [*Ashes*], 1903; *L'edera* [*The Ivy*], 1908; *Colombie e sparvieri* [*Doves and Hawks*], 1912; *Canna al vento* [*Reeds in the Wind*], 1913; *Marianne Sirca,* 1915; *Il segreto dell' uomo solitario,* 1921; *Annalena Bilsini,* 1927, and other novels and books of stories down to the posthumous tale *Cosima,* 1937. In her early novels she kept to naturalistic experiments, and Sardinia, with her people and their passions and their customs, takes up a good part of the psychological vicissitudes of the protagonists (although these are indeed strongly and dramatically stressed in *Elias Portòlu*). Starting approximately with *Colombi e sparvieri,* Deledda's skill improves. The psychological vicissitudes of the characters come more to the foreground, and a certain sentimental ambiguity, choked or compressed, is missing or is not merely an echo of the landscape and the obscure and mysterious customs of Sardinia but acquires its own independent power. In the last novels, the influence of Dostoievsky is evident, and in the last short stories, the influence of Oscar Wilde. It was this evolution from the "province" to European literary civilization that won her the Nobel Prize for Literature. The descriptive parts of her works are the least felicitous, revealing merely an able craftsmanship and a subterranean seam of chronicle or information. She achieved writing power in the presentation of secret, shy, reluctant sentiments, especially when they blur slightly with a touch of the elusive or the ambiguous.

Leonida Répaci was born at Palmi di Calabria in 1898. From *L'ultimo Cireno* [*The Last Libyan*], 1923 and 1928, through *I fratelli Rupe* [*The Rupe Brothers*], 1933–1937; *La carne inquieta* [*The Uneasy Flesh*], 1930; *Un riccone torna alla terra* [*A Rich Man Returns to Earth*], 1954; *Il deserto del sesso* [*The Desert of Sex*], 1957; *Il pazzo del casamento* [*The Madman of the Tenement*], 1959, he portrays a sort of epic realism, lighted and strengthened by its moral zeal, by an ardent love of liberty, by the hard and persistent battle undertaken first against fascism and later against conformism. In the last novels, the civil content itself has been resolved in grotesque fantasies, in a language that is full-blooded, sparkling, often satirical and polemical, occasionally farcical. An unreservedly involved artist, he is far from the experiments and the efforts of the avant-garde, he is not one of the decadents nor does he belong to the new realism. In his narration, which is quite alien to definite literary movements, one senses, as in few other writers, the presence, for example, of Imbriani, the narrative and stylistic tradition of Southern Italy. It is ardent, liberal, superabundant.

The Hermetic Poets

Ermetismo or *arcanismo,* that is, hermetic or obscure poetry, intends to express the most profound feelings through a lean and "essential" language. The images may be sublime or, on the contrary, withdrawn and restrained; in any case, they are always difficult, because they express their relationship with almost incommunicable intuitions from poet to reader. Often a single word tries to illuminate a complex, closed state of mind. The free meter makes use of refined meetings of rhyme and assonance and employs a huge metrical arc, from the traditional verselines (particularly the hendecasyllable) to the short verselines, of which Ungaretti has given us the most famous examples. It is also called *poesia analogica* or *un*logical poetry, because it brings a sentiment alongside an image which, at first sight, might seem alien to that sentiment. Therefore, to understand the analogy, the reader must strip himself of his common logic and try to grasp, intuitively, through the pure musical suggestion and the occult vibration of the word, the secret relationship between word and image, between image and image. It is also called "pure poetry," because it repudiates the common and traditional images, the grammatical and syntactical connections which are too visible and customary; eloquence, the old literary figures, at least insofar as they appear to be merely instruments of ornamentation and, in short, whatever refers to direct, immediate sensations and sentiments — to reality — is reputiated. Finally, it is also called "symbolist poetry" because for each word there is a corresponding inner situation of sentiment that is not brought into the image or the word by means of the senses, but gets there only by allusion.

The themes of the hermetic poetry refer to the problem of existence; therefore, it is not metaphysical poetry because it is not seeking philosophical truth in the classical sense, but, a way of existence, of being oneself and through being with others, of being able to open a human conversation. Often it is also a poetry of denunciation, that is, poetry which declares with stern sadness and firm positiveness how fleeting and vain are the illusions of power, conquest, and historic and civil progress; how conceited and fatuous are the ostentation of force, the pretensions of domination, the exaltations of scientific conquests. The hermetics sweep away the old Romantic myths which still – in a form henceforth empty and external – were thriving in D'Annunzio. They reject futurism and also the energetic, activist attitudes of a certain kind of irrationalism; they appeal, if anywhere, to the bemused poetry of Pascoli, to spiritualism and the fragmentism of the writers of *La Voce* and, as we have seen, to the existentialist and stylistic current of European symbolism, especially the French.

The hermetic language intends to be essential: a sparing use of adjectives, rhythmic isolation of words, free meter, renouncement of speech – even polemical speech – and the identification of lyrical language with utterly individualistic style. It is an intuitional language rather than one that is meaningful in the logical sense.

At this point let us trace some quick outlines of hermetic poets.

Arturo Onofri was born at Rome in 1885, and died in 1928. Originally a crepuscular poet, he then became involved in the search for a unity that would govern the relationships between beings. He thus passed from the *Liriche* of 1907 and 1914 over to the *Arioso* of 1921; then came *Terrestrità del sole* in 1927; and *Vincere il drago;* then *Aprirsi fiore,* a posthumous book in 1935. The yearning to discover the truth – the cosmic anxiety – sometimes is reduced to an obscure poetical discourse, ambiguous amid impulses of pure fantasy (sometimes even, of daydreams) and of absolute spirituality. Sometimes they attribute to the early images projected upon celestial space, an emotional fervor and a tense tragicalness. The work of Onofri, in its rough and impetuous spirituality, stands on the threshold of great poetry; it would have stepped over that threshold if, instead of submitting to the terms of an existential problem, the cosmic material had changed into open amazement.

Dino Campana was born at Marradi in Romagna in 1885. He died as an inmate of the insane asylum of Castel Pulci (Florence) in 1932. His poems were brought together in *Canti orfici* in 1914; the 1952 edition is entitled *Canti orfici e altri scritti* [*Orphic Songs and other Writings*]. Campana, too, sought avidly the primary origin of things, but not, like Onofri, for reasons of philosophical thirst, but in order to discover the image most hidden, most distant, most sensually coveted, out beyond the courses of the stars. His poetry was called impressionistic and visual, and in truth concerns the sensual possession of things with the sensibility of a painter, indeed, of a colorist, and with an innocence and purity of ardor such as D'Annunzio in his aestheticism and egotism never knew. The things and the colors which his poems present flee this world, moving unbound and free as if in a spatial and unreal atmosphere; yet they carry with them the mood of the earth and the sensual ferment which they inspired originally.

Giuseppe Ungaretti was born at Alexandria in Egypt in 1888, of parents from Lucca. He studied in Paris, contributing to avant-guard reviews, such as *Lacerba*. He underwent the influence of the crepuscular and futurist writers. Among the French poets whom he knew and liked, it was Guillaume Apollinaire especially who stimulated him to discover a deeper reality beneath common human reality, a reality truer, even though hidden, even though revealable only to the initiated, even though it might not be communicable by means of the traditional language of poetry. In a certain sense, Ungaretti was the master of Italian hermetic poetry, rather than Campana. But the earlier poems and those poems inspired by the war, in which he served as a soldier (*Il Porto sepolto,* 1917), still show a precise and definite situation, a situation of pain. In his poetry the war is felt as violence and martyrdom. The novelty of the short lines that break up the poetic period, isolating single words, is not such as to destroy the rhythmic continuity. Subsequently, Ungaretti went back to the musically completed hendecasyllable and to "constructed" poetry, but he deepened the intensity of the image that crosses over short-lived reality and discovers the reasons — hidden from most men, from the nonpoets — the reasons of the true and mysterious reality that was called *surreale,* supra-reality. Human situations and things are transformed into symbols of that reality, even at the cost of going beyond their common meaning and of being brought close to other things and situations which the profane do not see. When these symbols take over a philosophy of life fully, they resolve into true and proper allegories. The lexicon of Ungaretti is not difficult, in fact it is common rather than extraordinary and reveals his crepuscular training. The difficulty lies in the imagery which, to be understood, must always refer to analogy; that is to say, to the relationship of things with their super-meanings, with their projection and transfiguration into supra-reality. But, having explained the poetics of Ungaretti, the technique of his craft as a poet, it is necessary to add that the best of Ungaretti's poetry lies in the description of the feeling of sorrow (his own and that of mankind) both as a possession and as a capturing, often sensual, of reality. His verses are considerably more linear than scabrous: the poet compresses a charge of sensual possession, a disguised verbal thickness, into dry words. The inffuence of Apollinaire is more evident in his work than that of Valéry, even though his allegorical poems bring him closer to Valéry. His work shows a baroque tendency that gives him a sort of kinship to some part of Soffici, to something of Papini, and he himself interpreted in a baroque style that part of Petrarch which he favored. He also translated the poems of Shakespeare and of Gongora. He is a vigorous but fragmentary poet, even in his apparently most extended lyric writings. After the *Porto sepolto* [*The Sunken Port*] came *Allegria di naufràgi* [*Joy of Shipwrecks*] in 1922; *Sentimento del tempo* in 1933; *Il dolore,* which laments the death of his son and the violence of the new world at the time, the poet was in Brazil. His book appeared in 1947); *La terra promessa* [*The Promised Land*] in 1950. To these may be added the poetical translations of Shakespeare, Racine, Gongora, Mallarmé, and some volumes of prose: criticism, diaries, and recollections. His last book of poetry, *Un grido e paesagi,* of 1952, is also included in the nine volumes of the definitive edition of his works, *Vita di un uomo* [*A Man's Life*].

Eugenio Montale was born in Genoa in 1896. In Florence he was director of the *Gabinetto scientifico-letterario Vieusseux.* After 1947 he became the editor of the *Corriere della sera* and lives in Milan. To various dailies and reviews he has contributed and still contributes quite penetrating literary and musical essays. He has made translations from Cervantes. Shakespeare, and Melville. His four volumes of poetry are: *Ossi di seppia* [*Cuttle-fish* Bones], 1925; *Le occasioni,* 1939; *Finisterre,* 1943; *La bufera e altro* [*The Storm and Other Things*], 1956. In his poetry the sentiment of life as desolation and incommunicability is complete; in this sense the European poet closest to Montale is Eliot. Behind the colored and varied appearances of the world there is a falling of stones, a howling and hooting of horns, rack and ruin. Behind the exaltation of the senses and the will, disintegration not be controlled. The thread of memory unwinds, but brings thereby no memory, no affection. In comparison with the sea — which is liberty — the earth is chains and imprisonment. Men think that they rule earth and heaven, but they do not know even themselves; nor do they understand one another, nor make themselves understood. Time appears as an implacable, fatal succession of events that are all alike and meaningless, a "delirium of immobility" from which there is no escape. All is predetermined and at the same time unrepeatable, and it is useless and vain to wait for a hole in the net, for "the knot that does not hold," for "the fact that was not necessary." In Ungaretti, what prevails is the impulse toward a reality that supports the desire of man. In Montale what prevails is the denunciation of man's chains; hard to say whether it is denunciation that is more courageous or sorrowful. If Ungaretti presents things through the act by which they are possessed or in which they are craved, Montale, often with exactitude of terms and lucid linearity of words, presents things through dialectical contact with actual reality, which is the state and consciousness of exclusion, and of vanity. Finally, if in Ungaretti things rush into space, are cries, invocations, or ancestral coffers of far-off realities, in Montale, things: the parched summer, the gust of the sirocco, the cliff by the sea, the pole holding up the haystack, are the concrete chains of human imprisonment, the obstacles against which illusions and memories are shattered. In both poets, physical things are few and fundamental, but in Ungaretti they burn with human energies and ardors. In Montale they are the arid witnesses of the evil of living. The things of Montale stand out in our memory, those of Ungaretti do not; for in Montale they are in dialectical opposition to the evil of living, while in Ungaretti they participate in the human situation of the poet. The style of Montale's poetry is literary, stern, with an accent of quiet peremptoriness, of assertion with no shadow of doubt. The rhythm is slow, incisive, almost discursive; it opens to very measured melodic lengthenings, and therefore moves within a closed strophic structure. His analogies, difficult though they are because of the daring of the relationships between thing and thing, between thing and idea, have nevertheless an inner rationality of their own. Montale is the greatest poet, in the sense of the most "classical," of the twentieth century in Italy.

Salvatore Quasimodo was born at Modica (Siracusa) in 1901. He has contributed to almost all the avant-garde reviews. His first collections of poetry tend to isolate and to extol existentialist sentiments and the colors or even impressions of landscapes; then, slowly, after the translations from the Greeks (*Lirici greci,* 1940 and 1944) his poetry took on tones no less warm, but clearer and having almost the character of the fable. A new vision of a poetical South, of a Mediterranean and Hellenic Italy built even under apparently more distant images and ardors into a commemorative background and a continued lyrical utterance. Thus from *Oboe sommerso* [*Sunken Oboe*], 1932, and *Erato e Apollion,* 1936, we pass to *Nuove poesie* (1936–1942). All these collected poems are contained in the volume *Ed è subito sera* [*And Suddenly, It's Evening*]. Then the war came, and Quasìmodo yearned for a conversation with mankind, for the tragic desire of human relationship, beyond tyranny, beyond violence, and not with an indistinct humanity, but specifically with men, whether they may be free, oppressed, or killed. At the same time, his utterance as a means of communication, gains breath and vigor, as a result, also, of his often exemplary translations from Vergil, the Gospels, and Shakespeare. Thus we come to the books of dedicated poetry: *Con il piede straniero sopra il cuore* [*With a Foreign Invader's Foot on my Heart*], 1946; *Giorno dopo giorno* [*Day after Day*], 1947; and *La vita non è sogno* [*Life is Not a Dream*], 1949. This is poetry of frank emotion, of open emotional participation; it is intended to make man over, to express the intuition and the hope of a revival of man. Because of this chant, inspired by sorrow and by human renascence, he was awarded the Nobel Prize for Poetry in 1959. The more mature poetry of Quasìmodo is fond of the limpid melodies of the classical hendecasyllable, neither enclosed in the geometrical rigor of the strophe, nor too freely loosened in polymetrical verse, but presented in a series of unrhymed, or blank, verses. These are brought together, at intervals, by assonances, repeats, or reiterations. Quasìmodo has also written some keen critical articles which, for the most part, secretly refer to his own poetry or to his work as a poet.

Alfonso Gatto, born at Salerno in 1909, had a life that was lively but also pledged to literature. He contributed to the avant-garde reviews (*Italia letteraria, Circoli, Letteratura,* and so on) and with Vasco Pratolino founded and directed *Campo di Marte* [*Drill-ground*]. He started out with a closed *ermetismo,* unyielding and unflinching (*Isola,* in 1932, *Morte ai paesi* in 1937). Then his congenial inclinations toward impressionism (especially landscapes, seascapes, and cities in the polychrome tones of dawn, sunset, and moonlit nights) and toward fleeting, anxious human circumstances, culminated at last in *Poesie,* 1939 and 1941. These are supported by a frankly melodic line which is sometimes singable (some critics have made reference to the "airs" of Di Giacomo and even to the eighteenth-century *ariettas*). Then finally, as human events became more and more urgent, first, under the pressure of tyranny, then of the war, Gatto merged his impressionistic and melodic trends into the area of an utterance to which he was committed. He was personally involved, even when the vile deeds of violence and the consoling deeds of freedom appear changed into incidents and analogically transferred into distant, diverse, visions.

And so we came to *Amore della vita,* [*Love of Life*], to *Il capo sulla neve* [*The Head on the Snow*], 1949, and to *Nuove Poesie* in 1950. With some oscillations this fusion between the theme of sorrow and the impressionistic musical rhythm also declares itself in the last two poetical books of Gatto: *La forza negli occhi* [*Strength in the Eyes*], 1954 and *Osteria Flegrea* [*Phlegraean Inn*], 1962, which is a serene contemplation of death that the poet remarks, is, or should be, the wine of poets. Of his prose writings, let us mention those part narrative, part essays, contained in *Carlomagno nella grotta,* 1962, which seek the soul of Southern Italy.

Among the poets more or less connected to a "hermetic" experience, and they are numerous, we shall mention only some who seem to us to have won for themselves an independence of sentiment and of style: Piero Bigongiari (*La figlia di Babilonia,* 1942, and *Rogo,* 1952); Angelo Barile (*Primavera,* 1933); Attilio Bertolucci (*La capanna indiana,* 1951); Carlo Betocchi (*Realtà vince il sogno,* 1932; *Altre poesie,* 1939; *Notizie di prosa e di poesia,* 1948); Giorgio Caproni (*Finzioni,* 1941, and *Stanze della funicolare,* 1952); Libero di Libero; Luigi Fallacara; Adriano Grande (*La Tomba,* 1930; *Fuoco bianco,* 1950); Mario Luzi (*Avvento notturno,* 1940; *Un brindisi,* 1946; *Primizie del deserto,* 1952); Alessandro Parronchi (*I visi,* 1943; *Un'attesa,* 1949; L'Incertezza amorosa, 1952); Corrado Pavolini, who is also a fine translator for poetry; Sandro Penna (*Poesie,* 1939, and *Appunti,* 1950); Antonia Pozzi (*Parole,* 1939); the painter Scipione (Gino Bonichi), whose poems were collected in *Carte segrete* in 1942; Leonardo Sinisgalli (*Vidi le Muse,* 1943; *I nuovi Campi Elisi,* 1947; *La vigna vecchia,* 1952); Giorgio Vìgolo (*Linea della vita,* 1949); Sergio Ortolani, and so on.

Naturally, defining a current cannot level and unify poets as different as those we have mentioned. They differ in age, inspiration, and even in styles and rhythms. Religious inspiration allies Betocchi with Fallacara and allies both of them with Girolamo Comi, who in turn is bound to the poetry of Onofri. A use of affected wit, *concettism,* which finds satisfaction in extreme verbal economy (that is to say in the poetics of Valéry) constitutes the lyric manner of Vìgolo and of Sinisgalli. A certain propensity for the Romantic myths may be seen in the poetry of Libero de Libero, from *Solstizio* in 1933 to *Banchetto* in 1949, and it is his poetry alone which takes on the myth of paradise lost. Sandro Penna believes in a world populated by angels and limpid, marvelous things. Luzi and Caproni distill from their human encounters a firm inspiration into verbal essense. Others, like Bigongiari, find the very reason of their inspiration in a highly finished style, almost in the technique of poetizing. Almost all contribute to avant-garde reviews such as *Diana* of Naples, and *Letteratura, Corrente, Italia letteraria, Campo di Marte, Frontespizio, Quadrivio.* Two of these poets, Angelo Barile and Adriano Grande, founded the review *Circoli;* but the former is one of those poets who has said his say in a single volume, while the latter is one of those perennially prolific poets. The difference between them is not external.

Other poets, while inclined to arcane and analogical language, have adopted the spiritualistic tradition or that of the *crepuscolari,* and have thus changed to a broader, more spacious rhythm and language — one less densely analogical. They have charged things with more temperate and rational super-senses, indeed they often have a direct grasp of things. After all, poets like Gatto and Penna, because of their congenial, impressionistic attitude toward the world, are really poets on the fringes of hermetic poetry. Indeed, it is quite possible that in years to come the very institution of *ermetismo* may change its form to a point that poets such as Ungaretti and Montale will have to be, so to say, historically reconstructed on traditional foundations. Finally, as occurred in the cases of Quasìmodo and

Gatto, the sense of human responsibility, the impossibility of staying aloof from historical struggles, the tragic occurrence of the war and, later, the collapse of tyrannies in Europe, constituted a spur to renouncing the analogical evasions in favor of existential metaphysics or even unreality and to looking at man and suffering with him, or sharing in his hope of a revival.

Clemente Rèbora (born in Milan in 1885, died 1957), was first a melodious, impressionistic poet, with hints of the *crepuscolare* manner (*Frammenti lirici,* 1913). Then, after a religious conversion and after assuming the habit of the Rosminian monks, he was the poet of a stern lyricism that was inspired by religious images of life and death and by a watchful religious expectation (*Poesie,* 1913–1947; *Via Crucis,* 1955; *Canti dell'infermità,* 1957).

Camillo Sbàrbaro, (*Santa Margherita ligure,* 1888) is the author of *Pianissimo,* 1914; and *Trucioli* [*Chips, Shavings*] 1927 and published again in 1948. He was a rough poet, peremptory in his language, who sacrifices images in order to communicate what has to be said about mankind: virtue is powerless against the indifference of life. All this is set to the rhythm of denunciation and strong lament. He is a poet who in certain aspects is akin to Montale, a Ligurian like himself, and, like him, a poet of cosmic indifference and a user of rapid, denunciatory language.

Umberto Saba was born at Trieste in 1883 and died in 1957. He was a dealer in old books, his little shop being one of the themes of his poetry. He spent most of his life in his native city, and it was there that he died. He is the author of many books of poetry, which are collected in his *Canzoniere,* 1945 and 1951. To this must be added the last collections of his poems: *Uccelli — Quasi un racconto* [*Birds — Something Like a Story*] in 1951; and *Cose leggere e vaganti — L'amorosa spina* [*Things Slight and Rambling — The Amorous Thorn*] in 1952. Sometimes he has assumed the most daring forms of the twentieth century, but this is the part of his work which is unconvincing and will not become any more convincing in the near future. In his most congenial and felicitous poems he is fond of a tranquil poetic utterance in which the images arrange themselves fully in affectionate sentiments, in picturizations of things, in experiences of life. Contrasted to the sadness of living, to violence and deceit, the tender, loving usages console and indeed give happiness and vital ardor. This is why the most oft-recurring themes in Saba's poetry are his love for Lina his wife, love of Trieste, the city so dear to him and whose streets, squares, crowded little modest shops, the Triestine people, and the many races of which it is composed. He does not so much describe as interpret all this and, in short, everything which he loves in the daily round. Sometimes his membership in the external world seems simply to turn into a chronicle in verse form. His emotional reaction jumps with joyful, agile whimsicality from the moralistic epigram to the pathetic, the evocative, loving impulse. His style tends toward simplicity, toward the discursive, sometimes toward the humble, especially on the level of vocabulary, while its rhythm often avails itself of inversions and hyperbata and tends toward stiffness. On the whole, the poetry of Saba seems to fall between the nineteenth century and the twentieth. It is between the tradition of stylistic sternness and moral obligation, including the most recent naturalistic tradition and, finally, autobiographical exaltation. All is from the nineteenth century, either in the pace of the inward-slanted diary or in some concession to psychological introspection in a psychoanalytic key.

Sibilla Aleramo (1875–1959) is noted for her novel *Una Donna* of 1906, but more so for poetry (*Selva d'amore,* 1947, *Aiutatami a dire,* 1951, are her last two books of poetry). She attains lyrical expression that is lofty, inspired by tense affections, and she reaches a chaste and yet vibrant eloquence. Gustavo Botta, a Milanese, whose poetry is partially contained in *Alcuni scritti* [*Some Writings*], 1952, reveals an exquisite symbolistic, decadent training, matured, in his case, by the practice of interpreting and translating French symbolist poetry. A vein of the crepuscular, strengthened however by a warm and melancholy social sensibility, runs through the work of the Milanese dialectal poet Delio Tessa (1886–1939), author of *L'è el dì di mort, alegher,* 1932 and of *Poesie nuove ed ultime,* 1947. More personal, that is, shifted away from the naturalism of Tessa to "intimism," the inwardness of Corazzini is the crepuscular poetry rendered in Triestine dialect, of Virgilio Giotti (b. Trieste, 1885), the author, among other things, of the poetical books *Colori,* 1941 and 1943, and *Sera,* 1947. More faithful to the impressionistic tradition, in the dialect of modern Rome, is Mario Dell'Arco (b. Rome, 1905). Nicola Moscardelli grasps in things the poured-out presence of God; a native of Abruzzi, he lived from 1894 to 1943, publishing *Canto della vita,* 1938, among other pieces. The sentiment of childhood, which bedews the things and the present experiences of a virginal innocence, is perhaps the most congenial theme in the poetry of Elpidio Jenco (b. Caserta, 1893), the author of *Acquemarine* in 1929; *Essenze,* 1933, and other volumes. Raffaele Carrieri (b. Taranto, 1905) is a poet who passed through the experiences of the avant-garde, but who is especially fond of epigramatic moods whimsically combined with Hellenism — limpid landscapes, innocence of death. He is given to the fabulous irony typical of Palazzeschi in *Lamento del gabelliere,* 1945 and *Il trovatore* [*The Excise-man's Lament* and *The Troubadour*] 1953.

The Theater

The theater in the early twentieth century was still tied to the naturalistic and psychological tradition of the late nineteenth century. Nevertheless, two dramatists, Butti and Bracco, after their short naturalistic season, felt the influence of the spiritualistic aura that blew over Italy towards the end of the century. Enrico Annibale Butti (1868–1912) stated the spirituality of the real in a dramatic trilogy, *Gli Atei* [*The Atheists*], which was a hit. In another drama, *L'utopia,* he composed a satire of the worldly ideologies of his characters, contrasting them with the mystical sense of life. His drama, *Il gigante e i pigmei* [*The Giant and the Pygmies*], 1930, scored a success with its wordly interest; in it Carducci defends himself from the irreverence of the pigmies who are making fun of his senile love affair. Roberto Bracco (1861–1943), a Neapolitan, was a critic of art, music, and the theater, and was even a columnist and a dialectal poet. He started playwriting as a realist, with *Don Pietro Caruso, Sperduti nel buio* [*Lost in the Fog*]; and *Maternità.* He then turned to psychoanalytic investigation and surrealist research in *La piccola fonte* [*The Little Spring*], 1905, and *Il piccolo santo,* 1911. *I Pazzi* [*The Madmen*] was written in 1917 and published in 1922. He was a congenial writer for the theater since structure and scenic evidence are the internal motivating forces of his dramatic art. He therefore thought that his dramas might be read outside the theater without any loss of their dramatic strength, according to the formula "theater without theater." His best plays are those which represent a sacrifice: where society forces the humble and the unarmed to protect themselves with the shield of evil, sin, and violence.

The fame of D'Annunzio's theater was considerably less meaningful. We shall call it the declamatory theater of aestheticism; it was trailed by a few ephemeral imitators. The same may be said of the futuristic theater which seemed, in its time, a theater of experimentation and of which we have already spoken. Similarly, tragedy inspired by history or mythology declined, dragging with it the last aestheticisizing remnants. Among these followers or imitators, let us mention Ercole Luigi Morselli (1882–1921) with his *Orione* in 1910, and *Glauco* in 1919; Nino Berrini, with a *Francesca da Rimini* in 1924, and *L'ultimo degli Zar* in 1937. He also wrote some social dramas: *Una donna moderna,* 1912; *Aristocrazia nera,* 1917; *La luna guarda* [*The Moon is Watching*], 1930. Giovacchino Forzano (1884) wrote historical plays: *Lorenzino,* 1922; *Ginevra degli Almieri,* 1926; *I fiordalisi d'oro* [*The Golden Fleurs-de-lys*], 1924; *Madame Roland,* 1926; and *Danton,* 1930. Sem Benelli (1877–1949) brought into his theater too much (literary, e.g., the pedantism of copying the speech of the sixteenth century) historically evocative, and aestheticizing effervescence or inertia; his is a corrosive attitude that when it is freed from aestheticizing impediments, takes on effective and sometimes grotesque tones. Therefore the later style of Benelli, seen in *L'elefante,* 1937, *Il rangno,* and *La paura* [*The Spider; Fear*], 1947, is preferred today to the Benelli of *La maschera di Bruto* [*The Mask of Brutus*], 1908 or *La cena delle beffe* [*The Supper of Jests*], 1909.

The theater in dialect weakly drags on, seemingly having ended its splendid nineteenth-century life with the fall of naturalism. We mention the Florentine, Augusto Novelli; the Roman Luigi Zanazzo; the Neapolitan Roberto Múrolo (who of the preceding generation does not remember *Addio mia bella Napoli* of 1909?) ; the Veronese Giuseppe Adami and, closer to our times, the Venetian Renato Simoni (1875–1952), author of *La vedova* [*The Widow*], 1909, *Carlo Gozzi,* 1903, *Congedo* [*Leave, Furlough*], 1910, and also a critic of the drama. He may be described as an approximate heir of Carlo Goldoni. And certainly, especially on the technical plane, the dramatic work of Simoni is competent, lively, and genuine. The theater of Eduardo de Filippo, which we shall discuss a little further along, cannot be included under the heading of "dialectal."

The traditional theater, which is psychologically narrative and improperly called "bourgeois," still persists, or did at least until a few years ago. In addition to Simoni, we give here a list of names: Cesare Giulio Viola, Camillo and Giannino Antona Traversi, Sabatino Lopez, Nino Oxilia, Eligio Possenti, Alberto Colantuoni, Orio Vergani, Dario Niccodemi, Tomaso Monicelli, Alessandro Varaldo, Lorenzo Ruggi, Guglielmo Zorzi, Guglielmo Giannini, Cesare Vico Ludovici, Gino Rocca, and still more down to the most recent, Indro Montalnelli; and there are other talented and versatile writers. Comedies like *Addio giovinezza!* [*Farewell, Youth!*] by Oxilia (1911); *Felicità Colombo* by Adami (1935); *La nemica* [*The Enemy*], (1916), which is in Niccodemi's tense and tragic first manner, or his *Scampolo* (1915) ; and *La Maestrina* (1917) , which are in his more moving and elegiac style; or the descriptive comedies of Salvator Gotta (whose last, *Virgo Potens,* is dated 1952) that appear faded today because they were a part of a life which the Second World War swept away, away at any rate, from the taste of the new and middle generations.

The theater of Silvio Giovaninetti is considered to be introspective and psychoanalytic: his characters unfold their subconscious through close introspection. Its artistic limitations consist of too much scientific strictness and gratification of psychic disequilibrium; meaning, of course, literary gratification. We mention his *Ombre* [*Shadows*], 1929; *L'abisso,* 1948; and *Il sangue verde* [*Green Blood*], 1954.

Enrico Cavacchioli (1885–1954) also represented the "intellectual" theater. We mentioned him earlier as a futurist poet. Of his plays we shall mention *Pierrot impiegato al lotto* [*Pierrot The Lottery Clerk*], 1925, which approaches the grotesque.

Ugo Betti (1892–1953), whom we have already met as a poet, transferred the "human cases" that came before him to the theater through his capacity of judge and magistrate. The desolation of his themes is always redeemed on the human plane of pity—the same thing is not always true on the plane of art. Often the "theatrical machine" stiffens the characters and their very vicissitudes. The dramatist often yields more to the dialectics of facts rather than to the lyrical, dramatic theme. The fables, which are resolved in this more secret, but more congenial lyrical-dramatic world, appear to be more linear and rich in inventive strength. Among the dramas of the first group the more famous are *Frana allo scalo Nord,* 1932; *Corruzione al Palazzo di giustizia,* 1944; *Delitto dell'isola delle capre* [*Crime on Goat Island*], 1948. Among those of the second group are *I nostri sogni* [*Our Dreams*], 1941; *Favola di Natale* [*Christmas Fable*], and *L'aiuola bruciata* [*The Burned Flower-bed*], 1952.

The three dramatists mentioned above represent a sharp break with the old naturalistic and psychological theater. On the programmatic plane the break came about with the theater of the "grotesque," which made the characters like hallucinated ghosts or manikins, to assume so paradoxical a consciousness of their grief, of their human emptiness, of their consequent inefficacity, of their vainness, as to graze laughter. It is the supreme stylization of pain. These are the grotesque characters. Their founder, in a way, was Luigi Chiarelli, with *La maschera e il volta* [*The Mask and the Countenance*], 1916. In addition to Cavacchioli, the grotesque dramatists are considered to be Carlo Veneziani (*La finestra sul mondo,* 1918); Alberto Casella (*La morte in vacanza* [*Death Takes a Holiday*], 1924); Alessandro de Stefani (*I pazzi sulla montagna* [*The Madmen on the Mountain*], 1926); and more significant, Luigi Antonelli (1882–1942) and Rosso di San Secondo, (that is, Pietro Maria Rosso, 1887–1956). Antonelli (who was a storyteller) is the author of *L'uomo che incontrò se stesso* [*The Man Who Met Himself*], 1918; *L'isola delle scimmie* [*Island of Monkeys*], 1922; *La donna in vetrina*

[*The Lady in the Shop Window*], 1930; *Mio figlio, ecco il guaio* [*My Son, That's the Trouble*], 1935; *L'amore deve nascere* [*Love Must be Born*], 1943. Rosso, a writer of comedies and also a storyteller, causes passions to gravitate over his characters, whether manikins or puppets, and over his mask-faces (*volti-maschere*), until they assume a spectral, resigned, elementary sadness: *Marionette che passione!*, 1918; *Lazzarina tra i coltelli* [*Lazarina Amid the Knives*], 1923; *Una cosa di carne* [*A Thing of Flesh*], 1924; *Maniera d'amare* [*A Way of Loving*], 1935. Sometimes he shows the fresh breath of lyric grace: *L'avventura terrestre*, 1924; *Tra vestiti che ballano* [*Amidst Clothes that Dance*], 1927.

Luigi Pirandello

The Italian theater and, partially, the European theater in the early part of the twentieth century, is, however, dominated by Luigi Pirandello.

He was born in 1867 at Girgenti, today called Agrigento. He studied at Palermo, Rome, and Bonn. Returning to Rome, he taught at the Istituto di Magistero, occupying the chair that had been Capuana's. But he was, first of all, a writer. He was forced to face a serious economic crisis which overwhelmed his father and his father-in-law, who managed a sulphur mine. Then he was struck by a new family misfortune, the insanity of his wife. However, his fame as dramatist and theatrical reformer assured him of international stature, obliging him likewise to suffer the enticements and the official recognitions of the Fascist régime. In 1934 he was awarded the Nobel Prize for Literature. He died in 1936.

He began his prolific and untiring literary activity as an essayist and poet. While essay writing represented an enduring interest and resulted in two important books; *Arte e scienza* (1908), and *Umorismo* (1908 and 1920), today published in a single volume containing other scattered essays (1930, poetry turned out to be only a passing youthful phase: *Mal giocondo,* 1889; *Elegie renane,* 1895; *Zampogna,* 1901). He soon turned to narrative writing: his first book of stories, *Amori senza amore* [*Love Affairs without Love*] appeared in 1894; his first novel. *L'esclusa,* in 1901. His narrative phase lasted right down to 1936 and produced a good fifteen volumes of novellas, published from 1922 to 1937 as a single *corpus* under the general title, which he personally chose, *Novelle per un anno.* There are in fact 246 novellas, almost one for every day in the year. His interest in narrative writing also brought forth seven novels. After *L'esclusa,* they are: *Il turno,* 1902; *Il fu Mattia Pascal* [Engl. tr., 1923, *The Late Mattia Pascal*], which was published serially in *La Nuova Antologia* in 1905 and which made its author widely celebrated and marked the beginning of his literary fame; *Suo Marito* [*Her Husband*], 1911, was published posthumously under the title *Giustino Roncella nato Boggiòlo*; preceded by another novel published serially in 1909, *I vecchi e i giovani* [Engl. tr., 1923, *The Young and the Old*]; *Si gira,* 1915, which, in the new edition of 1925, became *Quaderni di Serafino Gubbio operatore* [*The Notebooks of Serafino Gubbio, Operator*]; *Uno, nessuno e centomila* [*One, None and a Hundred Thousand*], published by the *Fiera letteraria* in 1925 and 1926. The novels too have been republished in a single *corpus.*

His theatrical activity began in 1908 with *L'epilogo,* later renamed *La morsa* [*The Vice (Tool)*], followed by *Lumìe di Sicilia* [*Sicilian Limes*] in 1911, and *Il dovere del medico* [*The Doctor's Duty*] in 1912. Then, even more numerous, drama followed drama. These are the principle ones: *Pensaci, Giacomino* [*Think About It, Jimmy*] and *Liolà,* in 1917; *Così è se vi pare,* 1918 [Engl. tr., 1923, *Right You Are If You Think You Are*]; *Il piacere dell' onestà,* 1918 [Engl. tr., 1923, *The Pleasure of Honesty*];

I giganti della montagna (the first two acts in 1931) ; after which appeared the first four volumes of his plays under the title *Maschere nude* [*Naked Masks*]. Then one after the other, *Sei personaggi in cerca d'autore,* 1921 (Engl. tr., 1922, *Six Characters In Search Of An Author*) , *Enrico IV,* 1922 (Engl. tr., 1922, *Henry IV*) ; *La signora Morlì, una e due (Mme. Morlì, one and two); Vestire gl'ignudi* [*To Clothe the Naked*], 1923; *La vita che ti diedi* [*The Life I Gave You*], 1924; *Ciascuno a suo modo* [*Each in His Own Way*], 1924; *L'uomo dal fiore in bocca* [*The Man With A Flower In His Mouth*], 1926; *Diane e la Tuda,* 1927; *La nuova Colonia,* 1928; *Lazzaro,* 1929; *Questa sera si recita a soggetto* [*Tonight, Improvization on a Theme*], 1930; and so on to the third definitive edition of *Maschere nude* in ten volumes, 1933.

The youthful naturalistic experimentation of Pirandello affected only the first two novels and some stories, but it was already deeply etched and altered by a whimsical humor, by a bitter irony which resolves the characters and the happenings of the traditional regional (Sicilian) and naturalistic repertory into characters and happenings of an exceptional nature. They are exalted by the same cruel irony which, sometimes grotesquely, stylizes their painful life. Their pain is in being what they are, in being in such a condition in the world, among men. Therefore, the bitter and grotesque fable of *Il fu Mattia Pascal* is no surprise, but it is the elementary form of Pirandello's poetics which has already matured in the preceding works. The dramatic theme, even before the beginning of his theater, constitutes the pivot on which the structure of his stories and novels turns. It is the theme of the incurable contradictions of our life, of the useless weariness which we humans endure because we try to attribute logical meanings and rational construction to our thoughts, feelings, human relationships, and daily happenings; that is to say, to fleeting, elusive material completely dominated by irrationality. In his theoretical works, Pirandello made use of science and, so far as it concerned him, of psychology. He did so in order to discover, in the light of the reasoning process, the irrationality of what we men call the reality of history and, especially, the reality of our feelings and personality. The principle of the rationality of the irrational made its way into European decadentism chiefly through the theater of Pirandello. It is certain that Pirandello the dramatist had far more influence on European literature than Pirandello the storyteller. Yet not only does his narrative work already contain the themes and even certain motifs of dialogue and of scenography which would later be realized in the great theater of the *Maschere nude,* but, indeed Pirandello's theater was matured culturally and imaginatively on the structural decadence of the novel, on the impossibility of the author to resolve, in the slow narrative form of the novel, a creative situation or one of sentiment that required rapidity and tension. His theater, therefore, followed the novels, not the stories.

Pirandello's formula of *relativity* is well known. By making use of the title of one of his novels, we might say that each man is one, no one, and a hundred thousand, according to how each man is seen, judged, interpreted by himself and by any other person. In other words, each of us has thousands and thousands of personalities (therefore, rationally, he has none) according to how we feel at one time or another, how we stand in our make-believe, and according to how others feel about us, how they act toward us. Knowledge of oneself — the classic pillar of cognitive philosophy ever since Socrates — is an illusion, and the very reality of man in time and space is an illusion. Each of us measures himself and everybody else and the external world in his own way; he thinks he is getting hold of the world by judging it, and in truth it escapes him. The world is unknowable, and men can not communicate among themselves.

The danger of this poetics of rational irrationality lies in the system turning into sophism, mere play of the intellect. But fortunately Pirandello is a poet, and in his most exemplary tales, in his greatest plays, this desolate consciousness of the vanity of reality resolves into tones, happenings, and characters both tragic and sarcastic, in which madness, the exasperated exaltation of the mask, and broken and trampled illusion are tragically redeemed in sorrow. Thus in *Six Characters,* the protagonists of the drama would like the author to place them firmly in his art, but theirs is a bitter illusion which shatters when it appears that human existence in its everlasting flow in each individual is *life,* which cannot be stiffened into the *form* of art. Then the narrative and dramatic masterpieces flow out: when human life, always defined in individual characters and often congealed into socially evident surroundings and classes, is represented as a paradoxical reality, sometimes mad, sometimes grotesque, sometimes simply impious and therefore morally knowable and capable of being judged, then life is more often crushed and compressed by Evil. And it may occur even in the most airy, most whimsical novellas and dramas that Evil is transformed into a savage destiny, in the presence of which and at which it is even permissible to laugh and to grow hilarious, as though destiny itself invited us to a cruel and mocking game hiding ferocity beneath buffoonery.

The style of Pirandello in narration and drama is dry, with enchanting, landscapist transitions in the stories and in the stage directions (in which case they must be expressed by the producer, by the scenarist). It is lit up by the pressure of the logic of the unreal, by the subtle reasoning that triumphs and exults solely to defeat rationality — lit up, we said, and almost feverish. But the tragic meanings are deposited behind the action in the form of bleak facts, of wretched, wicked things, inert and at the same time expressive. For example, the shambles smoking beneath the sun under a cloud of flies, while the crow, the cause of the destruction, sounds again his free, blissful, and innocent little bell through the skies (in the novella *Il corvo di Mìzzaro* [*The Crow of Mìzzaro*]. Or the two hats, black and lonely on the parapet of the river, to mark the two splashes of two suicides.

If the technique of the story can remind us of some naturalistic Sicilian influence (which, indeed, is observable also in the Sicilian-inspired comedies), Pirandello's dramatic technique has absorbed something from the Russian theater (especially that of Andreev), and also something of the French "intimist" theater, the Italian futurist theater, and the German surrealist theater. But the rational development along the thread of frustrated duplicity is wholly Pirandello's. Also the linear and serried succession of scenes to the naked rhythm of the dialogue, the verbal limitating of expression, to bare essentials which however finally turns and swells upon itself, the vast play of interpretation left to the *regista* [producer, director], the stylization of the characters within the dialogue and of things outside of it, these are "Pirandellian" forms which have exercised a tremendous influence on the theaters of the world. Another thing in Pirandello that is fascinating is the scenic and structural vicissitude of movement and of cessation of movement, the rapid agressive pressing of lucid argumentation against the motionless ghosts of our absurd desires, of our dreary pretences. Above all, it is the denouncing of false piety, of falsehood, which gives strength and edge to even the most jesting fantasies.

The Storytellers and the Steps in the Dissolution of the Romantic Man

Alongside the theater of the irrational we may discuss the prose of the storytellers and essayists: ironic, perturbed, disenchanted, deconsecrating the most common and traditional human values and substituting for them the irrationality of dark instincts, such as cowardice, fear, and the burden and temptation of sin, or a corrosive intelligence that investigates, dissects, and reduces to absurdity by means of irony. The arc is naturally quite extensive and proceeds from writers still tempered by humanistic and Romantic tradition down to iconoclastic writers. These are carried to the extreme in their break with historical and moral values. It goes from Panzini, a writer in whose best pages irony is only a smile, a regret for the past or perplexity in the present and future; to Borgese, who was perhaps the first to write the story of a failure, a man to whom death comes as neither good nor bad but is useful only because it cuts a useless thread of life. Palazzeschi leaves a breath of necessary existence to his characters (in order to love and to remember, if for nothing else) ; and Buzzati dissolves man in a hallucinated wait for he knows not what.

Alfredo Panzini was born at Senigallia in 1863 and died in 1939. He was a teacher all his life until, in his final years, he retired to Bellaria, on the Adriatic, not far from Rimini, at the threshold of that Romagna so dear to him which was the land of his parents and of a cherished company of Romagnol writers from Pascoli to Serra to Marino Moretti. He is the author of novels, novellas, essays in the humanities, and a very successful *Dizionario moderno*. In a prose expressing bitter resentments, nostalgic recollections, astonished ironies, his experiences run the gamut of dismay between the old order and the new, between the old Italy of his teacher Carducci and the new Italy of the *decadenti*. All of this is through a veil of pathetic "intimism" that reveals the ambiguities of unfulfilled desires and wavering temptations. This is the spirit of novels such as *Io cerco moglie* [*I Look For A Wife*], 1920; *Il mondo è rotondo* [*The World Is Round*],

1921; *Il padrone sono me* [*I'm The Boss*], 1922; But we have his most congenial books where the irony is more humane and serene, where the humanistic remembrance of persons and writers and historico-literary places is more relaxed, where the filter of fine classical writing brightens the feelings: *La lanterna di Diogene,* 1907; *Santippe,* 1914; *I giorni del sole e del grano* [*Days of Sun and Grain*], 1929; *Il bacio di Lesbia* [*The Kiss of Lesbia*], 1937. *Il viaggio di un povero letterato* [*The Journey of a Poor Man of Letters*], 1919, is an important document on a crisis of conscience in the war years. *La Madonna di mamà,* 1916, is a war novel with crepuscular overtones. These last two books represent the extremes of the Romagna group: the *Viaggio* brings him close to the manner of Serra, and the novel to that of Marino Moretti.

Federico Tozzi was born at Siena in 1883 and died in 1920. After two books of autobiographical inspiration (*Bestie* in 1917 and *Con gli occhi chiusi* [*With Closed Eyes*] in 1919), Tozzi sought to pass beyond the limits of his writing for *La Voce;* that is, to change over to the objectivity of the novel from the lyrical-intimistic fragment. Thus in 1920 he published two novels, *Tre Croci* [*Three Crosses*] and *Il podere* [*The Farm*]. The first tells the story of three brothers; the second has much to say in describing people and things belonging to the sentimental old times of the Sienese countryside. Tozzi is sometimes a gloomy and tragical writer of angry and wicked states of mind and of closed, surly characters who have been compared to those of Dostoievsky. At times in more ardent and whimsical country idyls, he continues and accompanies the partly realistic, partly legendary narrative typical of Tuscany in the style of such writers as Fucini and Pratesi and Cicognani. But it is certain that intimistic decadence passed through his pages, just as the poetics of *La Voce* passed through them, which is especially evident if one studies his subtle prose with its tendency to dense lyrical patterns and to isolated and independent word groups.

Italo Svevo (1861–1928), whose real name was Ettore Schmitz, a native of Trieste, is the author of two famous novels, *Senilità* of 1898 and *La coscienza di Zeno* of 1923. They portray inner, closed vicissitudes complicated by psychological abnormalities. The descriptions come close to psychoanalysis but at the same time are supported by a certain robust harshness of style which tempers the introverted tone and strengthens the rational coherence of the confessions and the psychologies of the characters. Thus Zeno Conti, in his illness, prepares a psychic and psychological account of himself to be submitted to a psychiatrist for study. Zeno's malady is inertia, not mental but moral: he is aware of his malady, abulia, but he does not suffer on account of it. Therefore, the novel is the deconsecration to which the protagonist submits himself with the calm pace of unsorrowful renunciation. But the vigor of the style contrasts with the apparent detachment of the character as a result of his malady. This confers on Svevo's story the character of a strong, graphic ambiguity. Svevo was also the author of a youthful novel, *Una vita* in 1892, and some tales and theatrical compositions. The correspondence he had with James Joyce is interesting and reveals an affinity between the two writers.

Giuseppe Antonio Borgese (1882–1952), a Sicilian whom we met earlier as a cultural organizer and critic, is the author of *Rubé,* 1921. The best among his other novels are: *I vivi e i morti* [*The Living and the Dead*], 1923, and *Tempesta nel nulla* [*A Storm in the Void*], 1931). It is *Rubé,* however, that is a literary document of extreme importance. In fact, *Rubé* speeds up the bitter dissolution of modern man well beyond the temperate limits of crepuscularism, of the perplexity typified by Pascoli, of the irony of Gozzano. Man simply dissolves because he has nothing to communicate to other men, nothing to receive, nothing to believe in, or to work and suffer for. Rubé, intelligent, refined, scornful, and contemptuous, and therefore spiritually alone, has some little resemblance to the decadent heroes of D'Annunzio; but in *Rubé* the psychological analysis has become far keener and more pitiless, the style colder and more resolute. In the sophisms of Rubé there is announced the process, rational and sophistic, therefore subtle and coherent, which leads to the denunciation of the irrationality of life. He can make a game of his own life and that of others, and even of his death (he falls, overwhelmed by a charge of cavalry sent to disperse Fascist and Communist demonstrators who are fighting each other). His affections are false, even the attempt of his wife to restore relations with him is ineffectual, unpersuasive, and brings ambiguity and inertia in its train.

We have already discussed Aldo Palazzeschi. When his poetic vein ran dry with *L'incendiario* in 1910, he still kept faith with his odd impasto of intelligent play, irony, and legend by turning to narrative forms. His waggish and futuristic story entitled *Il codise di Perelà,* published in 1911, has a hero who is a man of smoke "light, light, light, light, light," and who by no virtue nor fault of his own is first praised by men and then damned. And then the great art of Palazzeschi matured and took form: in his memories of childhood, *Stampe dell 'Ottocento* [*Nineteenth-century Prints*], 1930; in his description of the vicissitudes of ancient figurines (old maids), dismayed and attracted by the open-minded customs of the new generation, *Sorelle Materazzi* [*The Materazzi Sisters*], 1934; in his stories of psychological paradoxes, *Il palio dei buffi,* 1937, in which inventive inspiration and paradox, keen and witty psychological studies move to a clear and elegant prose that by itself fuses a temperate irony and the whimsical inspiration for the strange fable. The succeeding novels were to lose the nimbleness and vivacity of invention and style; they would befog his supreme and elegant moderation and proportion — thus came *I fratelli Cùccoli* of 1948, *Roma* of 1951, and *Bestie del Novecento* of 1952.

Giovanni Comisso, born at Treviso in 1895, loved earthy things, among them men, and not necessarily men of any particularly marked qualities. He describes sensations and desires with innocence. However, his egoism, which is decadent, reduces everything to his own measure; but has nothing of the open and ranting Dannunzian manner, and is rather with a touch of ambiguousness that finally beclouds even his innocence which is like that of a happy earthy animal. He is the author of many books of war and of travels, having been a combatant in the First World War, a legionary at Fiume, and a newspaper correspondent in half the countries of the world. We shall mention only *Avventure terrene* [*Adventures On Land*], 1935; *L'italiano errante per l'Italia* [*An Italian's Wanderings In Italy*], 1937; *Gente di mare* [*Seafarers*], 1929; *Al vento dell'adriatico* [*In The Wind From the Adriatic*], 1928; and *Gioventù che muore* [*Dying Youth*], 1949.

Giani Stuparich (1891–1961), a Triestine with his literary roots deep in the Triestine tradition and the *Voce* movement, was the author of a war novel, *Ritorneranno* [*They Will Return*], 1941 and also of a war diary in 1931, *Guerra del '15* [*The War In 1915*]. He wrote the *Colloqui con mio fratello* (1925), which are conversations with his brother Carlo, a casualty at the front. Carlo too was an intimistic *Voce* writer, rather like Michelstaedter. Giani also wrote a vigorous novel of human portraiture, *Donne nella vita di Stefano Premuda* [*Women in the Life of Stefano Premuda*], 1932; and stories among which *L'isola* (1942) is especially remarkable. This work describes, with polished stylistic perfection, the restrained pathos of a son for his father who is condemned to death by an insidious, incurable disease. *L'isola* is set against a background of the Dalmatian coast and the sea.

The story telling of Carlo Emilio Gadda, born in Milan in 1893, is whimsically inspired, paradoxical, but nourished by a happy humor. He is the celebrated author of *Il castello d'Udine* (1934), L'Adalgisa (1943), and of the recent *Quer pasticciaccio brutto de via Merulano* [*That Nasty Mess In Via Merulana*] (1958): a novel that changes a detective thriller plot into real entertainment and is written in a very clever and amusing impasto of several dialects. In his inventive and stylistic inspiration we can compare Gadda with Carlo Dossi. Omiting Dossi's far more composed and dignified language, his satirical inspiration is also quite different from the elegiac and reminiscent inspiration of Gadda. Their styles are different too, Gadda's being elusive, Dossi's prehensile and clinging to things and to chronicles. Gadda grasps men and things with his language, and presents them as they are, but with a constant ironical twisting back and legendary inspirations that deform the initial reality or render it almost magical.

Magical realism also takes its inspiration from the irrationality of reality; however, it redeems the irrational with the amazed magicality of the dream, and, always, with a stylistic clearness of high craftsmanship.

Massimo Bontempelli was born at Como in 1878 and died in 1959. He participated in the avant-garde literary movements. He was the moving spirit of the review *900* in which, assuming an attitude much akin to futurism, he proclaimed that it was necessary to have done with "all the remains of the great art of the Ottocento . . . worm-eaten relics of psychologism, of naturalism, of estheticism, of lower-middle-class taste, of the damnable and fraudulent sentimentalism which tries to pass itself off as human art." Here he defined "magical realism": "to clothe in a smile the most sorrowful things, and with wonderment the most common things: to make art a miracle instead of a weariness: instead of the clearing away, the dispatching of some routine, an act of magic." And it was in magical realism that his fertile vein as story teller and essayist found its inspiration; however, it revealed through his careful and refined prose a distant classical education, an exact feeling for the word which means, or only alludes to, more distant senses and vibrations. His style is bright and clear, and yet rich in fascinating enchantment, even ecstasy. Whether he is narrating or reminiscing, his favorite theme is the fable. His magical tones, in his best pages, are touched with astonishment, wonderment, and melancholy. He made his debut in 1909. Among his stories are: *La vita intensa,* 1920; *La scacchiera davanti allo specchio* [*The Chessboard Before the Mirror*], 1922; *Giro del sole* [*A Round of the Sun*], 1941. Among his novels are: *Vita e morte di Adria e dei suoi figli* [*Life And Death of Adria and Her Sons*], 1930, and *Gente nel tempo* [*People In Time*], 1937.

Bontempelli was also one of the moving spirits of *Stracittà,* a movement in opposition to which *Strapaese* arose and found expression in two reviews: Mino Maccari's *Il Selvaggio,* and Leo Longanesi's *L'Italiano. Stracittà* stood for the refined life which was at the same time open-minded. *Strapaese* called for a return to wholesome energies, to sincerity, and took on overtones of the common man. In truth both of them were aestheticizing, artificial movements. Many writers took part in these movements and engaged in polemics. Among the "strapaesani" let us mention Curzio Suckert, whose pen name was Curzio Malaparte (1898–1957), a writer of paradoxes, a lively controversialist, as well as a story teller and essay writer in books such as *Viaggio in Inferno,* 1938, and *Donna come me* [*Woman Like Me*], 1940.

Corrado Alvaro was born at San Luca in Calabria in

1895; he died in 1956. He began as a poet, then changed to stories and the novel. He was also the author of travel books, but of travels reconstructed from memory. They were not on the plane of the factual chronicle, but on that of the spiritual atmosphere and sensations left in him by the men he had met and the landscapes he had seen. The following are some of his best works: *Itinerario italiano,* 1933; *I maestri del diluvio — Viaggio nella Russia sovietica* [*Masters Of The Flood — A Journey in Soviet Russia*], 1935; *L'uomo è forte* [*Man Is Strong*], 1938; *Incontri d'amore,* 1940; *L'età breve* [*The Brief Age*], 1946. But his most poetical book is the youthful collection of tales *Gente in Aspromonte* [*People in Aspromonte*] of 1930. Alvaro's power of recall is especially intense when it is inspired by his native Calabria; it is a storied, dreamy remembering, which repeats the imaginings of childhood. He himself wrote: "I wonder if it is worth while to travel so much, when after all what we see is always the same thing, is what we saw in infancy." A difficult theme is dear to him: the passing from dreamy childhood to youth, which forces the boy to become a man and take his place in life even at the cost of sorrow and disillusionment and weariness. This theme recurs in the *Incontri d'amore* and in *L'età breve* with the same lucid psychological wisdom, with the same harsh yet vague melancholy. Alvaro was also the author of a diary, *Quasi una vita* (1927–1947), and of youthful war poems: *Poesie in grigio-verde* [*Poems in Gray-Green*], 1917.

Magic and a fabulous amazement create a certain relationship between writers like Bontempelli, Alvaro, the contributors to *La Ronda* (think of Cecchi), and some of the writers who gathered around *Solaria,* a review founded at Florence in 1926 by Alberto Carocci and which lasted until 1936. Many of the writers we are going to discuss came from *Solaria.* One or them is Pier Antonio Quarantotti Gambini, born in Pisino in Istria [now Yugoslav territory] in 1910. The author of *I nostri simili* [*Our Fellow-men*], 1932, *La rosa rossa* [*The Red Rose*], 1937, and of *Trincee* [*Trenches*], 1942; he is a writer of careful psychological introspective studies, especially of the young. A surrealist writer of clear, firm prose is Tommaso Landolfi, born in Lazio (Latium) in 1908, author of *La pietra lunare* [*The Moonstone*], 1938, and of other stories, down to *Racconto d'autunno,* 1947, and *La bière du pécheur* [*The Sinner's Coffin*], 1953. The religious uncertainty of Nicola Lisi (born near Florence in 1893) gives an allusive sense to his stories, and we shall mention only *L'Arca dei semplici* [*The Ark of the Simple*], 1938; *Concerto domenicale* [*Sunday Concert*], 1941; *Diario di un parroco di campagna* [*Diary Of A Country Parson*], 1941; *La nuova Tebaide* [*The New Thebaid*], 1950. Romano Bilenchi (born in Tuscany in 1909) tells about vicissitudes from the interior of his soul. Two of his novels are: *Conservatorio di Santa Teresa,* 1940, and *La Siccità* [*Drought*] 1941. Alessandro Bonsanti represents, not the vicissitudes but something of the vibrations emanating from the vicissitudes. He was born in Florence in 1904 and is the author of *La serva amorosa,* 1919; *I capricci dell' Adriana* [*Adriana's Caprices*] 1934; and the *Introduzione al gran viaggio,* 1944. He served as director of the review, *Letteratura.*

Vitaliano Brancati (1907–1954), a Sicilian, is the author of *Don Giovanni in Sicilia,* 1942; *Il bell'Antonio,* 1949; and *Paolo il caldo* [*Paul the Hot*], 1952. He has related fabled and erotic doings with vigorous inventiveness and has also directed his sarcastic denunciations against Fascist usages in the short story collection *Il vecchio con gli stivali* [*The Old Man In Boots*], 1945. He is a pungent and humorous writer, with a wealth of vigorous images, and an inexhaustible creator of grotesque situations. He draws his material from his native Sicily, but he does so in a modern and universal key completely outside any old naturalistic and regional scheme.

Dina Buzzati of Belluno (1906) is customarily classified among the writers who have been influenced by the unreal and hallucinatory tones of Franz Kafka. A nightmarish atmosphere constantly rising toward disaster envelopes the characters within the hard, fearfully solitary and alpine landscape surrounding the military fortress in the novel, *Il deserto dei Tartari,* 1940. This remains his finest book, even after the appearance of *Sette messaggeri,* 1940, and *Paura alla Scala* [*Fear At La Scala*], 1949.

Literature After World War II

The penultimate orientation of Italian literature in narrative form is *neorealism,* which seeks to arrest the chronicle of our times on its page, especially the social and the political. It attempts to portray contemporary society within well-defined regional, city, and rustic limits in accordance with an often class-slanted "stratography": high, middle, and low bourgeoisie, workers, peasants, craftsmen, proletarians, jobless, under-employed, playboys, and attempts to study their formation through the vicissitudes of war, the throes of Fascism, the rise of new ideologies and political forces, the struggle of the resistance against the Nazi-Fascist invaders, 1943–1945. Ripened during the last years of Fascism, strengthened by anti-Fascism and by the Partisan struggle, by the last ruinous war, and by the ever stronger and more pressing enthusiasm of the Socialists and Christian-Socialists, neorealism exploded soon after the war, attaining its highest artistic results in cinematography and in the narrative art. The vigorous journalistic explosion, supported by the reviews of opinion, the generous and ardent inspiration toward a renewed and antiacademic culture, the psychological and cultural ascent of a people previously weighed down by ignorance and inertia and now called upon by the war of liberation to take an active part in political life, in trade-unionism, in culture — all this resulted in the creation around neorealism of the hearty and popular participation of the whole nation. To this add the broadening of culture beyond the boundaries of old Europe, especially toward North American culture and that of the Soviet Union, in a universal harmony of civilization, ever faster, almost lightning-like and vaster.

Within this framework, let us sketch quickly the profiles of some of the principal writers.

Cesare Pavese was born at Santo Stefano Belbo (Cuneo) in 1908. In 1930 he began to publish essays on American literature and to translate English and American authors (his translations are exemplary). In 1935 he was arrested for anti-Fascism and then interned. A vital fact in his life was his friendship with Giaime Pintor and Leone Ginzburg, both of whom were killed during the struggle for liberation in 1943. Later he lived in Turin, working for the publisher Einaudi. He took his own life on August 27, 1950. At the opposite extremes of his literary activity stand two books of poetry: *Lavorare stanca* of 1936, and *Verrà la morte e avrà i tuoi occhi* [*Death Will Come and She Will Have Your Eyes*], published posthumously in 1951. Later a bitter diary was published, *Il mestiere di vivere* [*The Trade of Living*] in 1952, and the book of stories *Notte di festa* [*Holiday Night*] in 1953. His three principal novels are *Prima che il gallo canti* [*Before The Cock Crows*], 1949; *La bella estate* [*Beautiful Summer*], 1949; and *La luna e i falò* [*The Moon and the Beacons*], 1950. Pavese's art took as its theme the realistic interpretation of a corrupt and cruel society (and Pavese either hoped or deluded himself into believing that he fought to cure it, as an anti-Fascist, as a Partisan, as a Communist). But his refined and pessimistic sensibility and his aristocratic and analytical intellectualism led him willingly to turn his social solicitude in sad and decadentistic directions. He was a poet and a writer who dug up from beneath the reporters' surface of facts and things the feelings of real grief, of the exhausting weariness of the occupation, the trade, which life is, of the uselessness of historical illusions, of the difficult or equivocal human agreement, in short, the senses of that anguish which will lead him to die willingly. The discouraged and disenchanted pages, the feeling of a lost past and a lifeless present, the yearning for an escape which proves fallacious, are poetically redeemed by his grief, a grief stripped of pathetic concessions, stern, angry, malign, but not irritated. His characters are logical beings and often speak in the first person because of Pavese's liking for the dramatic form; yet, all the while the Piedmontese countryside and the Piedmontese people, whom the reader divines in the background, insure that the structure of the story shows a dialectical relationship of the objective with the subjective. He translated and was one of those who brought North American narrative literature to Italy. This was anarchical and tragic literature, representative of a break with a certain formal America. His translation of Melville's *Moby Dick* is a masterpiece. Pavese's first novel, *Paesi tuoi,* 1941, stems from American realism, and especially from Faulkner.

Elio Vittorini was born at Syracuse in 1908. He is a writer who reveals an effective conscience in his work and who expounds and defends his realistic poetics. The narrator presents truth, using the spoken language, but he must discover it, divine it, reveal it, and drag it forth from the dark depths of consciousness into the light. Thus he succeeded in finding a lyrical realism, concerning which he spoke and wrote in a number of critical essays and appearances, and toward which he oriented his review, the *Politecnico,* and a string of new story tellers guided by him. The first of his novels to win fame was *Conversazione in Sicilia* in 1941, which was followed by *Uomini e no,* 1945; *Il Sempione strizza l'occhio al Fréjus* [*The Simplon Winks at the Fréjus*], 1947; *Il garofano rosso* [*The Red Carnation*] published in 1948, but written in his youth; and *Le donne di Messina* [*The Women of Messina*], 1949. He too was a model translator of English and American works. His own art seems to lie culturally between Verga and the Americans, from Melville to Faulkner. He was one of the most active and anti-Fascist intellectuals, and after the war, he was among the most active progressives of the in-between generation which was turning away from the "hermetic" period to that of realism without, however, repudiating his youthful decadentistic experiences.

Vasco Pratolini was born at Florence in 1913. He had a difficult life in his youth and tried a number of occupations. With Alfonso Gatto he founded and directed *Campo di Marte* in 1938 and 1939. Since the war he has shown himself to be one of the leading story tellers of the new generation. His characters come princially from the ranks of the poor; the settings of his novels are the poorer sections of Florence. He is a neorealistic writer, but possessed of an emotional fervor which is pathetic and tends to pour forth, even in objective or reportorial narration, an arrested autobiographical sense. Even during a painful episode it shows an irrepressible love of life, a higher, vital joy. The dialectal base of his language never sinks into the mire and never becomes self-satisfied, but goes its way musically and logically. With Pratolini the literary period of magical realism closes. There is perhaps a slight literary return here to Verga and the best naturalistic tradition. His first three novels are frankly autobiographical: *Via de' Magazzini,* 1942; *Il quartiere* [*The Neighborhood*], 1944; *Cronaca familiare,* 1947. The first novel about completely objective events is *Cronache di poveri amanti* [*Tales of Poor Lovers*], 1947, which would be a finished masterpiece were it structurally stronger and more rounded. Then, after some less convincing trials, there appeared the first novel of a narrative cycle which bears the title *Una storia italiana.* This novel is *Metello,* published in 1955. The trilogy was concluded with *Lo scialo* [*The Show*] and *Allegoria e derisione,* bringing the chronicle of Florentine life through later generations. As for the second novel of the cycle, *Lo scialo* which appeared in 1959, opinions are not positive: it might be the author's fullest and warmest book, if some controversially raw and angry pages did not spoil or interrupt the creative impetus. In any case, *Lo scialo* [*Waste*], because of its bulk and the great historical vicissitudes that are recounted therein [the struggles between the middle class and Fascism on the one hand, proletarians, socialists, and Communists on the other], that took place in and around Florence reveals the ambition of the contemporary historical novel.

The novel *Metello* reveals a return to the historical novel, in a model fashion and likewise the renewal in modern dress of an old literary genre so dear to Romanticism. In it history is interpreted, but on the ideological plane, on the line of a critical view; it is not merely dramatically recalled, nor are only everlasting moral judgments drawn from it. The two original and fertile motifs of neorealism are, therefore, repudiation of the aristocratic, stylistic language of the decadents; and the (Manzonian) restoration of the spoken tongue, of speech as language, as a national institution, to which the writer personally contributes a certain lexical and syntactical choice. On the other hand, there is the ideological interpretation of hisorical events. For one thing, neorealism has instituted identification of style with the common tongue and has given the literary language back to speech as it is spoken. It rejects both linguistic aristocracy and the speech of jargon; that is to say, it institutes a popular literary language. For another thing, it has placed in opposition to the independence of art (cognitive, not logical, autonomy according to the teaching of Croce), art with its content of problems and ideologies. Neorealism, therefore, not only definitively closes the calligraphic and existentialist experiences of decadentism, but also subjects the aesthetic and idealistic historiography of Croce to profound revision. It allys itself instead with Marxist philosophy and the neoilluministic European and American culture.

Francesco Jovine (1902–1950), born in the neighborhood of Campobasso, conjures up the images of his ancient province of Molise with epical fervor and nostalgic affection in *Signora Ava,* 1943 and in other less successful novels. But his masterpiece is the novel *Terre del Sacramento* [*Lands of the Sacrament*], 1950, the epic of the psychological and social evolution of an oppressed and depressed people that culminates in the occupation of the uncultivated lands by peasants hungering for bread and social justice. The novel is solidly constructed around the figure of the hero, Luca Marano, who stands at the center of the peasant insurrection against the absurd privileges of the ruling caste. His inward story is related with a wise and moving attentiveness, articulated and vibrant, down to the final holocaust that is decided by a moral and intellectual choice, prepared with all the melancholy fervor of youth.

The merging of realism and the personal diary is achieved in one of the most famous novels of the period following the war; that is, in *Cristo si è fermato a Eboli* [English tr. *Christ Stopped at Eboli,* 1947], published in 1946 by Carlo Levi (b. 1902), a doctor and artist of Turin. In it the author tells about his political confinement in a poor, secluded town in Lucania. The limitation of Levi's narrative (accentuated in the novel *L'orologio* [*The Clock*] is the lack of a finished structure. This difficult fusing of the ideological sense of reality with the effuse, insistent, and elegiac intimism weakens the story. However, especially in the former novel, there are pages of an idyllic freshness or of stern melancholy. Model essays are also to be read in two accounts or inquiries: the first, into the social conditions in the Sicily of today, *Le parole sono pietre* [*Words Are Stones*], 1955; the second, concerning Soviet Russia, *Il futuro ha un cuore antico* [*The Future has an Ancient Heart*], 1956.

Neorealism has produced a vast series of inquiries in the form of narrative essays: it suffices to recall Danilo Dolci who denounces present wretchedness in Sicily in several volumes inspired with a missionary zeal (Dolci is a Social Christian who left his native city of Trieste to go to Sicily to engage in the work of social redemption there); Leonardo Sciascia, a Sicilian and essayist, narrator of things Sicilian; Ottiero Ottieri; Palolo Volponi; Franco Fortini; Alberto Arbasino; Mario Soldati, and newspaper correspondents, and the television and radio commentators. Mario Soldati, reporter, journalist, and movie director, is also an able craftsman as an investigator. Born in Turin in 1906, a tireless author of stories and novels, of which two are outstanding for their mastery of structure, inventive liveliness, and whimsy: *A cena col commendatore* [*Supper with the "Commendatore"*], 1950, and *Lettere da Capri*, 1954. No longer does the reportorial, documentary background of the younger Italian writers lie dormant in the old naturalistic forms but tends toward inventive and, at the same time, ideological utterance of reportorial and documentary material. Here, alongside Soldati, we find Giuseppe Marotta, born at Naples in 1902, author of *L'oro di Napoli*, 1947, *A Milano non fa freddo* [*It's not Cold in Milan*] 1949, his two most successful novels; Cesare Zavattini, who, in his surrealist and humorous fantasies, condemns social selfishness (born in Emilia in 1902, he is the author of *Parliamo tanto di me*, 1931; *I poveri sono matti* [*The Poor Are Crazy*], 1937, and

Io sono il diavolo, 1942); Carlo Bernari, born at Naples in 1909, who has with his novels *Tre operai* [*Three Workers*] 1934, *Speranzella,* 1949, with *Siamo tutti bambini* [*We Are All Children*], 1951, and *Vesuvio e pane* [*Vesuvius and Bread*], 1952, brought into his stories a whole chorus of people while still keeping in movement some extremely articulate, self-contained, and whimsical happenings and portraits, so that the popular psychology is very real but subdued beneath the impetus of an untrammeled inventiveness; Giuseppe Berto, born at Mogliano Veneto in 1914, passing from "obligatory" novels, *Il cielo è rosso* [*The Sky Is Red*], 1947, and *Il brigante,* 1951, to the independent story, filtered through with critical sense and humor; Anna Banti, a Florentine who solves the psychological happenings of every day in situations, confessed openly, but in reality secret (*Artemisia,* 1947; *Il bastardo,* 1954; *La monaca di Sciangai* [*The Nun Of Shanghai*], 1957; *Le mosche d'oro* [*Golden Flies*], 1962; Giuseppe Dessi, born at Cagliari in 1909, author of tense novels and stories in which there is always a breath of the Sardinian saga, like *San Silvano,* 1939, *Michele Boschino,* 1943, *Racconti vecchi e nuovi,* 1945, *I passeri* [*The Sparrows*], 1955, *Il disertore,* 1961; Enrico Emanuelli, born at Novara in 1909, journalist, correspondent, travel writer in many parts of the world, the author of novels of penetrating and restless psychology, like *La congiura dei sentimenti* [*The Conspiracy of the Feelings*], 1943, and *Settimana nera* [*Black Week*], 1961; Gianna Manzini of Pistoia, who progressed from the autobiographical novel *Forte come un leone,* 1944, to the energetically motivated novel of inner vicissitudes, as in *Sparviera* [*Sparrow Hawk*], 1956. With these and other writers (Libero Bigiaretti, Ennio Flaiano, Carlo Coccioli, Giuseppe Longo, Ercole Patti, Silvio Micheli, Raffaello Brigneti, Beppe Fenoglio, Paola Masino, Anna Maria Ortese, Lina Pietravalle, Laudomia Bonnanni, among others) the Italian narrative of today freely gives utterance with prolific unfettered narrative impetus to news, political-social obligations, and ideological documentary. And here it is desirable to record writers of the middle and new generations who have developed in the last few years: Alberto Arbasino, a caustic writer who is more devoted to reactions in morals and usages than concerned with an ideological vision of present-day reality (*Le piccole vacanze* [*Short Vacations*], 1957; *Parigi o cara* [*Dear Paris*], 1960); Giovanni Arpino, who studies the difficult point at which, in his characters, personal sentiment meets the prejudice, the observance, or the rite of caste, presented in subtle, unhurried writing (his latest two successful novels are *Un delitto d'onore* [*A Crime Of Honor*], 1961, and *Una nuvola d'ira* [*A Cloud Of Anger*], 1962) ; Giuseppe Cassieri, from Apulia, who sketches the actions of the "exemplary" man, after having cut the last ties with naturalism (*La cocuzza* [*The Pumpkin*], 1960, *Il calcinaccio* [*The Rubble*], 1962); Natalia Ginzburg, whose preference runs to inner psychological stories, lucid and intimate, always on the edge of the anomalous (*Tutti i nostri ieri* [*All Our Yesterdays*], 1952, *Valentino,* 1957, and *Le piccole virtù* [*The Small Virtues*] and *Lessico familiare* [*Family Lexicon*], 1963); Raffaele La Capria, who brings into his novels the young people of the middle class at the critical point of historic and ideological crisis, youths impatient to escape from apathy through egocentrism, personal irresponsibility, eroticism (*Un giorno d'impazienza,* 1952, *Ferito a morte* [*Wounded Unto Death*], 1962); Michele Prisco, a tranquil and reserved narrator of common events (*La provincia addormentata* [*The Sleepy Province*], 1949, *Gli eredi del vento* [*The Heirs Of The Wind*], 1950, and more down to *La dama di piazza* in 1961) ; Domenico Rea, the imaginative writer of Neapolitan customs and atmosphere (*Spaccanapoli,* 1947, [the name refers to a populous section of Naples], *Gésu, fate luce* [*Jesus, Give Us Light*], and on to *Una vampata di rossore* [*A Flash Of Red*], 1959); Saverio Strati and Giovanni Testori, writers concerned with the portrayal, on an ideological plane, respectively with Calabria and the outskirts of Milan — the former is the author of *La teda* [*The Torch*] in 1957, *Tibi e Tascia,* 1959, *Avventure in città,* 1962, and the latter is the author of the stories *Il ponte della Ghisolfa* in 1958, *La Gilda del Mac Mahon,* 1959, the novel *Il Fabbricone* [*The Big Factory*], 1961, and two plays: *La Maria Brasca,* 1960, and *L'Arialda,* 1960. By their side let us mention the good narrative results of Nino Palumbo, Fortunato Seminara, Renata Viganò, Mario Schettini, Fausta Cialente, Mario La Cava, Sergio Antonielli, Oreste Del Buono, Lucio Mastronardi, Luciano Bianciardi, Maria Corti, Dante Troisi, Giorgio Soavi, Goffredo Parise, and many others. Particularly successful are the novels of a writer who is a psychiatrist and lives in Lucca, Mario Tobino: *Le libere donne di Magliano, La Croce di Biassoli,* 1956, *Il clandestino,* 1962; and successful also are the novels of Elsa Morante: *Gioco segreto,* 1941, *Menzogna e sortilegio* [*Lying And Witchcraft*], 1948, and *L'isola di Arturo,* 1957.

Neorealism therefore must be considered a durable movement because of its profound accomplishments in having formulated an ideological dimension, in having placed the stylistic use of everyday speech outside of jargon (and therefore the use and abuse of films in Neapolitan and Roman dialect have nothing to do with neorealism, while the use of language of deep dialectal and polydialectal constructions in narrative is neorealistic and is the language of a Gadda or a Pasolini). In this picture the heavy and sultry realism brought by Curzio Malaparte into his last novels since the war remains marginal (it will suffice to mention *La pelle* [*The Skin*] of 1949, a lifeless, inert reportage of Naples immediately after the war). But the novels of Piovene have a place there, those of Moravia, of Pasolini, Cassola, and even, for different reasons, those of Calvino and Bassani. Guido Piovene was born at Vicenza in 1907. He likes to provoke moral casuistry in his characters to the point of crime, or of complete apathy. These people are generally of high station and endowed with refined and corrosive intelligence. His books of this type, which are written in a lucid style, are *Lettere di una novizia* [*Letters of a Novitiate*], 1941; *La gazzetta nera,* 1943; and *Pietà contro pietà,* 1946. More recently Piovene has written essays and stories ideologically committed, like *La coda di paglia* [*The Straw Tail*] and at the same time has returned to the psychological autobiographical novel in which fantasy, reality, and recollections of reality are fused, and in which personal myths are reconciled with public myths (*Le furie,* 1963). Alberto Moravia (pseudonym Alberto Pincherle, born in Rome in 1907, with his very first novel, in 1929, *Gli indifferenti* [Eng. trs., 1932, *The Indifferent Ones,* 1953, *The Time of Indifference*] founded neorealism in his own way, not so much because of ideological commitment as by the reportorial vigor with which he portrays the stupidity and hypocrisy of the middle classes. In truth, he combats these evils only with the rights of intelligence, in the name of which he corrodes and wears down human values to a point where he makes indifference and boredom the only intelligent and possible instruments of life. A great writer, he knows how to sharpen his lucid, unhurried, and very coherent prose, how to smooth and spread it out on the plane of pure intelligence which contain no more sudden human shocks, no more adventures and surprises, not even thoose of chance. With Alberto Carocci he directed the review *Nuovi argomenti.* Among his novels which followed *Gli indifferenti* mentioned above are: *Agostino,* 1945; *La romana,* 1947 [Eng. trs., 1949, *The Woman of Rome*]; *Il Conformista,* 1951; *La ciociara,* 1957 [a woman of the Roman countryside; Eng. trs., 1958, *Two Women*]; *La noia,* 1960 [*Ennui;* Eng. trs., 1961, *The Empty Can-*

vas]. Among the short stories are: *La bella vita,* 1935; *I sogni del pigro* [*The Lazy Man's Dreams*], 1940; *Racconti romani,* 1954; *Nuovi racconti romani* [New Roman Stories], 1959; *L'automa* [*The Automaton*], 1962. Pier Paolo Pasolini, whom we shall meet as a poet also, born in Bologna in 1922, is the author of two novels: *Ragazzi di vita,* 1955 and *Una vita violente,* 1959. They are novels which show some superfluous pages here and there, an excess of the Roman jargon in addition to the literary-popular linguistic mixture, but the epic strength of many pages and of the religious aspiration to a reality different from the one presented and which is the reality of the soul squeezed, humiliated, abused in its intelligence, in feeling and in body, confers a stern sadness on their characters and their vicissitudes. A critic (*Passione e ideologia,* 1961), editor of the review *Officina,* a student and promoter of popular and dialectal poetry, and a movie director, Pasolini is representative of the young generation of artists and scholars committed to the social renewal and the ideological foundation of a new civilization. Carlo Cassola, born in Rome in 1917, but Tuscan on his mother's side, after having measured his abilities in some stories and prose writings, started with a novel based on the resistance against the Fascists and the Germans, *Fausto e Anna* (1952), one of the most solidly constructed novels of the many based on the same theme. Then he developed the love themes and the lyrical realities of that first novel in the stories *Taglio del bosco* [*The Cutting Down Of The Wood*], 1954 and in *La casa di via Valadier* [*The House On Valadier Street*], 1956, and then in the novels *Il soldato,* 1958; *La ragazza di Bube,* 1960; *Un cuore arido* [*An Arid Heart*], 1961. The short stories and the prose writings were finally published together in *La visita* in 1962. Cassola's prose, therefore, is precise but lightened lyrically. For him, realism lies in meeting, in a wood, not nymphs or shepherdesses, but woodsmen; it does not lie in reportage stripped of lyricism. Italo Calvino, born in Cuba in 1923, but who grew up in San Remo, published in 1946 his first novel, *Il sentiero dei nidi di ragno* [*The Cobweb Path*]. It was followed by *L'entrata in guerra* [*Declaration of War*], the novellas of *Ultimo viene il corvo* [*The Crow Comes Last*], and still more tales; *Il visconte dimezzato* [*The Viscount Cut In Half*], *Il barone rampante* [En. tr. 1959, *The Baron In The Trees*], *Il cavaliere inesistente* [*The Knight Who Did Not Exist*]; recently, in 1963, the story *Giornata di uno scrutatore* [*The Day of an Observer*]. He is a writer who is sometimes committed ideologically, but his most felicitous tales, the most congenial, are those which erupt from a happy, comic, storied inventiveness, to which constructive and psychological vigor is brought by the rapid moral and allegorical promptings, even though such inventions are consumed in a brief narrative round. Finally, Giorgio Bassani, born in Bologna to Ferrarese parents in 1916, a poet, a cinematographic scenario writer, the editor of *Botteghe oscure* and *Paragone,* is the author of the *Cinque storie ferraresi* [*Five Stories from Ferrara*], 1956, and *Gli ultimi anni di Clelia Trotti* [*The Last Years of Clelia Trotti*], in 1955; which were followed by *Gli occhiali d'oro* [*The Gold Spectacles*] and *Il giardino dei Finzi-Contini,* Eng. tr. 1962, *the Garden of the Finzi-Contini,* 1965. With this latter novel Bassano has defined his narrative pattern or norm: a slow development of inner psychological profiles in a dry, logical prose, relaxed by a tranquilly progressing expression, so that the realistic and reportorial pattern dissolves in the historical narrative which alludes to an ideological interpretation.

The posthumously published novel *Il gattopardo* [*The Leopard*], 1959, by the Sicilian Giuseppe Tomasi di Lampedusa, was a great success. The protagonist, Prince Fabrizio di Salina, watches the Garibaldinian undertaking in Sicily and the fall of the Bourbon monarchy with an elementary pessimism, with a "historic nausea," as the author aptly observed. The significance of the book lies in this debonair and temperate wearing away of the status quo, veiled in wisdom and in melancholy. This is perhaps the only frankly decadentistic novel to appear in this post-war period.

The narrative work of the "loner," Antonio Delfini (1908–1963), of Modena, belongs more to the decadentistic tradition than it does to neorealism. He is the author of stories now almost all collected in *La Rosina perduta* [*Lost Rosina*], 1957, and in *Racconti* [*Stories*], 1963. In them his keen intelligence sometimes leads human situations to the point of paradox, always dominated, however, by whimsical irony and by a remote, disguised human pity.

The more recent poetry also prefers the broad lyrical manner of expression, ideologically revealed, which tempers the melodic impetus and almost absorbs the musical trend in its rhythm which, for its part, is articulated either in a loquacious development or in rapid, characteristic, and repeated stylistic constructions and in epigraphical sayings. However, the "hermetic" and symbolist experiences have not disappeared. Thus in the poetry of Pavese, which we have already considered, the ideological expression betrays an ever so chastened suggestion of the allusive image, thus also the situation and the occurrence are mitigated, alleviated, in *Poesie* (1950) and in *Levania e altre poesie* (1956) by Sergio Solmi, of whom we have spoken above as a critic and essayist. The longing for a Christian and social renewal is expressed in the analogical poetry of distant hermetic teaching (Ungaretti's, especially) in *Udii una voce* [*I heard A Voice*], 1952, and *Gli occhi miei lo vedranno* [*My Eyes Will See It*], 1955, by the *Servite,* David Maria Turoldo. The hermetico-crepuscolar lineal ascendants persist in the poetry of Vittorio Sereni, also open to an ideological discourse, to a historical interpretation of the war and of human reality balancing on the wire of grief and perplexity, so that the hours, the seasons, the city suburbs are stressed (*Frontiera,* 1951; *Diario d'Algeria,* 1947; *Istruzione e allarme,* 1957). In the picture of this relationship between symbolistic analogy and ideology may be placed the new poets: Nedda Falzolgher, Francesco Carchedi, Marino Piazzolla, Elio Filippo Accrocca, Giovanni Giudici, Lino Curci, Tilde Nardi, Mario Tobino, Giorgio Bassani, Giorgio Orelli, Margherita Guidacci, Andrea Zanzotto, Renata Mucci, Gaetano Arcangeli, Francesco Leonetti, Franco Fortini, Elena Bono, Paolo Volponi, Alba Merini, Gilda Musa, Luciano Erba, Renzo Modesti, Nelo Risi, Alberico Sala, arranged along an arc which goes from the "social" poetry of Rocco Scotellaro to the neohermetic poetry of Renzo Laurano. The poet who has instilled into his poetry a more extended and pure eloquence is Pier Paolo Pasolini, the author of poems in the dialect of Friuli, the author of Italian poems which have passed gradually from a rigorous rhythmic and structural requirement (*Le ceneri di Gramsci* [*The Ashes of Gramsci*], 1957, and *L'usignolo della Chiesa cattolica* [*The Nightingale Of The Catholic Church*], 1958, to the epigramatic stylism and the eloquence of a laic, sorrowful, protesting religiosity (*La religione del mio tempo* [*The Religion Of My Time*], 1961).

In the last few years the theater has stressed "problematicity," either religious, although in equivocal ways, as in the plays of Diego Fabbri (*Processo a Gesù* [*A Trial for Jesus*], 1955; *Veglia d'armi* [*Armed Watch*], 1957; *Figli d'arte* [*Sons Of Art*], 1961), or in the ideological, satirical, realistic comedies of Giovanni Testori, Gian Paolo Callegari, Giuseppe Patroni Griffi, Ottiero Ottieri, and so on. But the only theatrical writing which today possesses its own elementary endurance is that of Eduardo De Filippo (born at Naples in 1900). The tragic and the comic are fused together and confer on Eduardo's realistic drama a psychological relief, a sad feeling about life, a coherent passage from the tone of farce to that of sorrowful sternness, from vital impetus to reflective withdrawal, from playfulness to ideological commitment; all of which are components that move free and articulated in the classical unity of the work. Eduardo is the dramatic poet of the poor, the overwhelmed, the oppressed people mocked by the mechanism of prejudices, by the use of that violence which wears itself out on the weak on behalf of the strong, and both of them ignorant of the position which they have been called on to assume. Theater of an implicit accusation, which is directed against that strange mechanism which is humanity. In this attitude, De Filippo picks up, in Neapolitan colors and tones, the rationality of the unreal which was Pirandello's. His language is the literary Neapolitan. Some of his plays: *Questi fantasmi* [*These Phantoms*], 1946; *Filumena Marturano,* 1947; *Napoli milionaria* 1950; *De Pretore Vincenzo,* 1957, have won him a well-deserved and worldwide renown.

In recent times, Italian literature has been coordinating in itself some fifty years of both decadentism and the brief neorealistic period and is tending in the direction of the ironic or fictional transfiguration of reality. Its limiting factor lies perhaps in an overabundance of corrosive intelligence, in a too hasty recapture of traditional poetic values (return to closed meters, to eloquence, to the historical novel), in an excess of ideology. Alongside the old European masters (Proust, Freud, Kafka) and the new masters, especially the Americans (from Melville to Faulkner to Hemingway), the younger Italian writers have lined up alongside the masters of European neo-decadentism, men like Beckett, Ionesco, Husserl, Musil, even though some of them still believe in writers who along with angry and sarcastic destruction nevertheless bring a message of human renewal, like Brecht. The industrial organization of culture has furnished an irresistible stimulus to literary production, which today is vast, enormous, backed up by journalism and radio-television media, so that narrative, poetry, and theater live today within the publishing and newspaper organization. Inventive writers have become journalists, and vice versa, with an all too facile process of intercommunication. Debates have taken the place of conferences; books roll off the production belt; patronage — support, subsidy, and protection — has become an instrument for advertising and for speculation. Nevertheless, the book as a work of art, and as a message, lives on, with its own uncoercible vitality. Even the younger critics have freed themselves from the pedantries of academicism and today flee the newspaper leading article, ward off the third-page article (of Italian newspapers), avoid the haste and carelessness of improvisation. Sometimes they succeed in producing books that are alive: committed, perhaps, but backed up by hard study, by the exigencies of historiography, and by that of the structural unity of their work. As for the inventive, the creative, writers, some of the oldest generation are still today living productively: Carlo Emilio Gadda has very recently published a volume of stories; *Accoppiamenti giudiziosi,* one of essays, *I viaggi della morte,* and a novel; *La cognizione del dolore;* and Riccardo Bacchelli is still active. Of the writers of the younger generation and of the one in between, while new works are being awaited from Vittorini and from Bilenchi, the following writers have been active: Vasco Pratolini with a new novel in his cycle *Una storia italiana: La costanza della ragione* [Eng. tr., 1965, *Bruno Santini*]; Dino Buzzati with a novel: *Un amore* [Eng. tr., 1965, *A Love Affair,* 1965]; Uberto Paolo Quintavalle with the novel *Rito ambrosiano, rito romano* [*St. Ambrose's Ritual, Roman Ritual*]; Alba de Cespedes with a novel of moralistic inspiration: *Il rimorso,* which has been compared to the work of Camus and of Simone de Beauvoir.

This section, on the twentieth century, deals with materials that have not yet been fully studied and is therefore more diffuse than the proportions of the entire work would require; we hope to be pardoned.

An Epilogue

A Brief Summary of Italian Literature During the Mid- and Late 1960's

(In this task of *aggiornamento* I cannot presume to extend the careful method nor emulate the highly individual tone of criticism and history associated with Eugenio Donadoni. The few summary remarks which follow will at least bring the brilliant panorama of Italian letters up to the year 1969. This brief epilogue will then cover several elements of the Italian literary scene: the literary life, celebrations, journals, discoveries, the novel, poetry, theater, and essays. The criterion of selection is the most debatable one of my own sense of what is important.)

R. J. C.

The Literary Life: During the 1960's, even as controversy raged over the value of literary prizes, Italy continued to award them annually with much fanfare. Even such small communities as Chianciano Terme (population 5,490) offered a million liras for the best Italian poetry of the year. The Etna-Taormina Prize provided the same sum each year, one of its happier selections during this period honoring Anna Akhmatova just before her death. The verbal campaign against literary prizes rose to a pitch in 1967, when the two top awards, the Viareggio and the Strega, turned out to be fiascos. Calvino refused the Viareggio which was then given to Libero Bigiaretti, and Antonio Barolini was disqualified after winning the Strega (on grounds that his prizewinning work dated from before the period of the competition).

The Italians always remember ceremoniously the anniversaries of their literary great. During this period the most elaborate programs were prepared for Michelangelo as artist and poet (fourth centenary of his death), Dante (700th anniversary), and Vico (300th anniversary), yet even such an unexpected writer as Seneca had his commemorative program.

One of the most significant events in Italian literary history was the abolition by the Roman curia of the *Index Librorum Prohibitorum* in 1965–66, four centuries after its establishment (1564). If many writers like Sartre and Unamuno benefitted by the demise of this outdated listing, Italian literature gained the most, for the vast majority of names on the Index were always from the Italian peninsula.

The Spoleto Festival of the Two Worlds continued successfully to attract visitors from the entire world. The final assessment for literature of this annual season will have to be made at a later date. Nevertheless Italians have always appreciated dialogue on literature, and Spoleto has afforded an important forum for this. It has encouraged as well the revival of non-commercial theater (e.g., the Renaissance comedy *La Venexiana*). Despite the brouhaha and the debated modernistic sculpture newly decorating this ancient monastery town, the excitement engendered each year by Spoleto is no doubt a beneficial and liberalising one for literature and the arts.

This period marked a few important changes in the area of literary journals. The highly-respected *Europa letteraria* disappeared for lack of funds. *La Fiera letteraria* was purchased by Rizzoli and became more conservative. At the other pole was *Quindici,* a New Left literary periodical favoring Che Guevara, Marcuse, and the many revolts of students and intellectuals in Italy and elsewhere. The most original and iconoclastic organ of new developments in the letters and arts was *Marcatrè,* founded by Eugenio Battisti and subsidised in part by Lerici. The neo-dadaist title (oil drillers' terminology for the deepest layers of petroleum) sets the tone for the essays, extremely vanguardist by authors under forty.

Several literary discoveries were made. Professor Victor Branca of Padua identified an autograph copy of Boccaccio's *Decameron* as well as the complete manuscript of the last work by Politian. A letter of Petrarch to Bernabò Visconti was discovered, and a long manuscript of Leonardo da Vinci was "discovered" in the National Library at Madrid, where it had lain unidentified for years. New information concerning the famous Monaca di Monza in Manzoni's *Betrothed* showed her to be a willful and evil woman. Diego de Donato unearthed and published an exchange of letters between Eugenio Montale and Italo Svevo, the Swabian novelist whom Montale had "discovered." The letters tell much about the young Montale, still displaying his critical acuity almost forty years after Svevo's death. They reveal even more about Svevo and his relationship to his own works: "*Zeno* is an autobiography, but not mine!"

The Novel. The Italian novel was undergoing sufficient

experimentation that Alberto Moravia could give a lecture at the Universities of Paris and Rennes on "The Death of the Traditional Novel."

Italo Calvino, storyteller, novelist, and disciple of the late Cesare Pavese illustrated Moravia's thesis and *his the bestseller rank* with a curious collection of fourteen fictions under the title *Le Cosmocomiche (Cosmo-comic Tales).* This curious work, falling somewhere between science fiction and an anti-narrative, makes a stunning rebuke to critics who had judged overly-realistic his 1963 novel *Giornale di uno scrutatore (Day of a Researcher).* Each piece is prefaced by the summary of some scientific or pseudoscientific theory.

Yet the experimentation displayed in the Italian novels of this period was considerably behind the revolutionary novelistic structures being tried out by the heirs of the new-novelists in France and the adventurous experimenters of Gruppe 47 in Germany. For the most part the more experimental novels in Italy fared less well with the critics and with the public.

Leonardo Sciascia continued to live a charmed life in Sicily writing novels about the Mafia without being gunned down by a *sicario* (triggerman). His damaging and depressing anti-Mafia novel *Il Giorno della Civetta (The Day of the Owl,* from Shakespeare) was followed by *A ciascuno il suo (To Each his Own).* In a small Sicilian town a professor accidentally discovers the background of the dual murder of a chemist and physician. The lawyer who arranged the slayings has the professor liquidated and marries the physician's widow. Once more justice does not pravail. As in his other indictments of an *omertà*-ridden society, Sciascia shows that most of the townspeople know the facts which the authorities seek in vain.

Vasco Pratolini's Florentine trilogy, *An Italian Story,* weaving together *Matello* (1955) and *Lo Scialo* (1960) was concluded in 1966 with *Allegoria e derisione.* Metello was an obscure socialist bricklayer whose sturdy body was to incarnate an entire society and period — that period when trade unionism won its first battle in Italy against industrialists, monarchists, and the police. The 620 pages of the concluding volume record an even more difficult period, up to that Liberation which left Florence so visibly scarred from World War II. Here Motello has given way to Valerio, also a worker but an intellectual coeval of the author with whom he obviously is identified. Thus the trilogy here assumes its greatest veracity, with Pratolini's own memory coming into play. Uncertain whether Pratolini had achieved a masterpiece, the critics were unanimously impressed by the sweep of his vision and the totality of his recall.

One of the international hits of 1964 was Giuseppe Berto's *Male oscuro* (translated into English as *Incubus*) which quickly took its place as one of Italy's best psychological novels. Over two years later Berto followed with a Freudian study on love, *La cosa buffa (The Ridiculous Thing)*. It traces the psychic and sentimental education of a young man during his first two liaisons. This tale, unlike *Incubus,* is related in the third rather than first person, but the narration is again free-association with the flow, rhythms, and syntax of a psychological confession. Berto demonstrates how women of differing types accede easily to their love affairs whereas the male partner remains ridden with guilt-feelings.

Mario Soldati's new novel, *La Busta arancione (The Orange Envelope),* was the chronical of a grown son's attempt to free himself from a domineering mother. He succeeds only at her death, after she has driven from him the one woman with whom he could have found happiness. The fine sense of mystery that runs through Soldati's novels, ably displayed also in *The Real Silvestro,* prevails here until the final recognition scene, when a fading letter in an old orange envelope tells Carlo that he was betrayed not by his vanquished mistress, but by his mother. The brisk pace, the unadorned prose, the objective depiction of the most poignant incidents may result from Soldati's parallel career in films and television, or, as likely, from his enthusiasm for Hemingway, who is widely thought to have influenced him.

Luigi Santucci's *Orfeo in Paradiso* recalls happy days in Milan between the revolutionary months of 1898 and the defeat at Caporetto in World War I. High on Milan Cathedral Orpheus encounters a bird which he recognises as his dead mother. He is encouraged to take a leap in time and space, finding himself suddenly in a Milanese neighborhood in the year 1892, just nine months before his mother is to be born. He lovingly watches her grow into adolescence and young womanhood. Though his memory tells him that the Austrians will break through at Caporetto, he enlists to protect signorina Eva. When he returns to Milan Eva is holding hands with Leandro, destined to become Orpheus's father. The ancient legend holds true. Orpheus is not to bring Eurydice back. This intricate conjuration somehow comes off well, even movingly.

Ignazio Silone continued to enjoy his rehabilitation among critics with one of his finest novels, *Avventura di un povero cristiano*. The story, which he has admittedly retold, concerns a humble man of the people who (like Pietro Spina in *Bread and Wine*) believes in a simple, almost evangelical Christianity and finds himself pitted against a hierarchical and parapolitical Church. In *Avventura* the "poor Christian" is a peasant born in Isernia in 1215 who succeeds in becoming a monk. While the Orsinis and the Colonnas compete to put a relative onto the papal throne, Celestine's attractive qualities and personality lead to his election as a compromise candidate. But the *Realpolitik* required of popes — the expedient forbearance of vice close to home, the abandonment of Franciscan ideals, the encouragement of warfare — compelled Celestine to abdicate. Even then he could not escape the system. He was murdered by his successor. Old Socialist Silone was obviously cautioning us that the same worldly perils and temptations hang over the Papacy today is in the thirteenth century.

Pier Paolo Pasolini's *Teorema,* an avant-garde novel exploring the curious theme of Mammon falling in love with God, appeared simultaneously with the film version. The film ran a few days in Rome before the censors caught up with it, but the novel fared better.

The major publishers, Feltrinelli, Mondadori, Einaudi, Bompiani, among others, continued their splendid campaign to bring out in Italian the best prose narrators of the Western world. Typical of the courage they displayed in this didactic endeavor was that of Mondadori in publishing the five novels of the American John Barth when that writer was barely establishing his reputation in the United States. Once more the publishers could boast that they were doing more than the schools and universities to make cosmopolites of their readers.

The ever-close relationships between cinema and novel, already suggested above, were not only debated in congresses at Sorrento and elsewhere, but were evidenced by the number of literary works which found themselves converted to film. Some classic plays were adapted as well. Despite continuing censorship, Alberto Lattuada produced Machiavelli's bawdy *Mandragola (Mandrake Root),* conscientiously preserving the authenticity of the original comedy.

Poetry. Italy's great triumvirate of poets, Montale, Ungaretti, and Quasimodo was finally broken up by the death of the latter. Aware that age was making haste more urgent, many agencies heaped honors on Ungaretti and Montale. The latter received a rare honorary degree from

Cambridge and was named a lifelong Senator of the Republic.

At his death Quasimodo was busy translating epigrams from Leonidas, writing on Hesiod, preparing an edition of his *Colloquies,* and readying for Mondadori the second volume of his essays on the theater. Shortly before his death appeared a small volume of verse, *Dare e avere (Debits and Credits).* Critics found therein that Quasimodo had entered a third phase as poet and as man. The first stage, which had produced such splendid self-discovery and description of nature (*Ed è subito sera* and *Giorno dopo Giorno*) was succeeded by the politically-committed poet, singing of Sputniks. The third phase was now one of stoicism, the *contemplatio mortis,* as death draws nigh. Yet the style and language of Quasimodo, nurtured on classical writers and honed by long practice as a translator, could not so easily be divided into phases. His images, consciously elaborated rhythms, and purist's concern for the poetic word kept him a poet even when he played at sociologist or politician.

In Ugo Fasolo's *Malumore (Bad Mood)* the source of the poet's black bile is our technological age, which can contradict or destroy man – an age, in fact, when the computer will probably end up writing a better Credo than the Apostles. Under the surface spoofing there lies deep seriousness. Fasolo, whose first verses date from 1935, is obviously impressing critics as one of the few veteran bards at home in the new world of IBM and Olivetti.

Novelist Elsa Morante abandoned the novel momentarily to compose a volume of free verse, *Il mondo salvato dai ragazzi (The World Redeemed by Children).* Among the topics treated are the Oedipus theme, the unspoiled universe of infants, and the myth of the Happy Few.

Theater. Italian critics like Giovanni Calendoli continued to worry over the old question of why there is no theater of consequence in Italy. Everyone had his own explanation. Calendoli attributes the sterility to the increasingly mechanical society which does away with personal contacts and communications in favor of mass media. During the mid- or late-sixties no playwright emerged to claim the mantle of Pirandello or Betti. Some of the country's best dramatic talents were devoting themselves to cinema, as were leading novelists like Moravia and Pasolini. Nevertheless, the period witnessed brilliant activity in production and acting on the part of the stable theaters, which toured not only the Italian provinces but other countries and continents as well. When measured by production and professionalism, the Italian theater had never attained the heights now attained by the Piccolo Teatro di Milano, the Teatro Stabile of Genoa, the Stabile of Genoa, and the uinversity-sponsored Commedia dell'Arte Theater in Venice.

Eduardo de Filippo, the gaunt and amiable author-director from Naples, saw his *Filomena Marturana* revived regularly and even metamorphosed into a hit film starring Mastroianni and Sofia Loren. For the reopening of the San Fernando Playhouse, rebuilt long after the bombardment of World War II, De Filippo wrote a new one-act play, *Dolore sotto chiava (Grief under Lock and Key)*. This concerned the Pirandellian situation of a husband kept ignorant for a year of the death of his invalid wife. De Felippo's contemporary Pirandello was being revived also, but less so the nine plays on which Marta Abba still held exclusive rights. The actress was under much censure in the literary journals for withholding these rights in a tight grasp.

Novelist Natalia Ginzburg, ex-Viareggio laureate, turned abruptly and busily to playwrighting, to a genre she had previously belittled. In 1968 she won the Marzotto Prize for the Theater with *The Insertion,* quickly put into English for Laurence Olivier. She completed as well two plays, *Strawberries and Cream* and *The Secretary.* Her first major hit, *I Married You for Joy,* was successfully filmed with the popular Monica Vitti as heroine.

Alberto Moravia himself turned to the theater, reviving an interest which had reached an earlier peak in 1958, when a volume of his plays had appeared. Like Gide, Cocteau, and others, Moravia wrote his version of the Oedipus myth, *Il Dio Kurt.* God Kurt, commanding a concentration camp at Sachsenhausen, stages *Oedipus Rex* for his inmates, with Nazi trimming and ideology. The young Jew Saul becomes Oedipus and his mother, Myriam, Jocasta. Kurt arranges for their real-life incest and then absolves the pair, but condemns them to continue working as German prisoners. Perhaps Moravia's playing of the Sophoclean drama in a German prison camp aided at achieving the stunning effect of Peter Weiss's *Marat/Sade.*

Essays. Alberto Moravia at the same time wrote a straight-from-the-shoulder corpus of essays in *L'uomo come fine (Man as the End),* informing the Russians that their unshakable attitude about *engagement* in literature is a dubious one at best, that the greatest genius matures most fully in a cultural and aristocratic state, that their aesthetic amounts to little more than a "suspension of art," and that, finally, if their idea of directed literature were valid, their own literary production is mighty feeble armament in the battle between East and West.

Another major essayistic work is Ignazio Silone's *Uscita di sicurezza (Safety Exit),* his first work since *The Fox and the Camellias* of 1960. This work is a mixture of narrative, essay, and autobiography. Silone's theme is — man's and his own — struggle with the religious and moral dilemmas of our times, a theme he was to return to in his later novel about Pope Celestine (see above). The tortured experiences of the author as an individual (at the age of 15 Silone lost his parents and five brothers during an earthquake) keep him concerned with ethical problems, the preservation of liberty, and indeed with the future of mankind. With this work Silone began to be praised as a perfectionist, and Italian critics who for some time had not only neglected but belittled him now outdid one another in rediscovering the talented author who had been there all along.

From the deceased Curzio Malaparte (1898–1957) came a posthumous work, *Diary of a Foreigner in Paris,* recording his 1947 return to that capital after an absence of fourteen years that encompassed imprisonment and sequestration on Lipari under Fascism. He captures the excitement of intellectual and daily life in the France for which in 1916 he fled his high school in the Tuscan Hills to defend it from Kaiser Wilhelm. Meanwhile Malaparte's *Accussed Tuscans* paved the way for a much more censorious and journalistic analysis of their countrymen, *The Italians,* by Luigi Barzini.

Another important collection of posthumous notes appeared. When Massimo Bontempelli died in 1960 he was working over an *Idearium,* a dictionary of aphorisms and notes. The work easily ranks the novelist and dramatist as an important aphorist. Some of the best items predictably deal with literary people: "What is missing in superior people are superior faults. It is surprising to see that a great poet, when envious, is envious like the merest of men; when greedy, greedy like an old maid." Or this following crystallization of the literary temper of his time: "I grant that in the matter of aesthetics it is necessary not to believe in Benedetto Croce; but it is absolutely indispensable to have believed in him."

Summary Statement. During the decade of the sixties the great, literate, international-minded publishing houses of Italy emerge as paragons of courage and preservers of the Italian literary tradition. During this period they published more book titles *per annum* than did the French, working in a more international language for a greater audience. The majority of the Italian publishers diversified their business interests and investments profitably, so much so that they could take risks in publishing works of merit and take losses with the consoling thought that they had nevertheless furthered the cause of Italian letters.

Index